About the author

Christa Wichterich is a freelance journalist for print media and radio, and a consultant on women's projects and gender policies. She is currently carrying out a study on women's empowerment projects in Asia and Africa.

The Globalized Woman: Reports from a Future of Inequality

Christa Wichterich

translated by
Patrick Camiller

Spinifex Press
AUSTRALIA

Zed Books
LONDON · NEW YORK

The Globalized Woman: Reports from a Future of Inequality was first published by
Zed Books Ltd, 7 Cynthia Street, London N1 9JF, UK and Room 400, 175 Fifth
Avenue, New York, NY 10010, USA in 2000.

Published in Australia and New Zealand by Spinifex Press, 504 Queensberry
Street, North Melbourne, Victoria, 3051, Australia
women@spinifexpress.com.au
http://spinifexpress.com.au

Distributed in the USA exclusively by St Martin's Press, Inc., 175 Fifth Avenue,
New York, NY 10010, USA.

Originally published under the title *Die Globalisierte Frau*
Copyright © 1998 by Rowolt Taschenbuch Verlag GmbH, Reinbek bei Hamburg

Copyright © Christa Wichterich, 2000
English language translation © Patrick Camiller, 2000

Cover designed by Andrew Corbett
Set in Monotype Ehrhardt and Franklin Gothic by Ewan Smith
Printed and bound in the United Kingdom by Biddles Ltd, Guildford
and King's Lynn

The right of Christa Wichterich to be identified as the author of this work has been
asserted by her in accordance with the Copyright, Designs and Patents Act, 1988.

A catalogue record for this book is available from the British Library

Library of Congress Cataloging-in-Publication Data
Wichterich, Christa.
    [Globalisierte Frau. English]
    The globalised woman : reports from a future of inequality /
Christa Wichterich : translated by Patrick Camiller
        p.   cm.
    Includes bibliographical references and index.
    ISBN 1-85649-740-2 (hc.) ISBN 1-85649-741-0 (pbk.)
        1. Women–Employment. 2. Unemployed women workers. 3. Labor
market. 4. Competition, International. 5. International division of
labor. I. Title.
    HD6053.W44713 2000
    331.4–dc21
                                                          99-056211

National Library of Australia Cataloguing-in-Publication Data
Wichterich, Christa.
[Die globalisierte Frau. English]
Globalised woman: reports from the future of inequality.
Bibliography.
Includes index.
ISBN 1 875559 67 1

1. Women in politics. 2. Women – Economic conditions – 20th century.
3. World politics – 1989– . 4. Economic history – 1990. 5. Women's rights.
6. Women – Government policy. I. Camiller, Patrick. II. Title.
305.42

ISBN 1 85649 740 2 cased
ISBN 1 85649 741 0 limp

Contents

Introduction

There is a lot of talk about globalization – but women do not feature much in it. The title of the standard French book on the subject, Philippe Engelhard's *L'Homme mondiale*, exemplifies the total lack of regard with which human beings are again defined as male in this connection.

Yet the effects of globalization are not gender-neutral: women are not caught up in it in the same way as men. In the planet-wide expansion of the world market that signals the victory of free trade, women find themselves being allocated special tasks and roles. It is high time that the effects of global developments on women's lives and work were systematically described and analysed, and the future prospects for women drawn out of the present dynamic of the globalization process.

Globalization tendencies, with all their disjunctures and unevenness of development, have highly varied and often even opposite consequences for women. They take hold of and change social systems, cultures and economies in different ways, powerfully eroding and revolutionizing societies in the East and South, while often provoking modernization and adaptation effects in the industrial heartlands of the North. All over the world, however, new forms of work, multiple strategies of social protection, different lifestyles and value-orientations are unsettling and reshaping women's lives.

Globalization means expansion of the neoliberal market economy to the remotest parts of individual countries and the most far-flung corners of the earth. Market economy and neoliberalism are Siamese twins in this global thrust, which is not the first in history but is certainly the most rapid. Space and time appear no longer to play any role; globalization and speed belong together. The US military strategist Edward Luttwak has condensed these two aspects in the notion of 'turbo-capitalism', where products, services and news, capital and labour-power, attain a new level of mobility and acceleration. Raw materials, semi-finished and finished goods are all transported at low cost around the globe, swamping real and virtual marketplaces and transforming cultures of shortage or scarcity into markets of overabundance. Currencies are made convertible, but jobs and labour-power are also more mobile and interchangeable than ever before. The world is like a chessboard on which corporations occupy squares in an unprecedented fever of business activity and rush from place to place with never a moment's rest. Multilayered flows of migrant labour are also on the move: people set off in search of jobs, and at the same time capital comes looking for cheap labour. A new degree of universal interchange-ability has been reached, just as mobile phones, pagers, baby monitors and other communications technologies have made individuals accessible in a way they have never previously been. All of this seems to be making distances shrink and fade.

The heart of globalization is abstract: it is a finance market made up of shares, currencies and derivatives which every day, to the tune of $3 billion, are speculatively moved around on dealers' computer screens in e-mail time. The financial exchanges are the world's new centres of gravity. When the markets cough, headlines grow bigger, companies shiver, and small investors work themselves into a frenzy.

If the global marketplace has a name, it is Wall Street. The control centre of finance capital is a tangle of communication cables weaving their way through a giant hall towards rows of computer terminals; it is a high-tech system in which fleet-footed dealers, guided by an invisible hand, scurry around the floor like an army of ants. The bell rings at 9.30 a.m., the seconds start to tick away, and within moments millions of dollars have changed hands. One transaction lasts ten seconds, so that five minutes is enough for the Dow Jones Index to rise, or to fall, by umpteen points. 'The world puts its trust in us', reads a digital ticker-tape above the market prices. This global marketplace is male and white. Very few women have so far been moved up into the sacred precinct of capital.

For women around the world, however, globalization is not an abstract process unfolding on an elevated stage. It is concrete and actual. Female textile-workers from Upper Lusatia in Eastern Germany are losing their jobs to women in Bangladesh; Filipinas clean vegetables and kitchens in Kuwait; Brazilian prostitutes offer their services around Frankfurt's main railway station; and Polish women look after old people at rock-bottom prices in various parts of Germany. Women in the Caribbean key in commercial entries for North American banks. In the Philippines, families who make a living by sorting through refuse cannot sell their plastic wares whenever a shipment of unbeatably cheap waste, collected by Germany's recycling scheme, arrives. And what is for the next meal is decided not by local women, but by multinationals specializing in novelty food and genetic-ally modified crops.

Across different countries and cultures, a number of parallel trends are making women's lives and work more and more similar. With higher levels of employment, but mainly in insecure low-paid jobs, they have to face greater social problems, more competition and sexist violence, a conservative rollback, a new culture of extravagant consumerism, and a quest for new identities amid growing social inequality.

'Only winners, no losers,' predicted Peter Sutherland, the last director of GATT, at the founding of the new World Trade Organization (WTO) in Marrakesh in April 1994. The liberalization of markets holds out a promise of equal opportunity, justice and democracy for continents and individual countries, for social classes and both sexes. And it is true that radical changes in the labour market, as well as the expansion of consumer markets, offer new chances and individual options for women by challenging traditional roles and patriarchal controls. Women are supposed to be profiting from world market integration, as it is they who are the main job-winners in labour-intensive or service industries. Cheap, docile and flexible, they have a competitive advantage over men in meeting the new requirements of the labour market.

More particularly, it is the US model of the free market that has prevailed. In Denver in June 1997, the summit of the seven major industrial countries turned into a celebration of this triumph. Lawrence Summers, US deputy secretary of the Treasury, declared that the contestants' corners in the new world order had already been occupied – by US corporations. As special gladiators of the 'global empire', he held up Disney in the entertainments sector, McDonald's in fast food, Microsoft in computer software, and Federal Express in postal packages. Summers showed no trace of embarrassment as he championed the US model and a kind of market totalitarianism. The global economy of the twenty-first century would take shape under US leadership, and this would ensure that welfare and growth were 'inclusive'.

The world market is meant to be integrative, as if everyone could gather freely and equally on the global labour, information and communication markets. Even share markets are presented as democratic and inclusive. 'Nowadays, to become co-owner of a Russian department store or a South American telephone company, all Lieschen Müller has to do is call her high-street bank,' wrote the investors' magazine *Börse online* in autumn 1997. The 'Top 97' women's fair in Dusseldorf showed that women are now being courted as a 'market segment'. Not only do they control 70 per cent of total household budgets in Germany; new investment clubs for women are making it easier for them to gain access to money markets and join the ranks of private shareowners.

In a much larger part of the world, however, fear of globalization outweighs any enthusiasm for investment and consumption opportunities, or for the age of information and high-speed transport. It is a fear of being overrun and devalued by outside products, norms and culture, a fear of losing old certainties without being able to glimpse new ones, a fear of being exposed to penetration and overhasty change. The dizzying fall of the South-East Asian tiger economies in 1997 confirmed both the legitimacy of these fears and the speculative, volatile nature of the new conditions. Through the mediation of money markets, local crises become global crises, and the shock waves from national economic declines make themselves felt as market instability all around the world.

The global age blesses us with records and superlatives: record corporate turnover and highs on the DAX and Dow Jones, but also record unemployment and erosion of the welfare state. It is a contradictory and desynchronized process that pulls in different directions at once. Corporate profits and job losses, wealth and poverty, appear as part of the same package. Women are integrated into the economy and the world market, but at the same time are immediately remarginalized.

Here today, gone tomorrow – throwaway products with built-in obsolescence of materials and designs keep the economy flourishing. But 'here today, gone tomorrow' also applies to the corporate pillage of natural resources without heed for the environment or the future, and to the whole use being made of labour flexibility. The prototypes of this development are, on the one hand, canned drinks, fashionable clothes or tamagochi toys, and, on the other hand, the exploitation of rainforest, lands and seas, as well as of young women in world market factories or of people working for DM620 in Germany. A 'just in time' mode of behaviour, geared to immediate market values, is thus taking the place of social and ecological responsibility.

Globalization cannot serve as a monocausal explanation for any kind of change. But it is a process that really exists, not just a myth constructed for the assertion of political and economic interests. Not every phenomenon described in this book is the simple and direct result of neoliberal globalization, yet it should be possible to identify the dynamic and perspectives of the complex process. It is a logic that stems from market economics and production, not from the household economy and reproduction that are still the centre of life for most women. It draws 'globalized woman' into a magnetic field between the attraction of saturated consumption markets and the destruction of social security, between hopes for new job opportunities and exploitation as an ever-available source of hard work, between the search for new cultural identities, networks of civil society and the currents of competitive individualization.

To my teachers

MARIA LAUBENTHAL
ANNELIESE GENSKE
MARIA MIES
CAROLA MÖLLER
EVA-MARIA BRUCHHAUS
EVA VON HERTZBERG

1

The Global Conveyor-belt

Women as a Comparative Advantage

In June 1997 one statistic sent a shiver down the spine of the representatives of international capital. In the first five months of that year, China had increased its exports by more than 26 per cent over the previous year. What a flow of commodities on to the world market, led by light industrial goods such as toys and clothing, shoes and microchips, electronic products and computer software! But also, what an outpouring of toil and sweat!

The boom figure is a sign of overheating in the globalization process. The present spurt had been preceded, since the 1960s, by a new international division of labour in which labour-intensive advances in production were shifted from the industrial heartlands to neighbouring low-wage countries: from Northern Europe to Portugal, Greece and North Africa, from Japan to South and South-East Asia, and from the United States to Central America. These competitive relocations changed the whole face of world trade, with the proportion of semi-finished and finished products rising *vis-à-vis* the share of raw materials and primary goods.

The comparative advantage of the new export economies was low pay without secondary wage-costs, plus weak trade unions and a powerful array of fiscal and investment incentives. T-shirts, shoes and microchips functioned as classical starter products for low-wage countries in the world market, and female labour-power as the most important 'natural' resource. In export factories, women accounted for between 70 and 90 per cent of the total workforce.

Labour-intensive production has always and everywhere been woman-intensive production; from the early capitalist period in England and Germany, through the economies of India or Brazil in the early part of the twentieth century, to the export factories that have sprung up in the South since the 1970s. Typically female industries have been the processing of textiles, leather and foodstuffs, the production of toys, electronic goods and pharmaceuticals, as well as certain occupations in chemicals, rubber and metal-working.

In the 'tiger economies' of South-East Asia, the widely trumpeted miracle of high growth-rates has mainly been due to the millions of women taken on and then dismissed by companies producing for the world market. A rapid turnover of labour was ensured by the hiring of young women with basic education at ridiculously low wages, who could usually be laid off after marriage or the birth of their first child. They served as the accelerator of economic growth.

In the countries that recorded the sharpest increase in exports and the highest growth-rates between 1970 and 1990, the percentage of women in the total labour force also shot up to new highs: from 25 to 44 per cent in South-East Asia, for example.[1] Export production and liberalized trade thus serve as the engine of female employment.

Women have accordingly been presented as the job-winners of world market integration, the United Nations even speaking of a 'feminization of employment'.[2] But women have paid a high price for this in the shape of appalling working conditions, few rights, meagre pay and no social security or sustainable livelihood. They are subject to exhausting and monotonous work routines that are often injurious to their health, for an hourly wage of between 16 and 60 US cents.

The greater the pressures to make ends meet and the fewer the alternatives, the more prepared are women to accept wretched working conditions and to be blackmailed into long hours. 'The boss said: If you don't show up Sunday, you needn't come in Monday either.' The methods that a Polish female textile-worker deplored in New York in 1909[3] are still quite usual at the end of the century in China, in Honduras or in Tunisia.

Why is cheap women's labour everywhere the means of launching into the world market? It is not only that their 'nimble fingers' have made them attractive to the bosses of light industry, in both the First and the Third World, at the beginning as at the end of the twentieth century; their starvation wages and easy dismissal have mainly been justified by the persistent myth that men are the 'family breadwinners' and women only 'supplementary earners'. Their 'impermanence', involving time off to give birth and care for small children, corresponds with requirements of flexibility by the companies.

Since the late 1980s, in the climate of intensified world-market competition, companies have been stepping up their various strategies to lower costs and maximize profits. This has involved a new wave of off-shoring, a drive to make labour more informal and flexible, and an expansion of automation. At the same time, the 'global players' have diversified by merging with companies from other branches, enlarging their product range and moving into the service sector. Out of monopolies have arisen mixed corporations.

At the present time, more and more firms are pulling out of the 'tiger economies' because of rising production costs. The new low-wage El Dorados are Bangladesh, Vietnam, Cambodia, Laos and China, whose entry into the world market proceeds through the same mechanisms of labour-intensive industry and female labour-power that affected other countries a quarter of a century ago. The Chinese boom figures, too, would be unthinkable without nimble and compliant young women.

Twenty years ago, a female factory-worker in South Korea earned as much in a month as her counterparts do today in Vietnam: roughly $60. Today the South Korean has more than ten times as much in her pocket. But in Bangkok the lowest daily wage in 1997 was just under $6, in Indonesia $2 and in China only half of that. The competition for markets knows no pity. Thai Underwear, a Japanese–Thai joint venture, gets roughly $1.25 on the European, Japanese or US market for each pair of its men's 'Jockey' underpants. Chinese firms supply a full dozen of the same brand of underpants for the same price.[4] Female workers in South Korea, Taiwan and Thailand are the losers, and women in the new low-wage countries are the winners.

Capital is much more light-footed than ever before. The relocations that took place in the first phase of the new international division of labour appear slow and ponderous in comparison with the new nomadic movements of employers. Today's competition operates not only between North and South but also between different low-wage countries and sites in the South. The global labour market has become a kind of shopping centre for itinerant executives, who help themselves to local labour, infrastructure and investment incentives according to where the greatest profits lie. The chairman of the North Rhine textile industry, Dirk Busse, thinks of the factory of the year 2000 as a ship that drops anchor wherever wage-costs are lowest.

Being docile, young women are the ace cards in these consumption goods industries. In the booming toys sector, for example, a million are employed in more than four thousand factories in South China alone. The Asia Monitor Resource Centre, based in Hong Kong, has established that the air in these toy factories is heavy with toxic chemicals released through the processing of plastic materials. The machinery and electrical fittings are antiquated, the fire safety completely inadequate. Overtime is compulsory and usually not paid in full. The women there are overworked and overtired.

Toy-factory fires in Thailand and China, which have claimed hundreds of women's lives in recent years, occurred in so-called 'three-in-one' sweatshops containing production areas, storage space and sleeping rooms in a single building. It all added up to a deadly trap for the workers. Doors and windows were locked so that the women could not take any toys out with them; passageways and staircases were blocked by materials and finished goods. Attempts by Chinese workers to defend themselves by organizing trade unions have been met with repression and the sacking of union leaders.[5]

Whether it is a question of toys given as birthday presents at McDonald's 'Happy Meals', or of Disney characters brought into children's bedrooms, the fact is that 70 per cent of the colourful world of Barbie, Lion King and Action Man is produced in Asia – 60 per cent in China alone. Childhood is a new boom market. The media and the toy industry have entered into an unholy alliance to make the new ranks of 'skippies' (schoolchildren with income and purchasing power) dependent upon them. The turnover of this sector has rocketed to $43 billion a year, with a growing part taken by electronic and video games.

On average, each child in Europe gets 230 dollars' worth of toys a year. The lion's share, however, is spent on boys – some 150 per cent more than on girls, in the case of Germany. Eighty per cent of all industrially produced toys are marketed in Europe, North America and Japan. The corporate Goliath is Mattel, the Californian Barbie producer, two of whose dolls are sold every second somewhere in the world; in 1995 this brought it a turnover of $7 billion. The global trade in toys is dominated by a single corporation, Toys R Us, whose turnover in the year 1996–97 came to 17 billion dollars.[6]

In countries such as India, many children used to enjoy a fascinating variety of playthings produced by village craft enterprise, often out of recycled material. But there too cheap imports from Taiwan and mainland China are flooding the market, depriving village and household producers of their former income and employment possibilities.

The growth in jobs for women on the global labour market should thus be set against the elimination of local goods by cheap mass-produced imports. This is how indigenous small-scale production is dying out, in sectors ranging from toys to the clothing industries of Nicaragua, India or Bulgaria.

Yesterday Upper Lusatia, Today Bangladesh, Tomorrow China

Germans seem especially attached to the belief that clothes make the person. Their average annual purchase of 26 kilogrammes certainly puts them in front when it comes to textile consumption – despite the losses incurred in this sector since 1991. By comparison, the average annual purchase worldwide is 8 kilos per head, and in the Cameroons a mere half-kilo. To make room for the new, 500,000 tonnes of old clothes are collected every year in Germany, almost half of which is exported to Africa and Eastern Europe as second-hand goods.

Still, we would all find ourselves pretty bare if we were asked to discard everything not produced in our home country. Our jeans may have ten thousand miles of travelling incorporated in them; our shoes may come from Vietnam and our blouses and shirts from Morocco, and were certainly produced by women's hands in the export factories of the South.

German clothing suppliers have more than 80 per cent of their goods produced abroad, nearly half in the countries of the South. This stark figure conceals the quiet death of the German textile and clothing industry, a trade so rich in tradition in Saxony and Thuringia, North-Rhine West-phalia and Bavaria. In the old *Länder* of the Federal Republic, nearly 70 per cent of the 900,000 (mostly female) jobs that it provided in 1970 had gone by 1995. The cull was even more stunning in the East after unifica-tion: only 24,000 out of 320,000 jobs remained by the end of 1995. The trend continues throughout Germany, with another 23,800 jobs lost in textiles and clothing. And the gross hourly pay of seamstresses – 16.75 deutschmarks – is at the bottom of the industrial scale.

This loss of hundreds of thousands of women's jobs has not caused an outcry remotely comparable to what is heard when redundancies are announced among male workers in the steel or shipyard industry, or in mining or construction. As in other sectors, the main reason for the dramatic collapse of the 'textile' labour market is increased productivity resulting from rationalization and technological change. Ever more produc-tive high-tech looms, and robots which can tie broken threads in circular spinning machines, are taking over more and more women's jobs. Cheaper overseas labour is thus only the second reason for the worldwide structural change in the textile sector[7] – which means that globalization cannot be the only explanation for mass unemployment in European countries.

On the other side of the global conveyor-belt, in the Bangladeshi capital Dhaka, the first light of dawn reveals more women than men on their way to work in the industrial districts. Fifteen years ago, hardly any women were to be seen in the streets at that time of day. Now they walk in small groups with flasks in their hands, towards huge blocks of houses jostling one another in an endless industrial monotony. On every floor there is a different clothing firm. In these large tailors' workshops, a few hundred girls and women stitch for ten to twelve hours a day on piece-rates, beneath glaring neon strips and in stifling heat. None of them suspects that she is a cog in the wheel of an international job off-shoring transfer, and that she is partly doing the work which, a few years ago, women performed 9000 kilometres away in Upper Lusatia to earn their daily bread.

In less than twenty years, nearly 1.5 million jobs (90 per cent of them for women) have come into being in Dhaka and Chittagong. The clothing industry is the big winner of the Bangladeshi economy. In 1995, with a growth-rate of 22 per cent, it brought in more foreign currency than any other sector: $1.73 billion.

The success story began in 1979. A businessman from Bangladesh signed a cooperation agreement with the South Korean corporation Daewoo and founded the Desh Company. Daewoo trained 130 Bangladeshis on the job in Korea, acquired machinery for Desh, sent across some managerial advisers and took responsibility for product marketing – all for 5 per cent of earnings. In this learning process across frontiers, the world-market novice was entrusted with all the import–export tricks for the avoidance of taxes and duties. Thanks to Daewoo's market openings and the transfer of know-how, Desh was able to take off in no time at all.[8]

Many of Daewoo's 130 apprentices left Desh in the 1980s, set up their own firms and even trained managers and women workers. Whereas there were forty-seven export-oriented clothing firms in Bangladesh in 1983, there were 2500 by 1997. Small businesses keep them supplied with labels, packing material and yarn. The luxury hotels of Dhaka and Chittagong, where buyers from Europe and the USA have set up permanent quarters, also get their slice from the boom.

Tasmin stitches collars to backs, sixty an hour, 700 a day. At 'Rhine Garments', a shirt takes half an hour from the first seam to the last button. Between the closely spaced sewing-machines, girls aged twelve to fourteen operate as a human conveyor-belt. Then comes the quality control, the shirt is ironed, pinned together and packed in transparent sheets. As a finishing touch, the Green Point (the seal of ecological approval in Germany) is affixed to it. The division of labour hits you in the eye: men cut out, iron and pack; women stitch. Each day the 450 workers produce 3500 gaudy shirts for the Baur mail-order firm in Bavaria. No other country produces as many shirts and T-shirts for the European market as does the land on the Bay of Bengal.

The equivalent of $290,000 that Shibli Rubayat-ul-Islam (the dynamic proprietor in jeans and shirts) invested in 'Rhine Garments' in 1991 had paid for itself just two years later. The sewing-machines he bought second-hand in South Korea. The material comes from Hong Kong, the buttons from Taiwan, the design from Germany. The clever young man in his mid-twenties makes a handsome profit, because he sells direct to firms in Europe, without intermediaries. He gets DM6.30 ($3.80) per shirt, freight costs included. In the Baur mail-order catalogue they are priced at DM29.90.

If clients exert pressure or order more of a top-selling line, explains Shibli, everyone has to get down to work twelve hours a day, often with no day off. But they do get an evening meal at the company's expense.

Tasmin earns $1.15 a day. With overtime she makes $37.60 a month, a little more than the official minimum wage. The women's pay-packets contain almost a third less than their male colleagues'. Tasmin learnt to sew by watching others and practising on their machines during breaks; 'on-the-job training', her boss pretentiously calls it. Only very rarely does a seamstress manage to become a supervisor. 'Cutting to size is too difficult for girls,' opines the smartly dressed Shibli, 'and anyway they usually stop working when they get married.' What he means is that proper training does not pay for a calculating businessman.

When Shibli leaves his small factory, two watchmen click their heels at the main door. When Tasmin goes home in the evening, she must open her bag to show she is not taking out any cotton reels.

Tasmin was fourteen when she came to Dhaka from a village 200 kilometres away. She had been at school for just six years. Her father, a peasant who had to hand over half his crop as rent to the landowner, was overwhelmed by debt and had no option but to let his daughter go. The relatives with whom Tasmin first stayed in Dhaka took her with them to the factory. Three-quarters of the women working there come from the countryside, and most of them will never go back.

Tasmin, like most of the other women workers, is not married. She wants to wait a bit longer, she says bashfully. Are her parents not pushing her, since she is already eighteen? Yes, but they live far away in the village, and she will have to save for her own dowry. 'I look after myself and also send my parents some money.' She was lucky to find a room to share with some fellow-workers in one of the rare hostels for women. Every morning she goes off with them to work, and with them too she comes home in the evening, goes shopping and sometimes to the cinema.

In the village Tasmin would live in purdah – behind the veil – her freedom of movement limited both at home and outside. She would be shut off from public space and the world of men, and her conduct would be strictly regulated by norms of shame and propriety. At first, city life and wage-labour were a culture shock that caused her feelings of anxiety more than of freedom. But now she says about her escape from the narrow peasant life: 'I have seen the world.'

The degree of independence that Tasmin displays far from the family represents, in the words of sociologist Salma Chaudhury, a 'clear cultural change'. Or, in the triumphalist expression of Redwan Ahmed, a member of parliament and chairman of the Association of Clothing Producers and Exporters, industry has brought about a 'social revolution for women'.

Yet the women textile workers have had to pay a high price for their own income and their new opportunities for action and movement. The job really takes it out of them. Like it or not, they have to work overtime, and that is when they complain most of being cheated – of being usually only half-paid. After a few years, many of the women suffer from eye complaints, headaches and a general debility, as dust in the air and chemicals in the materials seriously damage their health. Bladder problems result from too few toilets, and from the rule that the workers should not 'disappear' too often.

The women have two great fears: a fire in the workshop and rape. In June 1996 thirty-two women were burnt to death in two textile factories in Dhaka because there were no emergency exits or fire extinguishers. These incidents are still talked about everywhere. But there is silence about cases of rape.

Despite the blows delivered in this sector through the general strikes and political turmoil of 1996, the factory-owners hope that the boom will go on. There is a growing sense of insecurity, however, as the trump card of the world's cheapest labour cannot remain a trump card for long. Already China, Vietnam and Cambodia carry out work just as cheaply and, it would seem, with shorter delivery times, whereas the seamstresses in Bangladesh have the reputation of not reaching the peaks of productivity.

Employers' leader Redwan Ahmed sees two essential requirements if the country is to be secure from competition: 'We must do everything to keep our costs down'; and the proportion of value-added must be increased from its present level of 30 per cent or less (because raw materials and machinery have to be imported).

Bengali weavers, who could once produce fabric so fine that long shawls could be pulled through a ring, no longer supply the country's own textile industry. This absurd state of affairs is rooted mainly in the early phases of economic globalization. In the nineteenth century, the British colonial rulers destroyed the indigenous textile crafts in order to create a market for cloth from Manchester and Birmingham. After independence, the government of Bangladesh imposed import restrictions to protect national producers, but in the 1980s these were relaxed under pressure from the World Bank and the International Monetary Fund. Clothing businesses now buy material abroad, because foreign customers insist that fabrics of wholly Bangladeshi origin would not meet the quality standards of Western industrialized countries.

The world textiles agreement has been of some assistance to this poverty-stricken land, allowing it to export a lot of gaudy stuff to Europe without the usual quotas. For India, Pakistan and many other countries of the South, however, the agreement lays down maximum quantities of textiles that may be exported to the North, in order to protect the clothing industries there. This quota system is supposed to end at the latest by the year 2005, when the agreement expires and a regime of unfettered competition is due to come into effect.

Meanwhile, the Bangladeshi government is doing everything it can to entice foreign investors. In addition to Chittagong and Dhaka, it wants to establish two more free-trade zones exclusively for foreign capital. The special attraction of these enclaves is that good old national labour legislation does not apply there, and there is a ban on trade union organization and strikes. Oases are being cleared for the exploitation of cheap female labour, so that old-style Manchester capitalism can celebrate the millennium with a vengeance on the Bay of Bengal.

Not Every Eden is Paradise

Yaowapa Donsae goes straight to a pile of white T-shirts at Sinn, the well-known fashion store in Cologne. She looks at the seams and is sure that it was she and her fellow-workers in Bangkok who stitched them together.

In Thailand, Yaowapa worked for ten years at the Eden Group textile multinational, which supplied retailers in Europe and the United States. From Quelle to Kaufhof, from Horten to C & A, nearly every trading business and mail-order firm in the German clothing sector had Eden products on its shelves and in its catalogues.

The working conditions at Eden, however, did not live up to the promise in its name. The women workers there did receive a contract, but it could not be collectively negotiated. 'If you wanted to negotiate something, you weren't taken seriously.' In 1991, when the women created a workplace union because of the wretched conditions, the company tried various ways of reducing the workforce of 4500 women. First the management turned the screws on union members by constantly transferring them to other departments and raising their work norms. It was a tactic that had considerable success: a number of women became unnerved and resigned, and were replaced by non-contract temporary workers. At the same time, Eden farmed out some of its operations to producers in the informal sector. Illegal immigrants from Burma or Cambodia also work in these backyard sweatshops; women who, whatever the unions try to do, usually earn no more than a third of the average and form an underlayer that exerts a constant downward pressure on wages. Furthermore, the company has placed a number of orders in China, where lower wages and higher profit margins offer the prospect of another real paradise for capital.

Eden hit the headlines in Thailand and Germany in November 1996, when the suspicion was confirmed that children were working in the hovels and cellars of its subcontractors. Overnight the company quietly closed its doors in Bangkok, the management made itself scarce, and Yaowapa Donsae and her fellow-workers were left standing in the street. The compensation due to them under Thai labour law was not paid, all of Eden's accounts with Thai banks being overdrawn. 'Eden immediately transferred all its profits to its mother company in Hong Kong,' explained Somyot Pruksakasemsuk, head of the Centre for Labour Information Service and Training.

The German mail-order firm Otto, which holds 'acceptable social standards' as one of its 'explicit corporate goals', immediately ended its business connection with the Eden group, as did Quelle Schickedanz. When asked, however, none of Eden's long-standing German business partners said that it was prepared to contribute to a fund in support of the women workers.

The methods used by the Eden Group in Thailand are not untypical for transnational corporations operating in the tiger economies of South-East Asia and the newly developing countries of Central America and North Africa. When wage-costs increase and trade union organization is on the rise, these companies look for locations that will be more cost-effective.

What is not so typical, however, is that two of the laid-off workers suddenly turned up in Düsseldorf – in this case in April 1997 – standing in the doorway of their employer's overseas representative, Americanwear Europe GmbH. When they arrived, they could see chests and cardboard boxes lying around filled with T-shirts and pyjamas, their packing labels revealing Eden as the supplier and the Otto mail-order firm as the recipient. Naturally, these were spirited away by the office staff in double-quick time.

Though company boss Warren Brickell was hardly pleased at the visit, he was willing enough to speak and to shift all responsibility as far from himself as possible. There could be absolutely no question of his firm making any compensatory payment, especially as the public appearance of the women from Thailand had already inflicted such heavy losses that four of their fellow-workers in Düsseldorf had also had to be laid off. Very soon he would be forced to shut the business down altogether.

So two different losers in the transnational corporate sweepstakes were facing each other in that Düsseldorf office: a group of women made redundant in Thailand, and a group of German white-collar workers who had been told that profits had fallen so much as a result of the Thai women's impudent demands that lay-offs were now necessary in Germany. It was a classic scapegoating strategy, designed to obscure the company's aim of shifting social costs on to the backs of the workforce in both

Thailand and Germany. It is like the hit-and-run method of lumber firms, which fell whole forests in next to no time and then do a vanishing act.

When she is asked about her future, Yaowapa Donsae can hardly control herself. She moved to Bangkok ten years ago, when her parents' rice patch in Isaan in the desperately poor north-east could no longer support the family of eight. Yaowapa thought of the city and factory work as a temporary condition: she would earn some money fast, then return to her village and build a life for herself. The job at Eden seemed tailor-made for her, especially as she received the legal minimum wage that a half of all companies do not pay.

Today she realizes that she was used as cheap labour to fuel the Thai economic miracle. Her work was hard, and the wage of less than $210 a month was far from sufficient as the cost of living continued to rise. She shared a room in Bangkok with three of her fellow-workers. Most of what she earned went on rent, food and fares to work, so that only three times a year could she send half a month's pay to her parents. She is proud of having caught up on her secondary school education at Sunday classes. But at twenty-nine years of age, she is already seen as 'past it' and will probably not be able to find another factory job. 'I worked for them for ten years and was then just kicked out, as if I wasn't worth a thing.'

When the company closed down, forty women workers at Eden started picketing the government building in Bangkok. Yaowapa intends to keep on fighting for compensation: 'Thailand is a democracy, after all. These companies shouldn't just be allowed to destroy their workers' lives.' But the prospects are not good. The government is not ready to listen to small-time losers like the women from Eden. Since 1996 2 million people have lost their job from one day to the next, in thousands of companies. For after years of high growth averaging 8 per cent or so, the Thai economy has been in sharp decline, with export industry undercut by cheaper countries, currency and share prices in free fall, the finance and property markets in ruins, and countless small and medium-sized firms out of business. The government troubles itself over the major bankruptcies, not over a 'forum of the poor' and its pickets outside parliament. Indeed, these are seen as standing in the way of globalization.

The government hopes that the rural economy will absorb those who have been made redundant in the cities. Certainly many have returned to where they originally came from, once they were no longer able to afford the high cost of living in Bangkok. But the meagre proceeds of agriculture, which drove Yaowapa Donsae and so many others to leave the land in the first place, are still not enough to assure a living for their families. In many cases, a period in the city has aroused in women a desire to go into business themselves, perhaps by opening a village store. They lack the start-up capital, however, not having been able to save it during those years of exile working in Bangkok.

Agents are now roaming the north-east to hire these returnees as home-workers for clothing and electronics companies. Middlemen supply the material to their homes and come to pick up the half-finished products. The women earn only a fraction of their factory wage in Bangkok, and they have no work contract or employment rights. Unlike men in a similar position, who consider the lay-off as a personal fault and a severe insult and initially refuse any work they consider unworthy, women take up any opportunity to make some money, because they feel responsible for the feeding of their family. Some are recruited as fresh supplies for the international sex industry; others emigrate with new hopes of finding Eden.

Trampling People Down – Just Do It

What does the Borussia Dortmund football club have in common with Michael Jordan and a Vietnamese woman called Le Thi? They all work for Nike. But that is the only thing they share. For in 1996, whereas Jordan made $20 million for advertising work that was not really that arduous, Le Thi earned less than $500 for a great deal of hard work. And the corporation whose logo has made it truly the goddess of victory had a turnover of $6.5 billion in the same year, well ahead of its rivals Reebok and Adidas.

Le Thi produces sports shoes for Nike at the Sam Yang factory not far from Ho Chi Minh City. Sam Yang, a South Korean firm, made the headlines in Vietnam in April 1996, when a twenty-nine-year-old Korean manageress went berserk on discovering pieces of material in the factory garbage. She summoned fifteen Vietnamese forewomen before her and hit one of them over the head with a shoe. In Vietnamese culture it is one of the worst humiliations to hit someone on the head, especially with the sole of a shoe that is meant to collect dust from the street. So unthinkable was it that a thousand women employed at Sam Yang immediately downed tools. The manageress excused herself by saying that such disciplinary action would be 'no big deal' in South Korea. But public opinion and the government supported the workers' protests, and she was forced to leave the country.

Draconian punishments of one kind or another are nevertheless part of daily life in the factories where young Vietnamese women stitch together shoes for Nike, Adidas and Reebok. Nearly all the plants belong to South Korean or Taiwanese companies doing contract work for Nike, and they have exported the crude methods of regimentation characteristic of South Korea's industrialization of the 1960s and 1970s. Nike itself does not produce any shoes: it merely designs and markets the products.

To stand in the sun, to be kept moving round the factory in the midday heat, to kneel in front of superiors, to have one's mouth plastered up for talking too much, to drink water only twice or go to the toilet only once in an eight-hour shift – you are continually reminded of a punishment camp when you read the list of collective sanctions recorded in May 1997 by a representative of the US-based Vietnam Labor Watch during a tour of Nike's suppliers in Vietnam. In addition to these degrading tactics, the women were forced to do months of overtime and did not even receive the minimum monthly wage of $40.

'It's simply terrible,' Nike's press spokeswoman McClain Ramsey commented on the catalogue of abuses of human and labour rights. 'Nike is outraged that things like that could happen.' The responsibility is supposed to lie with the management of the firms in question, not with the corporation in the United States that hands out the contracts. In 1992, under pressure from public opinion, Nike already issued a code of conduct to improve working conditions in the Asian sports shoes industry, and now it simply washes its hands of the matter. The guidelines underlying its relations with Asian contractors refer in the main to the observation of national labour law. A thousand inspectors, mostly from the US firm Ernst & Young, are working full-time on the question in Asia, claims Nike's PR man Keith Peters. The company has also had its code of conduct printed in nine languages and distributed to the various factories. 'We look after our consumers, and we look after the people who produce our products,' he asserted in Bonn in September 1997. 'Nike treats its shoes better than its workers,' countered the US campaign for workers' rights.

Vietnam Labor Watch gets Vietnamese women workers to send it their pay-slips on a regular basis, so that it can check whether the minimum wage and overtime are being paid. Often the women have a sum docked from their pay because of 'mistakes' – for example, if a needle breaks while they are engaged in sewing. Huong Thi Khanh, a trade unionist at Sam Yang in Vietnam, reported that conditions in her factory had not significantly improved a year after the incident mentioned before. The women still had no contract, and the South Korean guards unyieldingly forced them to raise output. 'We often complain to the foremen that we are not machines. We are human beings.'[9]

Nike's stylish shoes are produced in thirty countries and in 350 factories, more than four-fifths of them in Asia. A total of 400,000 people – 90 per cent of them women – are employed in cobbling together the sporting status symbol in Asia, and of these more than two-thirds are in Indonesia and China. Phil Knight, one of the company's founders and its current boss, does not tire of stressing that Nike contracts helped to launch the economic miracle in South Korea and Taiwan some twenty years ago. Now it will help to lead China, Indonesia and Vietnam 'out of poverty'.[10]

Output is highest, however, in the shelter afforded by poverty and authoritarian regimes. Since the wages do not cover even the bare necessities of life, the women workers have to do overtime to make ends meet. In 1993, when the unionized workforce went on strike at Lotus Footwear (a South Korean company operating in the Bataan free-trade zone in the Philippines), the government sent in the police and army. In China strikes are forbidden, and the government has the right to take action against strikers. Yuen in China, with a workforce of 40,000, is by far the world's largest sports shoes factory and supplies all the leading brands. At the factory run by the South Korean company Kukje in Bandjaran, Java, the daily norm per worker was raised in 1996 from 200 to 300 (which obviously involved a lot of extra overtime), so that new orders from Nike could be met.[11] In April 1997 10,000 employees stopped work at another shoe factory working for Nike in Jakarta, when it tried to avoid paying the recently increased minimum wage. In September 1997 Nike broke off its business relations with four Indonesian companies, ostensibly because they did not want to pay the same wage rise. The campaign for workers' rights suspects that Nike will now switch these contracts to China.

The history of the sports shoes industry in Asia is similar to that of the textile industry. Phase One in the 1970s: selective production in South Korea, Taiwan and Hong Kong. Phase Two: production off-shored to the Philippines, Thailand and Indonesia. Phase Three: relocation to China and Vietnam, together with the growth of informal and flexible forms of employment (already 50 per cent of women producing sports shoes in the Philippines are temporary employees).

The greater the pressure on production costs, the more money is squandered on marketing. For example, Niketown on New York's 57th Street – one of Nike's top ten outlets in the United States – is not just a shop but a synthetic all-round experience. Round the corner from Disney World, Coca-Cola and Tiffany's, Nike lures hordes of young people with a combination of sport and high-tech, sound bombardment and cartoon films both on video monitors and on a screen stretching over three floors of the building. Every display of sports kits has a different acoustic and optical backdrop: a rally between Monica Seles and Mary Joe Fernandes, a dribbling action by a basketball star, running and jumping by Olympic athletes, rap and techno music. And always yells of victory, over and over again. Hundreds of photographs of stars, including such famous names as Steffi Graf and Michael Schumacher, insistently imply that those who succeed do so thanks to Nike. Among the customers who watch the explanations about the pivots and air-cushions of various kinds of shoe on the huge screen, or who call up a computer simulation of the optimal shoe for their own feet, the percentage of young, black, muscular men is conspicuously large.

But in front of Niketown, this temple of victory, there are often embarrassing demonstrations to recall those who belong to the Nike family without in any sense being victors. Of the $70 dollars that a customer may pay over the counter, the women workers in Asia receive only 3.9 per cent in their wage-packet. Around a half is swallowed up by the trade. The embarrassment was even greater in the autumn of 1997, when an anti-Nike campaign culminated in the piling up of innumerable cast-off Nike shoes in front of Niketown. The young protesters meant this to show that they no longer wanted to wear Nike shoes, now that they knew the conditions under which they were produced.

Under this kind of pressure, Nike commissioned a report from the former US ambassador to the United Nations, Andrew Young. He spent nine whole days travelling through China, Vietnam and Indonesia, had each of his conversations with Nike employees translated, found nothing but good working conditions, and did not inquire whether workers were receiving the minimum wage.

Although Young produced a glossy brochure full of smiling women workers, a protest campaign has been spreading from the United States as far as Australia and Finland – not because Nike shoes are produced under worse conditions than those prevailing at other shoe or clothing companies, but because Nike plays a special role as the market and image leader. Women's organizations in the United States reacted with particular fury when Nike mounted a series of TV ads in autumn 1997 to convince women that, if they wanted to be strong, healthy and independent, they had to do sport with Nike shoes on their feet.

The French sports shoes campaign *Agir Ici* has made the following calculation: 'If Nike were to reduce its publicity and promotion budget by just 3.5 per cent, it could double the pay of all employees working for Nike contractors in China and Indonesia.' And for its part, the Swiss-based Berne Declaration concluded in its 'Let's Go Fair' campaign that if a doubling of wages were passed on to customers, they would have to pay only an extra three francs on a pair of shoes costing 150 francs.[12]

Hollow Firms, Quota Hopping and 'Swallow' Companies

In December 1996 there was a strike in Cambodia for the first time since the country began to open up. Female textile workers were protesting against their starvation wages and their long hours of overtime without a day off. In Vietnam, a total of 3000 employees went on strike in 1994, but in 1996 12,000 women workers in Ho Chi Minh City alone put up a fight against wage-cuts and compulsory overtime. In Bangladesh, unionized women workers have been struggling since 1995 for one day off a week and a shortening of the working day.

Those who wound their way through the streets of Ho Chi Minh City, Phnom Penh or Dhaka were supposed to be the winners in the global market. For they have what many others would like to have: a job. The Vietnamese women workers are entitled to a monthly minimum wage of $40, a medium-grade civil servant earns $29, and a woman in a small local workshop makes around $11.50.

While these women protest at being overworked, others in South Korea, Taiwan and Thailand complain about the 'outsourcing' whereby big factories increasingly shut their gates and hand over to subcontractors in the informal sector. In outwork and backyard production, women toil under even more wretched conditions than in the factories: minimum wages, work safety and environmental protection can be more easily circumvented; the workers are isolated and hard for trade unions to reach; and there is no trace at all of health provision, maternity leave or other social protection. Here children can be used without anyone noticing, as can illegal immigrants. Informalization of the work process goes hand in hand with child labour.

All this means that the global conveyor-belt is becoming ever longer. The leading brands are, in fact, 'hollow firms'. They do not have factories of their own: they design goods, get others to produce them, and then take care of the marketing. In the industrialized countries of the North, producers have increasingly become traders.

Typically, the company will start by faxing or e-mailing its design and a production contract to, let's say, a Taiwanese corporation. This corporation then awards subcontracts to a number of Vietnamese and Indonesian concerns, which in turn distribute parts of production among local agents and small businesses in various provinces. The middlemen take the material to villages, where small family units or homeworkers finally complete the order. At the end of this production chain, women account for 70 per cent of the workforce in the textile sector, and as much as 90 per cent in the electrical goods industry. The rule of thumb is that the more decentralized and closer to home a job is, the lower is the wage, the less the control over working conditions, and the weaker the union organization.

The flexibilization and informalization of labour are ongoing strategies to lower production costs, in a situation where total wage-costs have been rising and trade unions demand more rights. In Vietnam private businesses do not want to take on board the labour rights of the socialist economic and women's policy, nor do they want to bear the additional costs for shorter working hours before and after childbirth, for maternity leave or time off to look after sick children. The informalization of certain stages of production provides the scope for evasive manoeuvres.

Women may, for example, be asked to work only at peak times, hireable and fireable at the employer's whim. It no longer even seems necessary to give them a contract in such cases. Just-in-time production is performed under high pressure when orders come in at short notice. It is expected that the female workforce will always be available and on call, as if there were no work that needed to be done at home and with the family. No heed is ever paid to this second occupation of women, and no support is ever given to children's crèches.

Awarders of contracts such as Triumph or Quelle, Hennes & Mauritz exert ruthless price pressure and are 'directly responsible for low wages, child labour and union bans', says Tony Tujan, director of the IBON research centre in Manila. It is current practice to have a Philippine firm design an article of clothing, to ask for a quote from Chinese producers, and then to put pressure on the Philippine firm to produce the item below that price. The producers pass on the price pressure to subcontractors, who apply it in turn to women workers. The producers' low prices mean that traders can enjoy very high profit margins. A pullover that the Otto mail-order firm buys in the Philippines for a little over $5 is advertised in its catalogue for nearly thirty.[13]

International cut-throat competition has accelerated the growth of subcontracting and temporary labour in the export-oriented clothing and electronics sectors. The sweatshop economy is spreading again. Labour organization is now decentralized and broken up among many small independent units. In 1995, according to the International Confederation of Free Trade Unions (ICFTU), 200 million people around the world worked in firms supplying export industry, whereas only 4.5 million were employed in various free production zones in sixty countries. To these should be added twenty or so special economic areas in China, with a labour force estimated between 14 and 40 million.[14]

Flexible employment structures were initially seen as 'female', but now 'male' industries are subject to the same imperative. Guy Standing of the International Labour Organization spoke in 1989 of a global trend to 'feminization through flexible labour'. In 1996 he modified his thesis and argued that, although the feminization of employment was continuing, flexibilization increasingly affected men as well as women.[15] The labour market is thus becoming insecure for both women and men, and the myth of the male breadwinner may be finally consigned to the dustbin of history.

At the same time, the processing industry in newly developing countries is stuck midway between low-wage manufacturing and the high-tech age. Rationalization is taking place not only through informalization but also through automation – the one being labour-intensive, the other capital-intensive. This restructuring process is especially characteristic of the employment market in South Korea and Thailand.

As in the first technological revolution that followed the early phase of industrialization, technology here displaces women. Men and machines lead a tandem existence in industrial history. The stonewash-machines in Indonesian clothing factories are operated by men, as are the knitting-machines in Indian Tirrupur or the cutting-machines in Bangladesh. Wherever capital-intensive production displaces labour-intensive methods, women shrink as a proportion of the numbers in employment. In South Korea, for example, women make up 62.7 per cent of those working in small businesses with four employees or less. In the early 1990s the pro-portion was down by 10 per cent to 29 per cent in firms with more than ten employees, and a mere 5.8 per cent in big enterprises with a large technological component.[16] In the traditionally female industries of Mexico, Singapore and Mauritius, the proportion of women has fallen since the mid-1980s from 80 per cent to 60 per cent.[17] Where automation, rationalization and downsizing are taking place, men are preferred to remain as the core workforce. Thus, the quantitative advance that women made in employment is now being lost in the transition to capital-intensive production, or else informalization means that, in most cases, their work is no longer capable of supporting them. The winners of yesterday or today will already be losers again tomorrow.

In the 1980s the axis of the South Korean economy was shifted from light to heavy industry in order to secure its competitive advantages. Public infrastructural development and various state subsidies supported the (typically male) steel, motor and engineering industries, and increasingly also communications technologies, fibre optics and precision synthetics. In December 1996 the South Korean parliament quietly took a further step down the same road, with new labour legislation that removed some protection against dismissal, permitted more flexible forms of labour, longer hours and the use of strike-breakers – measures deemed necessary to strengthen the country's competitiveness on the world market and to boost the already ample profits of the *chaebol*, the giant mixed corporations, in a situation where annual growth had slowed from 10 per cent to 6.8 per cent and export quotas were declining.

South Korea's unions responded with a four-week strike. Media photo-graphs focused on angry workers in the automobile sector or in heavy industry and shipbuilding. But nurses in the hospitals of Seoul, women workers in the textile and electrical goods industries and female bank employees fought equally against flexibilization of the labour market and the reversal of hard-won gains. Men saw the dream of lifelong full employment being dashed to pieces – a dream women had never dreamt in the first place. The curtailment of workers' rights is the price demanded by global competition: less security for workers makes corporate profits more secure.

Companies that are now leaving South-East Asia because of rising production costs find a number of advantages in the countries of Central America. Not only can they provide a surplus of cheap labour at a wage between 17 cents and $1.70 an hour; they also offer backdoor entry to the North American market. Half of Guatemala's textile exports to the United States, for example, are produced by South Korean companies. After Korean and Taiwanese companies had used up their national quotas for the US market, they turned their gaze towards countries such as Guatemala or El Salvador that did not fully realize their access potential, and settled down there. This is known in the technical literature as 'quota hopping'.[18]

The preferential access of Central America and the Caribbean to the US market involves the outsourcing of certain phases of production from the United States itself. Thus, ready-cut pieces of clothing are exported to Guatemala, where they are stitched together before being shipped back north. In colonial times *maquila* was the name given to money that a miller received for the grinding of flour; that is, for a part of the food production process. This is why the name *maquila* industry is now used for the assembling of half-finished goods into three-quarters or wholly finished items for export.

In Mexico, the first *maquilas* were already being established in the mid-1960s near the border with the United States. In Guatemala and El Salvador, the first export-processing zones appeared in the 1970s. Such initiatives lured foreign investors to the countries of the South, and the 'new international division of labour' spread through the development of export industries from Mexico through Tunisia to Sri Lanka. Nevertheless, the export sector remained an enclave in the context of an economic policy which, in Central and South America at least, centred upon import substitution and general promotion of the internal market. But then the credit trap landed country after country in the vice-like grip of the World Bank and the International Monetary Fund. Foreign currency had at all costs to flow more abundantly into the state coffers.

As the restructuring of the 1980s brought about the fateful neoliberal turn, the export sector became the hub of the new economic policy. In 1989 the Guatemalan government started offering export firms a tax and duty holiday, and after 1992 Violeta Chamorro's deeply indebted government in Nicaragua took up millions more in loans in order to expand its 'las Mercedes' free-trade zone. *Maquila* industry is today the region's largest employer.

In El Salvador, Honduras and Guatemala, the US development agency

AID functioned as a midwife for foreign investors and export producers. It built up infrastructure and laid pro-business foundations for the enlistment of foreign capital. For US-AID, job creation in the backyard of the United States is also an attempt to reduce migration pressure further north.

The export-processing zones in El Salvador look like army barracks, an extraterritorial area well fenced-in and guarded. Their attraction lies in the special regime as far as taxes, duties and administrative obstacles are concerned. Further sweeteners come in the shape of exemption from labour legislation, troublesome unions and environmental regulations. But the more that import and export duties in general have been removed through trade liberalization, and the more that bureaucratic hurdles and labour laws have been dismantled and tax incentives introduced for corporate profits, the more do the enclaves themselves lose their purpose. Entire regions – Mexico's whole border area, for example, since the creation of NAFTA – and even entire countries such as Singapore, Hong Kong or Mauritius have now been turned into free-trade zones. This great freedom for 'global players' is precisely what the twenty-nine OECD countries had in mind as they planned a multilateral investment agreement within the framework of the World Trade Organization. It is intended that foreign investors will actually have the right to invest on favourable terms in countries that are party to the agreement, and to avoid national legislation and regulation by the individual states.[19]

Maquila industry is supposed to ensure a 'link-up with globalization' and to promote development through technology transfer and various skill and employment effects – a kind of vitamin injection for domestic industry. In reality, however, liberalization and the resulting competition turn the screws on local sectors such as the clothing industry. Cheap mass-produced goods from Asia and old clothes from the United States flood the internal market. Local producers are unable to compete and can do nothing other than become suppliers for the *maquilas*. In Guatemala, the textile industry is already largely made up of small supply workshops and family sewers. Thus, on the hierarchically restructured world market, whole economies and regions change from self-sufficiency to externally-driven supply roles, while women become temporary and ancillary workers for distant markets with no legal rights.

Enterprises in the export-processing zones naturally seek to lower their costs as much as possible through flexibilization and the avoidance of social and ecological responsibilities. Women workers are often laid off before Christmas so that no seasonal bonus has to be paid, or before the birth of a child in order to avoid payment during maternity leave. In the *maquila* factories of Mexico, women do not dare protest against pregnancy-testing as a condition of employment, nor against questioning about their sexual behaviour, birth control practices or monthly cycles. Domestic employment, which is their only other alternative, is worse paid and comes with even less social protection. Most women are single parents or the main providers for their family, and so they put up with the humiliating checks on their body.[20]

Although a number of countries have legislated for sickness benefit and social security, women workers often find out in case of need that their company has simply not passed on the contributions deducted from their pay. Workers who fall ill may well be refused a doctor's visit. Thus, in March 1995 a seamstress in El Salvador died of appendicitis because she was not allowed to call a doctor to see her. In Mexico, where the social security system is partly financed by employers, the growing number of work accidents has recently led to a rise in their contributions. Therefore many firms try to hush up any accidents.[21]

The free-trade zone is yesterday's model. Today the mode of production is itself informal. If a trade union in Central America vigorously demands an improvement in wages and labour rights, the company can always pack up and head somewhere else – like a swallow. Women on unpaid maternity leave may be sacked or laid off. Sometimes a whole shed is emptied in a 'Night and Fog' operation, and the machines turn up a few days later in the hands of a subcontractor. Companies readily engage in cowboy-style poaching for cheap female labour.

The Third World in the First

In New York's Garment District, just behind the splendour of Fifth Avenue, time seems to have stood still – at least from the first floor up. On the ground floor are the storerooms for materials and accessories and the wholesale display rooms, fully air-conditioned, spick and span. As you move up the dilapidated high-rise buildings, however, you encounter the sewing parlours and halls of hundreds of small and large producers. The closely-packed employees sit bent over sewing-machines in the sultry air, hardly different from their colleagues in Bangladesh. The 25,000 people employed in the Garment District follow the usual gender division of labour and, in most places, are strictly segregated along ethnic lines. Men work on the design patterns, materials or cutouts on the upper floors, and other men load the clothing orders into giant articulated lorries; but it is overwhelmingly women who sit at the machines. Owners of Chinese firms hire Chinese women, Latinos employ Chicanas. For most of them, it is evidently their first job in the land of unlimited possibilities; they speak little or no English. At the minimum wage of $4.75 an hour, they work six days a week and eight, nine or ten hours a day, according to the state of the order book. Every building here is a one-world house, with the First World on the ground floor and the Third World above.

In the western states it is the same as in the east. In California, south-east of Los Angeles, nearly half a million immigrants from Mexico and Central America work for the lowest wages in the food, textile and furniture sectors. Many of the 150,000 female immigrants are on piece-rates with no tax or insurance, working in garage workshops that the big dealers play off against one another. What is special about this region is that the various local authorities have the constitutional power to pass fiscal, labour and environmental legislation of their own. Thus 48,000 people work but only ninety adults live in Vernon, a place whose local authority can issue laws that create extremely good conditions for profit. It is the Wild West within capitalism.[22]

Economists always used to describe the informal sector as a discontinued model characteristic of 'underdeveloped' economies in the South. Far from disappearing, however, it is booming more than any other branch of economic activity – not only in the countries of the South, but also in the industrial heartlands where the formal sector is evaporating in the heat of competitive relocation. The Third World exists in the First: informal and flexible, in sweatshops, garages and backyards, often staffed by new im-migrants. Homeworking – for example, as ancillary work for the clothing sector or for electronics or precision engineering – is a kind of black hole in the industrialized economies, with piece-rates equivalent to much less than the legal minimum wage. Women are often offered loans on favourable terms to purchase a sewing-machine of their own; they then have to cover all the electricity and repair costs.

'Homeworking', the ILO tersely states, 'is women's work almost by definition.'[23] Far from dying out in the industrialized countries, it is experi-encing a renaissance. Everyone knows why the United Kingdom stoutly refused to adopt the ILO Convention on homeworking in June 1996: homeworkers there do not have the same basic rights as other kinds of labour, and some earn as little as 45p an hour. In Australia, where the whole textile and footwear industry is organized around homeworking, it is estimated that companies farm out 75 per cent of their production. Sometimes homeworkers slave away more than twelve hours a day and seven days a week, for an hourly rate of around US$1.75.[24]

In Amsterdam there are several hundred small workshops that employ illegal immigrants to do sewing work. Clothing manufacturers have also returned to London, Paris, Rome and other big European cities, so that they can react as fast as possible to fashion changes and fluctuations in demand. 'Rolling orders' is the name for these high-value additions outside the regular spring and autumn collections. The 'new clothing industry', based on homeworking, is often organized by small firms run by immigrants – Turks and Moroccans in the case of the Netherlands. Both the owners and the supervisors are nearly always male. Their comparative advantage is the cheap supply of female homeworkers from their own section of the population. Especially for older-generation immigrants, homeworking is the only possible source of income. Besides, cheap mass production is meanwhile clattering along in the low-wage countries.

Unlike most immigrants, white homeworkers in England often have a good education but are unable to combine paid employment outside the home with the care of their children. Many women initially employed full-time at a large electronics firm in West Yorkshire switch to part-time or home-based work when the children come. They are just as skilled as the regular workforce but more of a bargain for the company.[25]

A German firm has telephone parts assembled by former 'Gastarbeiter' families who have become homeworkers back in their native Greece. There the sewing together of pieces of fur used to be 'skilled' male work, but now that it is done at home by women it is considered only 'semi-skilled' and is paid accordingly. The trend to homeworking can also be observed among men as the demand for cheap, flexible labour and the long-term unemployment make themselves felt.

Along with this domestication of industry, the global workbench is being stretched back from the South to the North, and with it come lower wages and a reduction in labour rights. Moreover, electronics and textile corporations from the South-East Asian tiger economies are themselves building production sites in Europe. They want to gain greater access to the European market and to have a finger constantly on its pulse. Their favourite areas are the highly subsidized 'zones' in Ireland, Scotland and England, where state support may contribute between 20 per cent and 35 per cent of investment.

In a strip of land between Glasgow and Edinburgh, all the big names in the electronics, computer and microchip industries of America, Asia and Europe have been establishing a presence in the last few years, from IBM through Samsung to NEC. Labour is in plentiful supply, given that the local steel and shipbuilding industries collapsed some years ago and left behind an unemployment rate of 15 per cent. Most of the newly created jobs are temporary or casual, controlled by specialist agencies and contractors. With no more security of employment or other rights to worry about, the high-tech investors find a veritable El Dorado of flexibility from which to supply the European market with PCs, microwaves, fax-machines, monitors and television tubes.

Similarly, in the vicinity of Newcastle, 450 companies with a total investment of £20 billion have created 60,000 highly flexible jobs. Siemens produces semiconductors here with a workforce of 1800, at 50 to 70 per cent of average German wage-costs. It is mainly women who have gained from this neo-industrialization: three times more men than women are now without a job in the region. The unions appear to be tamed, and investors are content that there are far fewer protests and strikes than in the past.

A cartoon in a British newspaper has two doors: one for men, one for women. On the first is written 'Pub', on the second 'Job'. If women here are so clearly the job-winners, it is because their hourly wages are a quarter less than men's and because they put up with part-time work without grumbling. They are quite simply more flexible. In booming Ireland, the 'Celtic tiger' where women have half of the new jobs, the industrial development authority justifies the high proportion of part-time and fixed-term jobs by 'the new levels of flexibility required if companies are to be competitive and profitable'.[26] In Wales, a number of activities already pay less than in South Korea.[27] The global conveyor-belt has come full circle.

Pushing Emancipation or Forced Labour?

Susan Joekes and other economists think it indisputable that no other group has profited as clearly as young women from the growth of world trade and production for export. Liberalization, in their view, offers women good chances to become free and independent economically; they are the winners of globalization.[28] 'Market forces and the policy choices underlying them have propelled women into a decisive position in much of the global and national economy,' concluded the United Nations on the occasion of the Fourth World Conference on the Status of Women in 1995 in Beijing.[29]

Economists often make a simple equation between women's employment and women's liberation, so that entry into the jobs market means access to a relatively secure income and, in principle, to a better life. 'An income of one's own' is thus seen as a chance to shake off patriarchal oppression.

Now, it is true that pay-day is the first time that many young women have money of their own in their hands. In Bangladesh, for example, the feeling of no longer depending on a man for food and clothing gives female textile-workers a new self-esteem. It is not only the way in which women see themselves that changes, but also the way others see them. 'Women are being transformed from representing economic burdens on their families into economic assets,' considers Naila Kabeer. At first, men in the village used to throw stones after the women workers as a sign of their disapproval, but now the earning of money has brought the women a bonus in terms of male respect. Their marriage value has increased. Some of them earn three times as much as an agricultural labourer. Earnings of their own, agrees economist Nasreen Khundker, 'empower women and increase their status by making possible the renegotiation of implicit intra-household gender contracts'.[30]

The judgement of society is ambivalent: on the one hand, women are respected because they make money; on the other hand, they are scorned because they offend against norms of seclusion by being out late in the evening without a male escort. Outside family control, they are immediately suspected of immorality and manoeuvred into the defensive position of having to prove their honour. Female industrial workers in other Asian countries also complain that they are accused of loose morals simply because they live a long way from the family. To ward off this suspicion back home, women often declare their most emphatic adherence to traditional norms and values. They stress that wage-labour and a relatively independent life are perfectly compatible with the morality they have brought with them to the city, and they violently dissociate themselves from women with 'loose morals'.

Young women who have been under the rigid control of their family and village do experience the way to the factory more as culture shock than as liberation. The principles of strictly regimented, Taylorized wage-labour in the proximity of men are fundamentally different from the communicative, integrated culture of work in the village, based upon strict gender segregation. Nevertheless, the industrial–capitalist mode of production uses precisely what is specific to the cultural disciplining of women: namely, their relative submissiveness. It is steered into new forms of work, but at the same time it is also reinforced.

This is why women sociologists in Bangladesh see the move from the village to the world of the factory as double-edged. They agree that it brings about a 'cultural change' or even a 'social revolution'. But Dina Siddiqi, for example, argues that the passage from a peasant to a proletarian culture involves the replacement of one form of regimentation and domination by another form, and that a convergence takes place between capitalist and cultural disciplining. There is a clear cultural break, yet women hold on to the morality and values of their village and family.[31]

Mobility and new space for action certainly contain opportunities, but they also introduce a sense of insecurity. Women textile-workers in Bangladesh break with the notion of lifelong male 'support'; they live in the city and move around without male guardians, their fellow-workers serving as protection and a kind of substitute family. The factory is perceived by the women as a protected area, the street as a danger zone.

It is by no means always true that the women can dispose of the income they earn. Female industrial workers in Honduras report that on pay-day their husbands wait to collect at the factory gate. Some men have even stopped work since their wives started earning money.[32] Many of the married women working at Eden in Bangkok were obviously being used in the same way; their husbands abandoned them when they lost their job and could no longer keep the family.

Women's wage-labour outside the home does not, however, entail much change in the family division of labour. Men still get out of doing the housework, and women find themselves with a dual burden. Every evening in Bangkok, the air outside the factory gates and workshops buzzes from the engines of countless mopeds. Young daredevils manoeuvre their way through the city's endless car and bus jams to ferry their wives home as quickly as possible, so that they can immediately get down to preparing a delicious evening meal. Married textile-workers in Bangladesh are happy that their husbands take on part of the housework. But most of them have to put in at least an hour and a half around the home, often after an exhausting twelve-hour day at the factory, and then are lucky if they get six hours of sleep – significantly less than their male fellow-workers. The result is a permanent weakening of their health.[33] Trade unionist Rosa Virginia Hernández from El Salvador reports that many women neglect their home and children because of the chronic strain imposed upon them: 'Husbands won't stand for it if we can take so little care of the home. So it is not surprising that 80 per cent of women in the *maquiladoras* are without a husband.'[34]

In the factory, too, the traditional allocation of gender roles has not broken down. Men work as supervisors and service the machines, while women tackle nimbly and diligently the labour-intensive stages of production. True, the World Bank considers that 'growth benefits women at large' and 'gender differentials in employment and pay are narrowing much faster in developing countries than they did in industrialized countries'.[35] But the wage differential remains between 30 and 40 per cent, and women still have little chance of further education or promotion within low-paid sectors of industry. Segmentation of the labour market into skilled and unskilled, well-paid and low-paid, is not breaking down. Indeed, the gender difference in pay is actually increasing over time.[36] Seniority rules, which reward length of service, often apply only to men and not to women.

Women's submissiveness in the factory does not mean that they accept the miserable working conditions. They are subjects with their own action strategies, even if they are also objects of capitalist exploitation. Often they take the first steps in developing subversive ways of fighting back. Thus, employers in Bangladesh complain that women workers hand in their notice and leave for another company precisely when the order-book pressure is greatest. In many other countries, a few years are all it takes for young women to come up with new forms of organization and resistance. In the 1970s in South Korea, for example, they engaged in conflicts over the freedom to organize democratic unions independent of the state. Their courage and militancy made them the driving force of struggles for better working conditions and human rights within the factory.

Experience soon taught them, however, that the male-led unions were geared to wage struggles and not sufficiently sensitive or combative when it came to women's issues such as compulsory 'retirement' after marriage, protection of pregnant women and new mothers, or the availability of crèches. Works committees also failed to stand up for women in relation to sexism and violence at work. In the 1980s, therefore, women set up alongside the mixed unions a number of organizations of their own that also included part-timers and homeworkers.[37] Their first step was to get a washing-machine and childcare facilities that would allow women to partici- pate in meetings – something of which male unions never seem to think. In Nicaragua, El Salvador and Honduras, women workers also felt left in the lurch by the old male unions and decided to start up organizations of their own.

Overwork combined with generally poor conditions tends to burn women up within a short space of time. In Thailand, damage to health and to the capacity to coordinate eyes and hands means that women can no longer be 'effectively used' after just five years of work in industry;[38] while in Central America, women last an average of seven years in the *maquila* factories. Doctors in the Dominican Republic report that women workers in the free-trade zones suffer twice as many miscarriages as women engaged in other activities, and bear twice as many underweight children and three times as many with deformities.[39]

Job security is everywhere proving to be a mirage. In most cases, factory work is a transition stage that many women leave exhausted or even ill, and hardly any with filled pockets. Rarely do they gain any qualifications that will be of use elsewhere. For, in keeping with the Taylorization of work, they learn only isolated routines or movements without any wider training. In fact, most of them learn by watching and imitating other women. 'We have not been trained,' says Rosa Virginia Hernández from El Salvador. 'Necessity is our instructor.'

At the same time it can be seen everywhere that women's marriage strategies and family plans are changing. What Aihwa Ong observed of women working in Malaysian industry in the 1980s is now being repeated in Bangladesh and Cambodia: they marry later, have their first child later, and generally have fewer offspring. More reliable than their brothers in sending money back home, they subsidize their family's survival in rural areas and at least temporarily check the trend towards its impoverishment and loss of social standing.

These women, Ong sums up, are 'neither classic proletarians nor classic victims'.[40] The models by which individuals plan and shape their lives are clearly changing. There is greater freedom and opportunity in the tense space between new-industrial and old-patriarchal dominance. But export-oriented industrialization and economic growth do not offer women a secure future or a lasting victory over poverty; still less do they guarantee the hoped-for equality or decompose the power relations between the sexes.

In a balance-sheet drawn in 1995, the United Nations maintained that 'economic growth is a necessary ... but not a sufficient condition for women's advancement'. As a result of globalization and world market integration, 'women were able to gain more jobs than men while losing in terms of equal pay and quality of employment. Women's economic position did not improve relative to men and probably deteriorated.'[41]

Global Counterforce – or Globalization from Below

'Those who don't resist end up in the kitchen': this, a few years ago, was the graphic slogan taken up by German women fighting for their jobs. In the export industries of South-East Asia and Central America, women workers are more and more often experiencing the opposite: those who do resist end up in the kitchen. When women organize and protest against pathetic wages, health risks and sexual harassment, they find themselves being sacked and placed on the blacklist that does the rounds among employers. When they demand human dignity and security, production is farmed out to little shoestring outfits or a network of homeworkers, and the employers turn overnight into nomads and disappear. In the global market, transnational corporations are as flexible and mobile as quicksilver: it is extremely difficult to lay hold of them. Instead of the classical conflict between employer and employee, strikers now run up against a wall that then moves away from them.

Change through trade – a slogan used by German politicians and economists in relation to China and its human rights abuses – has not been occurring to the advantage of individual rights and liberties. On the contrary. Marsinah and Titi Sugiarti, two Indonesian women workers, lost their lives in mysterious circumstances when their commitment to labour rights brought them to someone's attention. Marsinah, who was tortured and raped before her murder in 1993, will always be honoured as a martyr of the Indonesian trade union movement. In 1996, according to a report of the International Confederation of Free Trade Unions, ICFTU, 'harassment, intimidation and death threats against union members sharply increased'.[42]

At the same time, the effects of liberalization and cut-throat competition on the global market were put on the backs of the labour force. Rights at work were undermined, health and environmental risks ignored, and the production process made more intense. A publicity campaign for US textile dealers in 1990 boasted: 'Rosa Martinez produces apparel for US markets on her sewing-machine in El Salvador. You can hire her for 57 cents an hour.' A year later the publicity had been slightly modified: 'You can hire her for 33 cents an hour.'[43]

In late 1996, when women in Cambodia took to the streets for the first time against slave-driving practices in the textile industry, thirty firms from Taiwan, Hong Kong and Malaysia immediately threatened to pull out of that bottom-wage country if the government did not protect their investments from the labour unrest. Similarly, women working at a British textile factory in the free-trade zone of Bataan in the Philippines kept up a year-long protest action for payment of the minimum wage. In response, production was switched to another factory where the women were less well organized. Also in the Philippines, the firm Temic Telefunken Micro-electronic (a subsidiary of Daimler-Benz) sacked 1500 employees after a strike for higher wages and simply took on a new workforce.[44]

Women trade unionists in El Salvador report that there is such a surplus of cheap labour on the local market that, as soon as a firm lays off a hundred women, five hundred start queueing at the gates to be taken on.[45] For fear of dismissal, the women working at an electronics factory in Thailand did not make a fuss about the levels of chemical pollution, even though they could get through their shift only with the help of strong painkillers, and even though some women there actually died in 1993. The lack of alternatives on the labour market robs them of the courage to resist.[46]

In the conditions of market globalization, localized union struggles prove to be impotent revolts from which companies can escape simply by switching location. Indeed, the accelerated mobility of capital means that labour disputes that remain purely local are often counterproductive; resistance and defensive measures must rather be internationalized. But what can put a stop to the downward spiral of workers' rights and to the sapping manoeuvres of various companies? Which international instruments can workers deploy against them?

One possible answer is that governments could take responsibility for regulation of the liberalized market. The International Labour Organization (ILO) can already point to a variety of wonderful conventions on the protection of workers' rights. Yet they have proved to be so many paper tigers. For not only do many governments refuse to ratify them; the ILO cannot invoke any sanction if the conventions are breached. Debate in the past few years has therefore focused on the introduction of social clauses such as the freedom to organize, no compulsory labour, no child labour and no job discrimination. Such clauses, it is argued, should be incorporated into international trade agreements, so that trade sanctions can be imposed in the case of violations.[47]

At the first ministerial meeting of the World Trade Organization, held in December 1996 in Singapore, the US government and the ICFTU claimed to be spearheading the attempt to build social clauses into the regulatory framework of WTO trade policy. The governments of Malaysia, Pakistan and India vehemently rejected this as a new form of imperialism and protectionism, on the grounds that the industrialized nations only wanted to keep at bay the competition from low-wage regions and to torpedo the competitive advantages of the countries of the South. Soon the Damocles sword of unemployment – the threat that millions of women would lose the jobs in world-market industries that they needed for survival – was being conjured up and denounced. A series of trade unions and non-governmental organizations from the South supported this position.

The interest of the industrialized countries in maintaining jobs and living standards, and in shutting competitors out of the market, obviously cannot be denied. Unilateral measures have also been taken for purely political purposes, without the agreement of countries affected. The United States, for example, has used trade sanctions to punish countries not to its liking such as Cuba and Nicaragua, but not others with an appalling human rights record such as Indonesia. When it is a question of multilateral accords, universal standards should be applied that also command the agreement of the producer countries. But the South's critics of social clauses argue that their particular cultures are based upon different values from those of the industrialized nations.

Günter Rexrodt, the German economics minister of the time, supported these cultural-relativist objections in Singapore: 'Social issues have something to do with the political order of nations and their social values as a whole. We should not support any confrontation over cultural and social values within the WTO.' The World Trade Organization, midwife and catalyst of neoliberalism, thus insisted on a fundamental separation between trade and social questions, and referred the latter to the ILO. There the newly developing countries of Asia again appeared on the scene and declared their opposition to any linking of trade with social clauses. They wanted nothing to do with any international regulation of labour rights.

This political stand, together with the growing role of transnational corporations as 'global players', entailed that demands for minimum social standards were directed at companies rather than at the contending governments. In the age of deregulation, it seems more effective to hold companies directly accountable. Since the early 1990s, US consumers' groups and human rights organizations, trade unions and church-related groups, have been pressing the multinationals into voluntary codes of practice that commit them to produce without recourse to child or penal labour, to permit trade unions, to place limits on the amount of overtime, to pay at least the minimum living wage, and to accept equal pay for equal work.

Levi's and Reebok made a start – out of fear that their image would be harmed and boycotts organized against them. Many others then followed suit, and corporations in the United States can no longer say that they are responsible for product quality but not for the quality of working conditions. The Sweatshop Watch Campaign supported by President Clinton is preparing to launch a 'No Sweatshop' quality mark with the argument that 'in our global economy human rights are as important as business rights'.

The crux, however, is the question of monitoring. Who will check on the spot whether minimum social standards are really being observed? This obviously cannot be left to the contracting parties or to specialist firms: in China, those who award the contract do not even have the right to inspect conditions on the ground. Trade unions and other independent associations within civil society must be involved in monitoring at local level, but so far only one firm has ever permitted this: GAP. Its consent was given when the National Labor Committee organized broadly-based solidarity among the American population with the trade union at GAP's supply firm, Mandarin, in the free-trade zone of San Marcos in El Salvador. As in the case of Eden in Bangkok, the Taiwanese bosses of Mandarin gave everyone a hard time and sacked the women when they founded a union in 1995. Under massive public pressure, GAP then signed an agreement on the independent monitoring of production conditions in El Salvador – a success for the consumers' movement and for the policy of cross-border union links.

In European countries, a Clean Clothes Campaign is currently trying to get firms to sign a social charter. It does not argue that European companies should pull out if suppliers in the South fail to respect workers' rights, for that would very soon lead to lay-offs and shutdowns. Its aim, rather, is an improvement in working conditions. The campaign relies on the power of consumers, who are asked to choose in future the goods and brands that will have been given a seal of approval for socially clean production.

Another form of pressure is the purchasing boycott. Thus, a 'Toykott' campaign calls for a boycott of toys from China – so far with very limited success only – and similar measures have been temporarily threatened against other products. The effectiveness of these campaigns is open to question, however, for if the consumers of a well-known brand switch to a cheaper and less familiar one, their purchases will probably be of goods that have been produced under even more degrading conditions.

Most workers in the relevant companies of the South are afraid of losing their job and therefore reject the idea of the purchasing boycott as a means of international pressure.[48] They call for consultation and agreements between campaigns in the North and the people concerned in the South. In Guatemala and Bangladesh, for instance, women trade unionists have also opposed campaigns in the United States against child labour and the employment of young girls. Of course, they know all too well that it is better for children to go to school than to slave for starvation wages at a sweatshop bench. But so long as their income is indispensable for their family's survival, the earning of money has to be the priority.

Most women's organizations support the principle of minimum social standards, on the grounds that women are especially affected by poor working conditions and are therefore in especially great need of regulation of the global employment market. Nandita Shah from Bombay argues that the rights of women workers should not be played off against the principle of national sovereignty, as the Indian unions tend to do.

But there is also scepticism on the part of some women. Angela Hale from Manchester, who, together with the organization Women Working Worldwide, has supported local struggles by women in export industries, has considerable reservations about the ICFTU campaign. Women's priorities, she points out, are often different from those of male workers and the male-dominated unions. When textile-workers in Bangladesh were asked what was their biggest problem at work, they said it was the journey home in the dark after hours of overtime. Job security, maternal rights, childcare and protection from sexual harassment were other of their major concerns, but none of these has yet found a place on the list of minimum standards.[49]

Minimum standards may be attainable in the formal sector. But it is incomparably more difficult to monitor their observation by subcontractors and local agents, in small supply workshops and homeworking contexts. Regulation of the informal sector would be all the more important for women, since it is there that most of them work. But the passing of social standards without an awareness of the interests and forms of employment of working women would tend to marginalize them still further.

The debate is only just starting on these issues in women's trade unions and international women's organizations. And even with the alliances across frontiers and economic blocs, women's and consumers' organizations are only just beginning to show support for the struggles of women workers in producer countries. Still, the new regional economic blocs are opening up various possibilities. Within NAFTA, new alliances have already come into being between Mexican trade unions and US networks of human rights groups, trade unions and consumers' organizations.

In the global marketplace, the cause of international women's solidarity requires new directions and new instruments. ILO conventions, investment rules, social clauses and voluntary undertakings by employers are not enough to disturb either the structures of the world economy or the gender inequality. All they can do is restrict the crudest injustices and social evils. These international means of protecting workers' rights must be combined with transnational cooperation among trade unions, consumers' and women's organizations, so that a countervailing force can be created against the increasingly uncontrolled power of the 'global players', and so that social and ecological limits can be set to the logic of the market. Such new alliances among the forces of civil society are all the more necessary because, according to ICFTU figures, trade unions have lost half their global membership in the last decade and suffered a decline in both effectiveness and credibility. Without countervailing forces that are at once stronger and more concentrated, neoliberal globalization of the labour market and commodity flows could be followed by a loss of rights all around the world.

Notes

1. United Nations (1995), pp. 19f.
2. Ibid., p. 48.
3. Documented in the immigration museum on Ellis Island, New York.
4. IPS (International Press Service), 20 November 1996.
5. *ila* (1995), p. 7; *epd-Entwicklungspolitik* 21, 1996, pp. 21f.
6. *Tageszeitung*, 3–4 February 1996; IPS, 3 April 1997, 12 May 1997; DGB (1997).
7. International Labour Organization (1996), *Globalization of the Footwear, Textile and Clothing Industries*, Geneva, p. 119.
8. Yung Whee Rhee, 'The Catalyst Model of Development: Lessons from Bangladesh's Success with Garment Exports', *World Development 1990*, 18/2, pp. 333–46.
9. *International Herald Tribune*, 24 June 1997.
10. IPS, 30 October 1996.
11. IPS, 15 April 1997.
12. Berne Declaration, *Let's Go Fair*, 1/97.
13. Südwind e.V. (1997).
14. IBFG (1996), p. 35; Pamela Dar and Jenny Säve-Söderbergh, 'Women and Men in the Era of Trade Liberalization and Globalization', *ICDA Journal* (1996), pp. 26ff.; DGB (1996a), 46, p. 14.
15. Guy Standing (1989); and 'Revisiting Global Feminization through Flexible Labour', speech at the Conference on Employment and Women, ICRW, The Hague, 18–19 September 1996.

16. Maria Rhie Chol Soon (1997), 'Das Ende der Sanftmut', *Frauensolidarität* 1, pp. 22ff.

17. Joekes (1995), p. 23.

18. See Ökumenisches Büro für Frieden und Gerechtigkeit (n.d.); Forschungs- und Dokumentationszentrum Chile-Lateinamerika (1996); and *ila* (1995).

19. At present, new rules and regulations for the elimination of 'trade constraints' are discussed within the World Trade Organization and the Transatlantic Economic Partnership. See: *Le Monde Diplomatique*, December 1998 and May 1999.

20. Human Rights Watch, *Women's Rights Project, Mexico*, 8/6, August 1996, pp. 2ff.

21. *ila* (1995), p. 9.

22. Ibid., p. 5; Edna Bonacich, 'The Labor Behind the Label – Die Arbeit hinter der Marke. Wie die "ModemacherInnen" in Los Angeles/USA arbeiten', in Musiolek (ed.) (1997), pp. 144–58.

23. *Soziales Europa: Heimarbeit in der EU*, supplementary issue 2, 1995, p. 67.

24. *Clean Clothes Newsletter* 7, February 1997, p. 14.

25. Sheila Rowbotham (1993), *Homeworkers Worldwide*, London; *Soziales Europa*, p. 71.

26. Denis O'Hearn, 'Free Trade and Workers' Rights: A Contradiction in Terms?', in Oxfam (1996b), p. 19.

27. Uwe Jean Heuser (1997), 'Oase für das Kapital', *Zeitpunkte* 1, pp. 80–5.

28. Susan Joekes, in *WIDE Bulletin* (1996), p. 21.

29. United Nations (1995).

30. Naila Kabeer (1995), 'Necessary, Sufficient or Irrelevant? Women, Wages and Intra-Household Power Relations in Urban Bangladesh', working paper no. 25, IDS, Brighton; Susan Joekes, 'Does Trade Liberalization Carry a Gender Price Tag?', in Oxfam (1996b), p. 26; Nasreen Khundker, 'Gender Issues in Export-based Industrialization in Bangladesh', paper prepared for CPD-UNRISD workshop, Dhaka, 27–28 October 1995.

31. Dina M. Siddiqi (1991), 'Discipline and Protect: Women Factory Workers in Bangladesh', *Grass Roots*, October–December, pp. 42–50.

32. Gabi Fischer, in Ökumenisches Büro für Frieden und Gerechtigkeit (n.d.), pp. 24f.

33. Pratima Paul-Majumder and Salma Chaudhuri Zohir (1995), 'Empowering Women: Wage Employment in the Garment Industry', *Empowerment*, 2, pp. 83–112.

34. *ila* (1985), p. 27.

35. Zafiris Tsannatos, 'Growth Helps, Inequalities Hurt and Public Policies Matter', speech at the Conference on Employment and Women, ICRW, The Hague, 18–19 September 1996.

36. Joekes (1995), p. v.

37. Chong-Sook Kang and Ilse Lenz (1992), *Wenn die Hennen krähen ... Frauenbewegungen in Korea*, Münster, pp. 107ff.; Maria Rhie Chol Soon (1997), 'Das Ende der Sanftmut'.

38. Rachel Kurian, 'Women, Employment and Poverty Alleviation', speech at the Conference on Employment and Women, ICRW, The Hague, 18–19 September 1996, p. 19.

39. IPS, 30 April 1997; IBFG (1996), p. 28.

40. Ong (1987), p. 99.

41. United Nations (1995), pp. 27–8.

42. International Confederation of Free Trade Unions (1997), *Annual Survey of Violations of Trade Union Rights 1997*, Brussels, pp. 5f.

43. Wee and Heyzer (1995), p. 22.

44. *Clean Clothes Newsletter* 7, February 1997, p. 19; Angela Hale, 'The Deregulated Global Economy', in Oxfam (1996a), p. 10; *Tageszeitung*, 3 April 1997.

45. *epd-Entwicklungspolitik* 5, 1997.

46. Sally Theobald, 'Employment and Environmental Hazard: Women Workers and Strategies of Resistance in Northern Thailand', in Oxfam *(*1996a), pp. 16–22.

47. DGB (1995c); Margareta Kulessa, 'Handelpolitische Sozialstandards zum Wohle der "Dritten Welt"?', *INEF Report* 12, 1995; Kreissl-Dörfler (1995).

48. See *epd-Entwicklungspolitik* 5, 1997.

49. Hale, 'The Deregulated Global Economy', p. 44; and 'The Rights of Women Workers in the Global Economy', in ICDA Journal (1996), pp. 10–17.

Postindustrial Work

Postindustrial society is a service society. The service sector is booming
and expanding like no other, with the finance market, data-processing and
tourism high up the growth ladder. The United States is in the vanguard
of this 'tertiarization of the economy', which accounts for 72 per cent of
all US employment as against a world average of 46 per cent.[1] Recently,
services have been booming even as an export sector – from insurance
through commercial cleaning to telephone sex. Bed-linen from German
hospitals is sent to Poland to be washed, while Polish women pick gherkins
on the other side of the River Oder for five marks an hour, and German firms have their computers serviced by engineers in India. Fierce
competition in the global market takes place not only over national telecommunications systems, but also over local transport services, refuse collection
and water supply. The value of cross-frontier services is already equal to
that of traded goods, but is growing at a much faster rate.[2] Whereas heavy
subsidies are necessary to keep parts of the 'material' economy afloat, the
'immaterial' and the 'virtual' economy are enjoying a definite boom.[3]

The world of services is everywhere mainly a women's world. Does this
mean that the service society is the great hope of equality for women? It
is true that expansion of this sector is the chief reason for any statistical
feminization of employment, and that in the EU, for example, it en-
compasses 79 per cent of all economically active women. Only 17 per cent
work in industry and 4 per cent in agriculture, with a downward trend in
both cases.[4]

Services have more and more developed into a female segment of the
European labour market, and globalization has in no way reversed this
process. Occupations continue to be allocated by gender with astonishingly
little change. Thus, in Germany 80 per cent of women are concentrated
in twenty-five of the 376 trades requiring an apprenticeship, and the
Federal Republic brings up the European rear in respect of the proportion
of women employed in 'male' occupations.

In Greece, Spain and Portugal, offices and administration departments were still overwhelmingly male in the early 1980s, but there too women have since taken the lion's share of jobs, as they had already done in the health sector, education and public employment. In the catering trade, too, they have been gaining ground through the spread of big, modern fast-food chains and the like, although in France and elsewhere in Southern Europe it is still mainly men who cook and wait at table.[5]

The changeover to a market economy in Eastern Europe is strengthening the gender division on the labour market. In Russia, at the end of the 1980s, women accounted for 60 per cent of highly skilled labour and were well represented in the natural sciences and engineering. But when the collapse of the state-socialist economy eliminated half of all industrial enterprises, the women formerly employed in them were offered retraining in the classical female services: physicists and chemists were pushed into becoming hairdressers, cosmeticians and secretaries.

So, has the rise of the service sector cleared the way for women to join the labour market? Yes, but … If we are to speak of increased employment, then the growth of 'atypical' forms must also be pointed out. Of course, this concept still takes lifelong full employment as the norm, from which part-time and temporary work are deviations. But in reality, various forms of temporary, casual and (seemingly) independent work are more and more becoming the norm as a result of world economic restructuring. Informalization and flexibilization, in services as well as in productive sectors, represent the future of paid labour.

These forms signal the end of the Fordist social contract, a deeply patriarchal model built around the breadwinner/housewife polarity. To his (male) workers, Ford promised a wage high enough to put their family on wheels, so that the 'normal labour relationship' would generate the purchasing-power necessary for industrial mass production. The premise, then, was lifetime employment and social security for the male industrial worker and breadwinner. Both of these conditions have now been overtaken by history: the vocabulary of full employment and a guaranteed job is destined for the economic and social archive of industrial nations.

Women are the pioneers of the new flexible forms of work, but men will be following in their trail. This is already evident in the 'jobs miracle' in the United States, with temporary staff and techno-nomads part of life even in highly skilled occupations.[6] A joke is doing the rounds that when President Clinton boasted at a campaign meeting of having created 8 million new jobs, a woman in the audience chipped in: 'Yes, and I've got three of them!' For it is a fact that 3.6 million women in the United States have more than one job, because one is not enough to live on. Individual patchwork and mixed economics, of a kind familiar from the countries of the South, is becoming a widespread way of making a living among the 'working poor' of the industrial heartlands.

Women in the service sector are the prototype of the stand-in worker: the 'temporary help' who is called in at busy times to the supermarket check-out; the telephonist who works at home taking mail orders and is expected to keep herself 'available' outside the agreed working time; or the Japanese air stewardess who is employed on a short-term contract and who earns only a quarter of a full-time employee's salary. In view of these 'unprotected working conditions', the Cologne sociologist Carola Möller calls the growth in female employment an 'illusory gain'.[7]

There are 5.3 million part-time jobs in Germany. Women make up 89 per cent of part-time workers, against a European average of 78 per cent. But in this respect the front-runner among industrialized countries is the Netherlands, where 37.4 per cent of all jobs are part-time. Bill Clinton recognized this at the G-7 summit held in June 1997 in Denver, when he invited the Dutch head of government Wim Kok to dinner to report on the success of the 'polder model'. The Dutch land reclamation on the labour market, the miracle of 100,000 new jobs created in 1996, is overwhelmingly due to a greater sharing out of jobs. In addition, the introduction of a two-day waiting period before sick pay can be claimed has lightened corporate liabilities by reducing wages and incomes, and cuts in welfare payments are also forcing the unemployed to consider jobs far below the level of their skills and previous pay. In all of this, the gender division remains intact: 66 per cent of economically active women work part-time, but only 16 per cent of men.

The growth of jobs in Britain is also largely based upon declining wages and social standards, and the replacement of fixed relations of employment with cheaper, temporary arrangements. More than two-thirds of the jobs added since 1993 have been part-time, and women account for 90 per cent of these.

National legislation has adapted to the deregulation of the employment market, relaxing the legal protection from dismissal in Spain, for example, or removing the ban on female night-time work in Japan. In December 1995, the European Court of Justice in Luxembourg ruled that insecure minor employment as well as Germany's DM620 jobs do not involve discrimination against women. Conservative estimates made by the Cologne Institute for Social Research and Social Policy put the number of these jobs at 5.6 million, involving 3.3 million women.[8] And since shops in Germany were permitted to stay open longer, the retail trade has further reduced its number of full-time employees and introduced more and more DM620 jobs. It has been calculated that 70 per cent of all saleswomen are employed on a less than full-time basis.

Does the need of the economy for flexibilization match women's interest in discontinuous work? Ex-Federal minister Claudia Nolte considered that part-time work was opening up new opportunities for women's employment. Too true! More than a hundred German companies now have 'women promotion programmes', which mainly (to the tune of 90 per cent) offer young mothers flexible models of part-time work. Any real 'promotion', any real advancement in their career, is thus denied to part-time workers.[9] Most of them find hourly-paid jobs in the lowest wage-groups, often outside the framework of national wage-bargaining, and women in particular constitute the cheap and mobile reserve at the bottom of the economic pyramid. Since part-time work is still unthinkable in top positions within a company, it cannot fulfil the equalizing potential that it would have if it applied to men and to bosses. This is why trade unionists at the DGB Women's Conference held in Magdeburg in November 1997 discreetly pointed out to the chairman of the DGB that his job too might be shared – as a pointer in new directions.

The economist Sibylle Raasch from Hamburg thinks that concepts of flexibilization in Germany are mainly geared to corporate interests, and do not involve a negotiable 'widening of options' to the advantage of women. 'What the employers would like is to have labour on call to suit changing requirements, but not to have the shape of part-time work decided by the employees.' By a 'widening of options', Raasch understands a modular system of different forms, places (home or factory) and times of employment, which would also include rotation between companies and the possibility of sabbatical leave.[10]

The whole organization of paid labour changes with the development of 'atypical' forms. Work abandons its former physical location, which is no longer distinguishable as a place of work. From commercial cleaning through book-keeping to sales, services are being outsourced and privatized. Stocks and personnel are run down, materials and labour called up and delivered 'just in time'. 'Buy rather than make!' is the cost-cutting strategy of service firms too: they limit themselves to core functions, and everything else is farmed out. IBM Germany, for example, has handed over the whole management of its corporate offices to outside contractors.

Higher up the skills ladder, too, this outsourcing is often associated with a downward spiral of social standards. Whole occupations are being deskilled, whole fields of work given the chop, permanent employment converted into temporary or fee-based contracts. For example, the outside companies to which West German Radio entrusts its production contracts are not bound to the rules and regulations of public institutions for the purposes either of wage-bargaining or of affirmative action programmes. In the new forms of online editing, search and surf skills on the Internet are more important than traditional journalistic expertise. The occupation of radio technician is a thing of the past. In future, editors' offices will be equipped with digital cutmasters on which they can produce finished broadcasts. Freelancers will be expected to have their own equipment and to deliver material ready for use by the radio station.

As a new wave of mergers creates powerful financial monopolies, flexibilization and fragmentation are tending to make individual market actors independent of one another. The labour-market equivalent of the limited liability company is the 'fractured business' with a small corporate core that is able to call upon decentralized independent units, or else upon an outside network of small or medium-sized firms or self-employed individuals. Every member of the chain is expected to show the highest level of motivation as pressure grows for speed-up and quality control. Success of the controlling corporation is a matter of survival for the small businesses and freelancers who depend upon it; and if their performance is not satisfactory, no more contracts will come their way. This pressure demands new skills or interdependence-competence within the work process and gives birth to new occupations such as information management, quality advice or process optimization.

The victors are known as the 'Olympic team', the chiefly male core of permanent employees around whom small suppliers, casual workers and freelancers revolve like satellites on part-time or outside contracts – at once dependent and autonomous. The slimmed-down corporation and the new forms of employment are the breeding ground for job arrangement agencies and professional 'head-hunters', as well as for the older type of agency dealing in temporary and casual labour. Using the register on their database, they can put together all manner of virtual 'skill teams' whose computer-linked members complement one another from different parts of the same country or of the world.

Along with these work teams, whole firms are pulled in for a fixed period of time. 'Virtual companies' are networks of independent businesses which work together only for a temporary and particular goal. Such 'glocals' (*glo*bally lo*cal* companies) may establish a 'presence' for themselves 'without physically being at the place in question'. There it is local firms that take care of adaptation to the particular clientele and of regional distribution of the company's product-range.[11]

The public sector, too, operates in more and more countries as a competitively-oriented corporation with the triple goals of attracting customers, raising efficiency and lowering costs. The frontrunner here is the New Zealand government, which employs top ministry officials as managers on a five-year contract, who may then put together a team of administrators and specialists for a fixed period. Routine labour and accountancy services, economic studies and political advice, are purchased by the ministry on the open market. In Germany, eighty-two city councils have been modernized since 1995 with the aim of raising efficiency and productivity, and a New Control Model has been tested out. Work in the new team hierarchies becomes more intense and stressful, but individuals also have greater opportunity to affect the shape of things. The type of the stolid official who just obeys orders has had its day. When the federal ministries move to Berlin, this will be used as a further opportunity for systematic rationalization with the help of 'electronic throughput', reductions in staffing levels and an intensification of work.[12]

Personal services such as care of the sick, old or disabled are also subject to the rationalization dogma. As in a Taylorized industrial process, units of time are bureaucratically fixed for particular movements and nursing functions; there is no room for personal comfort, advice and acts of tender loving care. Indeed, the long-term care insurance system in Germany treats independent providers of welfare work as equivalent to private-sector companies. Cheapjack outfits find ways of getting round the agreed pay levels for skilled labour. For example, the services of a trained nurse normally cost DM40 an hour, but Polish women come to Germany on a three-month tourist visa and work for an hourly wage that might be as low as DM10. Such competition puts pressure on the quality of care, as well as increasing the stress on nurses and reducing their job satisfaction. On average, a skilled nurse does not last ten years before quitting the profession.

'The labour market of the future will tend towards a situation where there is one person to each company,' predicts industrial scientist Walter C. Zimmerli. He also thinks that the multimedia environment will create an open world labour market. 'A big corporation is no longer needed to offer one's skills and knowledge world-wide. All that is required is an internet hook-up.'[13] The future labour market, then, will be a global cyberspace in which economic subjects are scattered around. Facing them will be capital opaquely networked and concentrated in big companies, whose recruitment tentacles will stretch horizontally and vertically right across the world.

The winner on this type of market will be the 'tiger' – flexible, unfettered, highly competitive, always poised to spring. Specimens already much in demand are financial advisers, equity specialists and high-tech innovators. Quite a few 'tigresses' will also be appearing on the scene, young, dynamic, single, with an excellent education, but the prototype is definitely male. Being conscious of competition and career pressures, he is prepared to put in longer hours at the office or in front of a computer – so long that, if he has a family, his wife will have already put the children to bed by the time he gets home.

The gains in female employment due to the service economy have not shaken the gender distribution of jobs and income. For the realm of women is one of cheap jobs and flexibilization; they hold today, as they have held for years, no more than 6 per cent or so of jobs within the male managerial cartel. Although their qualifications are often higher than those of men, and although their social skills are highly valued in leadership situations, neither of these has brought them equality. In fact, an earnings schism is once more opening between the sexes in the industrialized countries. According to figures issued by the German Association of Working Women, the prospect of equal pay for equal work has again receded far into the distance, with women now earning only 70 per cent of the income of male colleagues.

In Sweden, a midwife lodged a complaint in 1996 that a male technician in the same hospital as hers earned nearly $600 more than she did. But the court ruled that the work of the two categories was not comparable, that it was quite by chance that the woman happened to earn less. In the United States, where the pay differential between men and women had narrowed to 100:77 by 1992, the gap has again begun to widen. Moreover, women are still divided into three age groups: young women 'still capable of bearing children'; middle-aged women 'who have children'; and those who are 'too old'. Between the ages of sixteen and twenty-four, women earn 90 per cent of men's income; in middle age, three-quarters; and above fifty, only 65 per cent.[14]

Women Fending for Themselves

After a break for several years because of young children, Gaby Menden started looking for a way back in to her occupation of care-worker.[15] She was appointed by a notary to look after people in need of help: young, old and sick. For some she took on the duties of a guardian, submitting applications for welfare payments or pensions; for others she organized admission to a home, helped with the packing and moving, and cleared out their old accommodation – a range of tasks including those of bureaucrat, psychologist and home help.

Gaby is self-employed. She has invested DM7500 in her work (roughly $4330), including for a PC, a metered telephone and an answering machine. After five months she can draw up a balance-sheet of her work. She compiles a list of the assets belonging to the person in her care, writes a report motivating each of her own activities, and applies to the notary for reimbursement of her expenses. Then the wheels of the bureaucratic machinery start to turn. If the person in her care has no assets, the court cashier's office makes the payment. But sometimes not every activity is recognized as necessary – for example, a personal conversation or the purchase of some clothing. Some of Gaby's colleagues are still waiting for payment, a year or eighteen months after submitting their claims. Gaby must therefore assume that her first money will come in only two years after she began self-employment.

Gaby likes the variety of her work and the fact that she is responsible for it herself, although she often feels she has been left alone to make difficult decisions. Once a month she meets a friend to discuss particularly hard cases – something else she cannot include in her claim to the court cashier.

In future, flat rates per case are supposed to make calculations less troublesome. But the Association of Professional Careworkers argues that it is impossible to predict how much work a particular case will require. Up to now, the scale of payments has ranged from DM30 to DM75 an hour, according to the level of the worker's training and experience. Competition is growing from unqualified labour, however, and further squeezing incomes.

Gaby is one of a million freelancers in Germany who occupy the grey area between independent entrepreneurs and dependent employees. Examples of such 'illusory independence' are the demonstrator who runs a jewellery stand in a department store, or the 'waitress' who serves a small section in a restaurant on her own account, buying drinks and dishes at the counter and selling them at 'her' tables. There are more and more people who do translation or design work on a freelance basis, who offer temporary replacement or financial advice, or who practise a craft, publish or drive a vehicle. They work for an employer and follow his instructions, without receiving anything from him by way of social insurance contributions.

Today, 57 per cent of the new small enterprises are 'established' in services, 30 per cent in trade. A third of all the self-employed are women. Corporations such as Blumen 2000 (Flowers 2000) or Body Shop manage to lure women into business with offers of a franchise, but they have to put up at least DM40,000 to DM60,000 of their own capital. For this they get a fully equipped shop and a certain amount of training. They are allowed to sell only goods supplied by the company, which takes a 5 per cent cut for itself. Often lacking relevant experience, women take on the risk in order to escape from unemployment.

Especially in the new eastern *Länder* of Germany, it is economic necessity and a lack of alternatives that push women to be 'inventive' in setting up new businesses, says social scientist Gisela Notz. In more than a half of cases, these new businesses consist only of the woman who founded them. Nearly a quarter of women newly working on their own account have to manage on a net monthly income below DM1000, and a half can only pay themselves less than DM1800. Only a third of women in the old parts of the Federal Republic have an income above DM3000, as against three-quarters of self-employed men. Not least because of their modest income expectations, women are more likely than men to keep going for five years or more, even if this means living a hand-to-mouth existence. Nevertheless, the self-employed woman who wants to forge her own destiny is held up as the paragon of neoliberalism; she is prepared to take the risk and believes in the opportunities afforded by the market.

When women set up a business they tend to be 'emotional and oriented to use-values', says Eva Wonneberger, who organizes regular get-togethers of female founders of companies in Upper Swabia. They start with little capital and few status symbols, they are cautious in their business operations, and they carefully avoid the risks of large loans. Their priority is to make their lives secure, not to make maximum profits at any price. They want to do meaningful work, and at the same time to be 'their own boss'.[16]

The Global Office

Far-reaching technological change has always been Janus-faced: jobs have been mechanized out of existence, but new ones created at the same time; work has been made less back-breaking, but new health risks introduced; productivity has been increased, but traditional skills put to one side and forgotten. 'Computer technology is no exception to this tradition,' considers Swasti Mitter, professor at the New Technologies Institute of the UN University in Maastricht. She compares the present controversies over the introduction of modern information and communication technologies to the conflicts at the time of the first technological revolution in the late eighteenth century. More still than industrial production, office work by hand and machine is being transferred to microchips and megabytes. Already people are imagining a fully electronic, paperless office.

Malaysia, the Caribbean islands, India and China saw that the new communication technologies gave them an opportunity to catch up in the service sector that would be incomparably less costly and problematic than a similar manoeuvre in industry.

Lufthansa and Swissair have all their booking records – including passenger cancellations, stopovers, seating and meal preferences – entered a second time by keyboarders in India, so that they can better plan for in-flight habits and purchasing trends. And in 1989, when new databases had to be installed everywhere in Britain because of changes in municipal tax legislation, many local authorities decided to award contracts for this work in the Philippines.

Since the mid-1980s, some islands in the Caribbean have been built up into secondary cash registers for the US market. With the help of new computer technology, a systematic record is kept of trade and services in the world's largest consumption area. First in Barbados and Puerto Rico, then in Jamaica, the Dominican Republic and St Lucia, offices were relocated for US companies and, to some extent, for municipal authorities. Private insurance companies are able to draw on these data-processing offices to analyse their loss reports and compensation payments, while the public health and welfare services use them to classify in various ways their records of sick leave, applications for reimbursement, and actual social security payments. Department stores and mail-order firms want to establish their patterns of stock turnover, and to analyse complaints, advertising response and the effects of direct-mail special offer vouchers, so that they can plan ahead for trade cycles and customer preferences. Credit card firms keep a record of their holders' use patterns and habits, and libraries and archives store the computerized results. Tape recordings of court proceedings are transcribed. Banks systematically file account transactions, savings and loan behaviour, and repayment standards among certain groups of customers.

At first, the data were mainly sent by air freight from the United States to the Caribbean, and then back again by e-mail. The functioning of this telecommunications service had two prerequisites. First, technical infrastructure had to be in place for the computer-assisted communications, as well as transport by means of a digital telephone network, underwater glass-fibre cables, satellites and modern airports. Second, women's nimble fingers had to be available to feed in endless data, and the women themselves had to be both highly productive and prepared to accept low wages.

In Jamaica, whether in foreign-owned firms operating in the Digiport free trade zone or in national companies operating outside it, women make up more than 90 per cent of those who sweep their hands across the computer-cabled keyboards and perform labour-intensive services for export. Young women aged seventeen or eighteen, fresh from high school, are tested for skill, accuracy and ability to work under pressure, and the successful ones are then given a course in typing. Most of them are hired on a three-month contract. Average output in the offices is around 12,000 keystrokes an hour, with 99.8 per cent accuracy. Those who no longer meet the norm have their employment terminated.[17]

In Jamaica women are better educated than men, but, in general, 'male' employment is clearly differentiated from 'female' employment: men work in better conditions, earn more, and are more often unionized. In the export-oriented high-tech offices, women key in data alongside male systems analysts. Their opportunities for promotion and further training are as limited as those of women in the export-oriented textile industry. Keyboarders do earn more than textile-workers, yet after two or three years most of them have had all they can take of the monotony and constant stress, which often results in disturbed vision, back trouble or the new occupational disorder, repetitive strain syndrome. Many go on to work as 'normal' secretaries.

Ruth Pearson, in her study of data-processing in Jamaica in 1993, still hoped that keyboarders might gain further qualifications and come to form one of the occupations of the high-tech age. Instead of that, however, women working with computers have undergone rapid marginalization. The technological revolution is faster than they can type. Their manual labour is increasingly being replaced by scanners and by software that automatically links everything up to the cash desk and bank counter, records and appraises everything from the processing of insurance documents to the airport check-in. Many small businesses in Jamaica that were run by young Jamaicans have had to cut back drastically their operations, or even to close down altogether.[18]

Stana Martin, communications specialist at Texas University, calls it a question purely of business management whether it is more cost-effective for a firm to employ women in India, Malaysia or Barbados or to purchase an expensive octogo-character scanner. Routine office work will, in her view, first be further redistributed around the world; this will sharpen the pressures of world-market competition on women in the industrialized countries, and create new (insecure and non-unionized) jobs for women in the low-wage countries. The more labour-intensive their work, however, the more susceptible it will be to automation.

In Malaysia, too, where office work has been booming as a result of new computer technologies, there has been a further polarization between stereotyped repetitive activities and administrative or organizational tasks – in other words, between manual and mental labour. Most women are employed in low-skilled, low-paid online activities, as data keyboarders, bank cashiers, switchboard operators or flight-reservation clerks. None of the women with this kind of job, in either public or private enterprises, thought that suitable career opportunities were open to her.[19] For the most part, these jobs are in danger of being replaced by customer-operated machines, such as bank ATMs or electronic reservation systems, and so new additions to the workforce in this domain are recruited only on fixed-term contracts that allow of easy dismissal. Similarly, the very high intensity of work on computers makes the employment of part-time labour an attractive proposition.

Most women working on and with computers in Malaysia thought that they had improved their skills level and increased their productivity. But computer work fixes the great majority at the bottom of the office hierarchy, and the objective compulsion of the machine subjects them to the stress of constant monitoring. If, at the end of the day, the keyboarders have not fulfilled their norm of 12,000 strokes an hour, the evidence of their shortfall is churned out by the computer and displayed on the office wall.

Switchboard operators have a quota of 3000 connections a day, which means that they have to complete each one within seconds. They too are computer-monitored and are given a report on their performance each month. At an airline company, the women who take telephone reservations have a quota of 150 calls a day, of which none should last longer than three minutes. The computer prints out hourly reports of the number of calls, and in addition supervisors check the women's ability to communicate during them. It is a truly Orwellian system: big brother, little sisters.

The hope that modern technology would redistribute mindless routines and break up office hierarchies has not been fulfilled. Most women have become data and keyboard drones of the information world; only a small group have acquired new skills, broadened their range of activity and started working for themselves. By no stretch of the imagination can it be said that the computer age has brought equality for women.

In Europe, outwork relying on telecommunications has been hailed as the key opening to a new organization of labour, especially as far as women are concerned. 'It is no longer people who go to work but work that comes to them. Human labour is too valuable to be wasted in overcrowded rush-hour traffic.'[20]

The Integrated Services Digital Network is presented in publicity as the springboard for teleworking, allowing the online worker to pat the baby on her lap with one hand, while she waits on the computer with the other. What an idyllic harmony between job and family! And it is true that there are 250,000 such jobs in Germany, most of them done by women. A computer situated midway between cot and stove is part of the corporate strategy of relocation and decentralization; it saves a considerable amount in rent, electricity and telephone costs.

Insurance and trading companies, among others, increasingly equip their sales representatives with a portable terminal or 'office', so that they can keep working even in a car, at a client's or in a hotel.[21] In fact, they no longer have a desk of their own at the company offices but only one that they share with others – two others in Germany, already ten in the United States. 'A free choice of workplace really means that I can run my virtual office anywhere': this is how IBM project leader Werner Zorn cracks up mobility and flexibility as freedom and a new 'culture of work'. 'Sooner or later,' he adds, 'we will all have a network link-up at home, just as we all have a telephone today. Then we will all be teleworkers.'[22]

Other decentralized forms that have become increasingly common are satellite offices located closer than company headquarters to the workers' homes, and 'tele-cottages' in cheaper parts of the country. Eight million Europeans are already engaged in teleworking. In the United States, roughly 10 per cent of the economically active population now work for their company within their own four walls. According to the Bonn research institute Empirica, the figure could rise as high as 2.5 million jobs in Germany.[23]

Wordbank, a firm with offices in twelve European countries, offers a package of translation, design, editing, desktop publishing and printing, so that brochures, reports and catalogues can appear simultaneously in a number of languages and countries. The work is mainly done at home by freelancers, as and when the orders come in. They have no job security at all.

The volume of work is equally uncertain and irregular in a '*société de services*' in the South of France, which passes orders on from local firms to homeworkers. It started by creating a database of suitably qualified women in the area, and then offered them work at home as well as the opportunity to buy second-hand computer technology.[24]

The transfer of jobs from a workplace within the premises of a company to online private homes is hailed as an opportunity for women to achieve autonomy and control over their working time. In reality, however, baby still cries when mother is sitting at the computer, the nursery child brings measles home without caring about the presence of a terminal, and the mother-in-law in need of care wets the bed even when a microelectronic task is waiting to be done. The teleworker must herself draw boundaries where private life is no longer clearly distinguished from work. Again she has to perform a continual balancing act between the two.

Most teleworkers are either self-employed or on DM620 a month. All know that remuneration depends upon performance, and that those who commission their work do not concern themselves with sickness benefit, pension contributions or the protection of new mothers. Firms increasingly prefer freelancers, because they make more of an effort and have a direct interest in productivity and efficiency.

The German Otto mail-order firm has most of its telephone orders taken by homeworkers in the Netherlands. The women are assured of at least twenty hours' work a month, including weekend or nighttime duties. But they have to be available for five hours a day. The peak times are at midday and in the evening.[25] The Netherlands, with a third of all Europe's call centres, are what one might call the telecommunications control centre for the continent – above all, because of the country's high number of immigrants and the language skills of the population. The main competitor in this field is Ireland. Hertz, UPS and Lufthansa all hire students of German from Dublin University to take telephone orders and reservations.

Most women want to do computer homeworking only for a limited period – for example, when they have to be around to look after young children. They experience it as a really testing time, when they have to grapple with isolation for want of social and workplace contacts. Only highly qualified IBM specialists, who can afford to pay for childcare or move backwards and forwards between home and office, are satisfied with their work situation. Others tend to work as electronic recluses well into the night (when the children are asleep), and to suffer from a guilty conscience as well as tiredness and overwork, without making up for it in their leisure time.

Trade unions everywhere call for ergonomic standards to apply to homeworking, with breaks of at least ten minutes an hour to relieve physical and mental stress. In Germany, experts in the field argue that a job which alternates between home and workplace would be a more 'considerate' variant.[26]

'The introduction of computer technology has reinforced the numerical dominance of women in office work,' maintains Swasti Mitter, an expert on questions of women and technology.[27] But an international conference of women computer scientists, held in Bonn in May 1997 on the theme 'Women, Work and Computerization', concluded that the new information technologies had by and large produced no equalizing effect. In the global office, women are still overwhelmingly locked into uncreative, low-paid and insecure routine jobs. It is true that computerization offers fresh opportunities to a small number of women, but this rather confirms the hierarchical gender division of labour.[28] In Brazil, for example, it has been shown that women and men with the same training in computer programming have very unequal career opportunities.[29]

The majority of medium-grade programmers, systems analysts and managers are male, even if the proportion of women has increased somewhat. The half-life of qualifications for jobs in computing and information sciences is so short that constant updating is required. Anyone who takes time off to start a family and care for children will lag behind and soon be written off, and of course it is almost entirely women who experience such interruptions. In short, children and housework are harmful to women's qualifications, reputation and career. The image of fast-moving computer careers combines with traditional role allocation to yield a preference for men in highly qualified technological jobs.

'Women are at an automatic disadvantage because of the breaks in their work record,' concludes Stana Martin. The cultural software involved in this is 'the myth of men's competence in technology and women's remoteness from it'.[30] The figure of the hacker gives heroic form to the male as master of technology. In Germany, women comprise only 10 per cent of Internet users. They are also once again declining as a proportion of students of information science: roughly 10 per cent in 1983, now no more than 5 per cent.

Isle of the Blessed

'Isn't that a nice photo?' asks Hans Krafka, chairman of the board of directors at Siemens Communications Software,[31] as he looks with un-concealed paternal pride at a group picture of the workforce: women in colourful saris and salwar kamiz in the first two rows; behind them, on the entrance steps of Raheja Tower, the male team with the beaming founder in their midst. Since 1994 he has taken on 340 employees. They write software on a contract from the 'mother company' in Munich, which supplies the programmes on the international telecommunications market.

Siemens does not want to miss out on the action where IBM, Motorola, Digital Equipment and Hewlett-Packard are jostling for position. Bangalore, in the mid-1990s, is dominated by a gold-rush mood. In the air-conditioned corporate headquarters in the city centre, and further out in Electronic City, the representatives of foreign companies knock on one another's doors. 'Do you also want to set up in business?' I am asked by the receptionist at VeriFone, an international communications technology firm.

After Silicon Valley in California and Silicon Island in Penang, the city with 5 million inhabitants in the South Indian state of Karnataka calls itself Silicon City. In the first half of 1996, the Indian software industry increased its turnover by an impressive 61.7 per cent. Of the total, 40 per cent remained in the national market, while 60 per cent ($1 billion in 1996) went abroad.[32]

'Presence' on the South Asian and South-East Asian market, at a time of intense international competition, is the first reason given by Krafka for the choice of Bangalore as a software 'dislocated development branch'. The excellently trained computer engineers, who speak English at break-neck speed, are the second reason. The favourable wage-costs, he quietly adds, are the third: the equivalent of $6,000 a year, a pittance in comparison with German levels. The running costs for the business in Bangalore, however, are hardly different from those in Hong Kong, New York or Frankfurt. As to the question of trade union organization, Krafka merely shrugs his shoulders: 'There isn't any, and no one wants it either!'

Apart from the cheap skilled labour, India also has time on its side. As its time zone lies between the European and the North American ones, Indians can be working on software while their German colleagues are still fast asleep; and if a US firm reports a programme crash at the end of office hours, Indian experts have a few hours to get the data up and running before their counterparts in Detroit or Chicago switch on their computers for the day.

'Our offices here are not a whit behind those in Eschborn' – as deputy-head of Deutsche Software India, a subsidiary of Deutsche Bank, Henning Steinbrinker is certainly to be believed. The building is grand and spacious, flooded with light, clinically clean, decorated with a gallery-like collection of contemporary masterpieces, and boasting a small but immaculate canteen at the back. The work stations on the eighth floor of the Raheja Tower are like a virtual reality high above Bangalore's city centre filled with noise, dust and fumes. Some of the software engineers have rolled their desk chairs next to one another and are discussing something in hushed tones; others gesticulate from one screen to another, or are working by themselves on a programme. It is here that programmes are elaborated for electronic banking, in cooperation with Deutsche Bank in Singapore and the head-quarters in Eschborn. 'When Mercedes Benz in Stuttgart or some other Germany company wants to check the state of its account in New York, Vietnam or Singapore, it can do so with one of the programmes we have developed,' explains Steinbrinker.

Those who have a job here are young, highly specialized and career-oriented, India's yuppie winners of the growth economy who look as if they have stepped out of a mail-order catalogue of the Brave New World. The average age at Deutsche Software is twenty-seven and a half, and two floors higher, at Siemens, it is two years less than that.

In Bangalore's high-tech firms, a fifth to a quarter of the workforce is female. 'The software industry is a great opportunity for women to make a career for themselves,' opines Shadiba, with the confidence of the better-paid. She is project manager at VeriFone, where she is currently 'helping' Citibank in Frankfurt to organize its bank entries better. She is not sup-posed to say any more – it is confidential.

Most of the women come from good homes and high-caste families. The way they reel off their educational and occupational history is quite breathtaking: a degree in computer sciences, mathematics or electrical engineering at the age of twenty-one, next a couple of courses in pro-gramming or systems analysis at a private institute, and then into the race in the overtaking lane of the Indian economy.

Like Shabida at VeriFone, women programmers at other software firms are convinced that they have found their way into an oasis of equal opportunities. For them discrimination is a foreign word; their career chances at management level are better than anywhere else. Shobha, a director's secretary at Siemens, also once asked herself: 'Why not me? I've got what it takes, after all!' Of her colleagues working in computers, she

says: 'Women are getting ambitious now. They want to be somebody, not
just lead a protected life inside their own four walls.' These self-assured
young people are doing what most Indian women can only dream of: they
are planning their own lives. Only nine of Siemens's female employees are
married, although at twenty-five years they have long passed the age for
marriage in India.

Lakshmi at VeriFone wants her intended to be quite clear about what
he is letting himself in for. She wants to continue working and to have one
or at the most two children (whatever the sex) – and he had better know
that he won't be able to treat her badly, as his father did his mother. Will
he play along? If he doesn't, she says without batting an eyelid, she'll have
to look elsewhere.

'When you are financially independent, you are also independent in
other respects,' says Vinutha from Deutsche Software. And what about
husbands or men friends? There's a problem if the woman's income, career
position and prestige are higher than the man's. 'It doesn't exactly boost
his ego.'

Despite the verbal rebelliousness, all the women shy away from a confrontation with their family. If the parents live in Bangalore, the daughters
(as well as the sons) live with them as a matter of course – even if they
could afford to have a place of their own. They hope that their parents will
gradually change their attitude to the way of life of the high-tech generation. The inner revolt is looking for ways of gentle subversion.

The dream income of $6,000 – three times more than that of a building
engineer and twice that of a professor in India – is one attraction of a
software job; the prospect of a period abroad is the other. Some of India's
software exports involve what is called 'body shopping', the lending of
people to write, adapt or correct programmes in another country.

It was 'body shopping' that got the Indian software boom started in the
late 1970s, in California's Silicon Valley. But when the US trade unions
stepped up pressure for a tightening of visa regulations for Indian workers,
the computer giants began to open branches in India, to negotiate joint
ventures or to issue contracts to Indian firms. In 1992 the Indian government moved to attract foreign investors with a number of 'technology
parks' that combined customs and tax benefits with laid-on infrastructure.
Bangalore has been booming ever since.

Despite the seductive pay prospects, however, parents allow 'body shopping' of their daughters only when conditions are 'safe' and a trustworthy
firm is keeping an eye on things. Well-known German companies evidently
fit the bill; Siemens is considered 'part of the family' as a slogan in German
ads of Siemens says. If the company wants to send a female programmer
to Germany, she would never go against her parents' will or without their

approval. Before she leaves, she respectfully touches their feet, and they place their hands upon her head.

The demand for qualified software staff is holding up. In Bangalore earnings increased by up to 30 per cent in 1996. Firms lure away one another's employees by offering bonuses or additional benefits such as a fitness centre. This explains the often high staff turnover. 'It's not so bad in our case,' says Henning Steinbrinker, adding that Deutsche Software's social benefits are 'like in Germany ... The same standards apply throughout the company.' Nevertheless, even German employers sometimes find their top staff falling prey to head-hunters from the United States. After all, they can pick up as much as $40,000 a year over there.

VeriFone offers its employees round-the-clock flexitime – any eight hours they like. If, by way of exception, a valued software specialist has a baby, the company will even install a computer in her home so that she can help out when the deadline pressure is greatest.

Bangalore will keep booming for a few more years, thinks Hans Krafka of Siemens. But many companies already find its air too sticky, its traffic jams too time-wasting, its property prices too high, and its daily power cuts of four to six hours too long for their own batteries and generators to bridge. And so now they are eyeing up cheaper regions such as China, the CIS countries, Costa Rica or Malaysia, where a whole reserve pool is already in its starting blocks. The vast new 'technology park' on the edge of Bangalore, which an army of building workers, including many women, helped to build for a wage of little more than a dollar a day, is standing two-thirds empty.

In perspective, the software engineers who still bask in the assurance of being a scarce commodity on the world market are actually working themselves out of a job. For they are developing new computer languages and programmes that will themselves be able to carry out the future tasks of writing and adapting – without the zealous, self-confident yuppies who now get shoeshine boys to polish off the street dust, and without the equally talented and upwardly mobile young women who think they can outsmart the arrogant Indian patriarchs.

Towards the Self-service Society

'Look at the latest thing in,' a cashier tells me in a Bonn supermarket, pointing to a chequecard and a smartcard machine lying next to the scanner. 'More and more technology!' Every little bit is helping to make redundant that same cashier who for the moment still finds time to refill the shelves, to ask a student if he's throwing a party or a pregnant woman how much longer she's got to go.

Since the scanners were installed, the woman at the checkout no longer needs to keep track of the prices. In return her arms and back ache more often, as she has to hold each item up against the barcode laser. There is no future in that.

Soon the customers will be able to scan their own goods and pay for them with a piece of plastic – if, that is, they still go to the shops instead of doing it all on the Internet's electronic marketplace. Karstadt has already announced an online warehouse called 'My World', which will of course never have to respect any closing hours. 'Cyber-shopping' has also arrived in Malaysia, where mouse-click ordering will do away with thousands of jobs in the retail trade. Self-service is replacing the provision of services. On New York's Upper West Side, there is already a virtual emporium with a thousand computers that can sell you old Soviet Army uniforms, Gucci or Fiorucci perfumes from Italy, or a hand-painted Madeleine Vionnet scarf from France costing $500. The global mall is open for business. At Christmas 1997 Internet shopping made its first decisive breakthrough, with a total world turnover of a US$1 billion.

The Internet can be used to book a flight, to pay for it by giving a credit or airline card number, and even to choose a seat. A traveller with only hand-luggage can skip the check-in counter and get a boarding card straight from a machine.

In the cyber-economy of the future, customers will be present on virtual marketplaces by means of tele-shopping and Internet banking. Teleworkers will cooperate online, as digital workplaces come to be staffed by global networks of engineers.

Since September 1995, Bank 24 in Bonn has offered you a 'personal declaration of independence' – twenty-four hours a day, seven days a week. This straightforward subsidiary of Deutsche Bank has no branches or counters; its 'up-to-the-minute access' takes place by telephone, fax and Internet. The company projects an 'uncomplicated' image and a 'customer first' philosophy, which together make up the new 'culture'. In an old grain mill in Bonn's river port area, the workplace scene is dominated not by smart bankers in collar and tie but by stylish women in T-shirts. 'We are rather American here,' explains head of personnel Christine Enterlein. 'It may be that someone has previously been to Australia for three years or had a job in a bar, so they'll come to work either in stilettoes or in shoes with thick wooden heels. That doesn't concern us at all.' What does concern them is how the staff of 550, more than half of them women, perform in their work. Their average age is twenty-seven years, a little less than the customers' average of thirty-three.

What they mainly do at the call centre is speak to customers; it is the 'point of intersection between customer and bank'. The 'customer' experiences the bank as a voice, which must therefore not only carry out the particular tasks but also add a personal touch that makes the customer feel in good hands. 'Women get on easier in a world where the customer comes first,' says Enterlein after two years' experience. All the supervisors at the call centre are women. On the top floor, men have the executive rooms all to themselves. Obviously they get on easier in the world of management.

The planning of shift cover at the call centre involves 'a constant learning process'. On a normal day 8000 customers phone in, but the figure is higher when shares are being offered for Deutsche Telekom or some other well-known company.

American, too, is the system of remuneration: no wage contract, performance-oriented, from DM18 an hour up, extra for night work but not for Sundays and holidays. After four weeks' training, new members of staff are set to work in a team with a loose hierarchy that provides 'special coaching'; conversations with customers are monitored and 'rated' according to standard criteria, from the first greeting to the final words of goodbye. They are also always recorded, both for security back-up and for random checks.

Above the work station, an illuminated display shows how many customers are being held in a queue. Three callers have already been waiting 2:58 minutes. 'That's too long,' says the head of personnel, 'I'd have hung up by now.' The telephone workers are supposed to adjust the length of their conversation to the strength of the incoming flow. She denies that this is a big-brother system, it would only provide a 'quality guarantee'. 'If you're good at it, you can develop fantastically,' Enterlein assures the other women, including a number of mothers with small children who are pleased with the flexible working hours. One reason for the choice of Bonn was its supply of well-qualified and motivated women 'released' by the public authorities.

Since autumn 1996 the bank has offered a 'HomeLine 24' service: 'the whole bank at the touch of a button'. Already 17,000 of the bank's 150,000 customers operate online their own giro account, making payments and deposits and even dealing in securities. The trend continues upwards; fewer and fewer teleworkers will be needed in future.

While the new technologies make workplaces redundant, they also function as instruments of socialization. Regardless of location, they can be accessed by people in distant places as well as by the handicapped, and can serve as means of social integration and democratization of education and health. Online medical practice, for example, will allow patients to be diagnosed and monitored over any distance. X-rays and tissue samples will be scanned and e-mailed for evaluation by specialists. In the same way, training and further education will be possible by means of remote learning, through mouse clicks in libraries, archives, museums and research institutes.

Politicians, of course, still sell information technologies as the great hope for future jobs. But that is a naive miscalculation, because far fewer jobs are being created than automated out of existence. Rainer Thome, a computer economist at Würzburg University, has calculated that over the next decade 6.7 million service jobs will be rationalized away in Germany; and that half of the 3.4 million jobs in the retail trade may also disappear as a result of automated checkouts, electronic payment systems and Internet shopping. Not only private businesses but also public departments are beginning to make the leap into automation. 'Advice computers' in the halls of job centres and social security offices are just the first step: 46 per cent of the 2.6 million jobs in public administration may be in danger in the years to come. In the banking sector, the corresponding figure may be as high as 60 per cent – wherever a job involves repetitive and varying tasks.[33] Between 1993 and 1996, under the watchword of 're-engineering', Deutsche Bank reduced the number of its jobs in Germany by nearly ten thousand, to 43,000 – and, at the same time, recorded the highest turnover in its history. Banking is currently passing through a phase of merger euphoria, and this will obviously be stoked up further by the decision of the World Trade Organization to clear the way for cross-frontier financial services from 1999. The basic calculation is that personnel costs can be cut to two-thirds of the existing level if two branches are fused together. The introduction of the euro will make further downsizing possible, because the international currency trade will become much simpler.

It is still uncertain whether the TIME industries (telecommunications, information technology, media and electronics) will pick up some of the labour shed after the year 2000. But the trend towards a self-service economy would seem to contradict such a prospect.[34]

The International Army of Cleaners

To clear away the daily refuse is a dirty business; not only because women (and it is mostly women) get their hands dirty, but also because the employment practices are not usually spick and span. For cleaning is overwhelmingly part of the grey economy, 'invisible' and therefore lacking in social esteem. It is insecure and unprotected work, a continuation of household labour in the jobs market, a 'natural ability' of women that is one of the worst-paid of all activities.

In Germany, the cleaning of buildings is probably the most common female occupation. But only 5 per cent or so of the workforce is employed full-time. Whether they clean private homes, big offices or hospitals, more than three-quarters are hourly-paid workers with no social security.

Since the early 1980s, private firms and public institutions have increasingly turned to private suppliers for services such as office cleaning and maintenance, monitoring and security, and the provision of food and catering. The outsourcing and privatization of cleaning have also led to the formation of transnational corporations in this sector.

The largest German corporation is Pedus Service P. Dussmann, which has branches elsewhere in Europe and North America and records an annual turnover of more than DM1 billion. But the international market-leader is the Danish firm International Service Systems (ISS), which has even been making headway in the markets of the South. Service diversification is typical of this process, and the various companies now offer not only cleaning and guard duties but also the provision of food for airlines.[35]

At the same time, a quasi-industrial splitting of activities has been taking place, each with rigid time and output norms subject to strict checks and a gender division of labour. The cleaning of windows, façades and streets is better-paid men's work, while the cleaning of interiors is mainly women's work.

Along with the internationalization of the cleaning business, there has been a parallel internationalization of the workforce. In Germany, three-quarters are now migrant workers. For many women who have recently come to Germany and do not have a work permit, cleaning is in fact the one and only way of earning some money. They form a category that keeps replenishing the occupational hierarchy from the bottom up, and the same mechanism is repeated within each team of cleaners. Newcomers must start by cleaning the toilets, thus allowing others to move up a rung on the ladder.

Female immigrants to the industrialized countries have also brought back an occupation that seemed to have fallen victim to the technological revolution: namely, the housemaid. Working women in well-paid households treat themselves to a girl to look after their home or their children. The neoliberal policy of offering 'career women' the extra privilege of tax relief on domestic help substitutes a labour-market device for the old feminist demand for a redistribution of paid and unpaid labour between the sexes.[36]

Unlike the servant girls of old, who came young and single from the impoverished hinterland, most domestics at the end of the century are married and have children of their own. If they come from border regions – as do Mexicans in the west and south of the United States or Poles in Berlin – they try to travel back at weekends to see their family. Others live for years on end separated from their children.

Some problems faced by domestic servants are similar to those of a hundred years ago: low pay, long hours and sexual harassment. What is new is that their work often involves actual deskilling, since many have had a good education. Edna, for example, used to be a teacher in the Philippines. She gave the job up when an employment agency promised her a post as a private teacher in Rome. Her family sold some of its land to raise the $2300 for her air ticket and the agent's fee. But Edna's plane first stopped in Prague, from where she was driven in a hollowed-out lorry across the Austrian border and then smuggled into Italy. Now she is a quite ordinary domestic servant in Rome, without documents, without rights, and without some of her former illusions. But despite everything, she has enough in her pay packet to send more home each month than she used to earn in the Philippines. And back home, her family remains with debts and great expectations.

The Frankfurt-based Institute for Women's Research has calculated that Philippine domestic servants who live in an employer's home in Germany earn between DM320 and DM400 a month, while those with accommodation of their own receive between DM600 and DM1500. If their papers are not in order, they live in constant fear of a police raid. Many still have an open-dated air ticket, because they would otherwise have to stay in prison prior to deportation.[37]

To look for statistics in this area is to stumble into a thicket of shady figures. Officially, 3.5 million Philippine citizens currently work abroad, but other sources speak of 7 million, 60 per cent of them women. No other Asian country exports so much labour. A total of 1.5 million are in the United States, 1.3 million in Saudi Arabia, and more than half a million in Europe. Most of the women are employed as nannies, cleaners, cooks or all-purpose servants.

No one is quite sure whether it is one-third or two-thirds who have no residence or work permit. But legal or illegal, in 1996 immigrants transferred nearly $7 billion to their native countries; each one supported an average of seven others back home, financing the education of children, hospital care for uncles and parents, and attempts by an unemployed husband to make a living as a street-trader. For many countries, migrant workers are thus the number-one earners of foreign currency and a hugely important factor in the economy.

Amy Cheang is a career woman living in a double-salary home in Hong Kong; she has two children and two Philippine servant girls, 'so that someone is always there at weekends to look after the kids'. An agency gave her a video offering an endless supply of filipinas ready for export. Amy chose one on a three-month right-to-return basis, but she was quite satisfied with how things worked out.

For nearly twenty years now, filipinas have been part of the Sunday scene in Hong Kong: they go together to church; they sit in groups with shopping bags and picnic hampers on the central squares and street corners; they chatter, laugh and sing – uncertainly. For since Hong Kong was handed back to China, they are threatened with cheap competition from the huge and poor mainland to the north.

So long as women earn more from housecleaning and childminding overseas than from teaching in their homeland, they will tend to set off and leave their own country and children behind. This is why women go from Sri Lanka to Japan, from the Dominican Republic to Madrid, from Sierra Leone to Lebanon, from China to Thailand, from Thailand to Malaysia – the list of migration flows grows longer and longer. And in Sri Lanka and Indonesia as in the Philippines, emigration has for a long time involved more women than men.

Most of the women do not realize beforehand that not only the pay but also the cost of living is much higher abroad. But they do tend to be warned by others already there who have been humiliated, exploited or violated. They listen to stories of an underpaid day's work that begins with ironing at six in the morning and ends around eleven at night with babysitting; they hear of the loneliness in a strange land, which sometimes ends in tragedies such as that of Flor Contemplación, convicted of murder and hanged in Singapore, or of the fourteen-year-old Sarah Balabagan, who killed her eighty-year-old employer in Saudi Arabia when he tried to rape her. When, following this incident, former president Ramos of the Philippines announced a clampdown on the exodus at least to Arab countries, a cry of outrage swept across the land. For along with the tales of horror, there are success stories of migrant workers whose money transfers may even have been converted into building stone for their families back home. 'Tempting fate' is a common idea with which women set off from the Philippines.

The migration business is also a lucrative sector in the domestic market. Each year, would-be emigrants pay several million dollars in their own countries to agents and route organizers, to clinics for the issuing of health certificates, to training centres for crash course diplomas, and to their national authorities for passports. President Ramos himself did not mean his warnings to be taken too seriously, for his government cannot do without the foreign currency transfers from abroad any more than it can forgo the mitigating effect on unemployment. The export of women is by now a well-calculated item of economic planning, an indispensable raw material plundered all the more ruthlessly, the heavier the external debt burden grows. In January 1998, the Vietnamese government announced in turn that it would promote the export of labour.

The conditions in which this selling of human capital takes place have nevertheless been deteriorating. Europe is not the only region that is sealing itself off. As a result of stagnant employment, ongoing rationalization or economic disasters, Thailand, Malaysia, Saudi Arabia and Singapore are also making their markets hard for migrants to enter. The Thai government is aiming to show the door as soon as possible to more than a million immigrant workers, mostly from Burma. And Malaysia, which would like to rid itself of nearly three million (mostly illegal) immigrants, has already deported thousands upon thousands of Indonesian immigrant workers and is driving newcomers from the coasts. Hong Kong has frozen the income of domestic employees at a low level, in the hope that they will soon pack their own bags and leave.

In 1990 the UN General Assembly adopted a convention on the rights of migrant workers and their families, to come into force once twenty countries have signed it. So far, however, only seven states have ratified it, and every one of these – from Sri Lanka to Mexico – is an exporter of labour. As an example of what is happening in host countries, Saudi Arabia is actually whittling away the few rights that immigrant domestic servants have hitherto enjoyed; in future they will have to surrender their passport at the moment of arrival. In Britain and Malaysia, women's rights of residence are tied to a particular job, so that they are unable to change their employer however they are treated. In Taiwan, women arriving to take up domestic service are subjected to a pregnancy test. Rights violations are part of the rules of the game on the global migration market. The law lags far behind the other aspects of effective globalization.

Body Markets

In 1910 the National Committee to Combat Trafficking in Girls, then based at Lützowplatz in Berlin, warned 'emigrant girls' in a poster: 'Don't take any job abroad without first making reliable enquiries!'

As the century draws to a close, this warning has lost none of its relevance. Take Anna, for example, whose life-story sounds like a stereotype. In 1993 she saw a job for summer domestic help advertised on a street column in her hometown of Szczecin, Poland. Hardly had she started working as a kitchen assistant when a similar job was promised her in Berlin. But there she was forced into prostitution and beaten when she protested. Constantly guarded by a man who had taken away her passport, she had clients brought to her all through the night. Finally, after being sold to 'Café Casablanca', she received DM10 a trick. Brothel-owners from Berlin and West Germany usually pay between DM300 and DM5000 for women like Anna; it depends how attractive they are. A stolen car, by comparison, brings in DM10,000.[38]

The transnational and transcontinental traffic in women is nothing new.

But it has been given a boost by the opening of frontiers, the establishment of trading rings, the faster means of transport and the new communications technologies. When governments promote tourism as a currency-earning growth strategy, they usually count prostitution as part and parcel of it. Local young women are seen as a sexual pool for tourists, regardless of the social consequences or the risks and side-effects for the women themselves. It is considered officially admissible, indeed desirable, for the national economy, that women's bodies should be thrown on to the world market at a knock-down price.

As in the past, the usual trade route is from poor to well-off regions – within the South, from South to North, from East to West. And, as in the past, accurate figures for the flesh trade are hard to come by. Perhaps half a million in Europe, two million worldwide? Exploitation of the female body is an international industry, maintains Radhika Coomaraswamy, a Sri Lankan legal expert and UN special rapporteuse on violence against women. Women 'are tricked, coerced, abducted, sold and, in many cases, forced to live and work under slavery-like conditions as prostitutes, domestic workers, sweatshop labourers or wives'.[39]

Colombia is a control centre for dealers shipping women to Venezuela, Ecuador and Panama, but also to the USA, Spain and other EU countries. The cocaine traffic is useful for good foreign trade contacts, even if the women have nothing to do with it themselves. Kenya, as a tourist and transport centre, is the hub for East Africa, with a constant supply from Uganda and the civil war regions of Central Africa.

Cambodia is a trans-shipment centre for young women not only from the poor hinterland but also from Burma, Laos, Vietnam and southern China. In 1992, when 20,000 men went to Cambodia as part of the UN peace mission and to prepare elections, a hugh new market developed overnight for commercial sex. One study found that more than 20 per cent of the prostitutes were between twelve and seventeen years of age.[40]

After the peace mission ended, the number of prostitutes fell again. But Phnom Penh had by then established itself, together with Bangkok, as the centre for human smuggling to Japan, Europe and the United States, because things are less hot there and the authorities easier to bribe. The complicity of state officials is everywhere what keeps the prostitution racket so well oiled. Whether en route from Bangladesh to Pakistan or from Burma to Thailand, and often even in the brothels themselves, the protection of corrupt officials is extended to the dealers rather than the women.

The recruitment of fresh supplies happens in a number of ways. In the 'two-stage model', the racketeers look for their commodity in local red-light districts. In the 'one-stage model', made more common by the fear of AIDS, young girls are directly shipped abroad from their native village and initiated into prostitution with an act of rape.[41] Everywhere the age of 'new models' keeps tumbling. Girls dancing in the sex clubs of Bangkok are often no more than ten years old. And each year, a million children become victims of sex tourism, organized prostitution and so-called paedophilia.

It can be assumed that in Nepal, Bangladesh and Burma parents are more and more often aware that their young girls are being sold into the sex industry, but that poverty leaves them with no other source of income. In Albania, however, armed gangs descend on families and carry off their prettier daughters to work as prostitutes in Italy.

Much of the traffic in women's bodies is controlled by transnational syndicates, which make profits by the billion. The trade is an integral part of international crime, often linked to the drugs and automobile rackets. Indeed, in Eastern Europe the payment for stolen cars is often made in women.

Poland has become a supply region for Western Europe, because poverty and unemployment there form a disastrous mix with lack of education and the myth of getting rich quick in the West. The rate of female employment in Poland fell from 78 per cent to 54 per cent between 1985 and 1994, and twice as many men as women are being hired for new jobs. At the same time, Poland is a major transit country for Russian women heading west.

Apart from the traditional forms, new types of weekend prostitution have drawn in students and young women from Eastern Europe who want to earn some spending-money; another new variant is the so-called TIR (Transport International Routier) prostitution along lorry routes near the German–Czech and German–Polish frontiers. In Poland, telephone sex has increased disproportionately since the expansion of the telephone network.[42] At the Black Sea in Turkey, fair-skinned 'Natashas' from Russia and Georgia offer themselves to tourists and nationals alike. The Thai embassy in Moscow receives nearly a thousand visa applications every day from Ukrainian women, who are much sought-after in the Thai and Japanese flesh and marriage markets where novelty is always at a premium.

In Germany, East European women constitute the fourth recent wave in the prostitution racket. The first, in the 1970s and early 1980s, came from South-East Asia; the second from Ghana, Nigeria and Zaire to Western Europe; and the third from Latin America, especially the Dominican Republic.

Anna, whose story was researched by Radhika Coomaraswamy from the UN, might just as easily have come from the Czech Republic or Ukraine, from Nigeria, Burma or the Dominican Republic. Prostitution odysseys are all pretty much alike. The need to pay off 'immigration debts' ties the women to oppressive contracts, and their lack of valid papers means that they are trapped in a dual illegality: as sex workers and as immigrants. Japan, for instance, does not allow any 'unskilled' immigration, which is the category under which prostitution falls. If a Japanese mayor wants to pose as Mr Clean, he orders local brothels to be combed through for foreign women and has them deported. All over the world, raids in red-light districts hit the women, not their pimps or the dealer mafia. And when the women return to their country of origin, often infected with HIV, they may no longer be taken in by their family. Finding themselves in direst need yet in a social vacuum, they are then forced again to take up prostitution.

Decriminalization is a demand that unites prostitutes' organizations and support groups from Brazil through Bangkok to Berlin. In Brazil as in Germany prostitution is not illegal, but it may become criminal at any moment because it is not recognized as involving a relationship of employment. The DAVIDA self-help centre in Rio de Janeiro, for example, where female and male prostitutes work side by side with non-prostitutes, campaigns against violence in red-light districts, arbitrary police actions and discrimination involving the children of prostitutes. It offers legal advice, provides appropriate health care, and organizes its own AIDS prevention. For Gabriela Silva Leite, however, a co-founder of DAVIDA and herself a former prostitute, the aim is also to demystify prostitution and to have it accepted as an occupation.[43]

Prostitution is the choice made by those who have no choice; such is the conclusion from a survey of prostitutes in Recife, a boom town of sex tourism. In most cases, it was an experience of violence in the family or in a circle of acquaintances that first drove the women into commercial sex work. They are helped to get through the 'programme with a gringo' by the dream of a 'fairy prince', preferably from Germany, and by drugs that deaden their feelings of repulsion. More than half the girls had already been once to Europe with a client, in the hope that a marriage might come out of it. Of those who remained, quite a few would learn that marriage is no protection against discrimination, violence or even prostitution.

'Ask them yourself', says Chantawipa Apisuk from the 'Empower' organization, who has been working for more than ten years with prostitutes in the Patpong district of Bangkok that is especially popular with sex tourists. 'They will tell you that they want good working conditions, fair pay and better health care. They do not want to be told that they should stop working because it is immoral.'

The sex industry in Patpong and in Frankfurt's station district are mirror images of each other. Both are products of the glaring difference in living standards between North and South, and of the exotic fantasies that mark sexual consumption behaviour on the part of men. In one case it is the clients, in the other it is the working women, who travel halfway round the globe.

Thai women are still being enticed to Europe with the promise of a good job or a marriage – to Berlin, for example, where the authorities estimate that they account for 3000 of the city's 7000 prostitutes. The introduction of a visa requirement for Germany sent the commission of 'immigration agents' rocketing up to as much as DM40,000 per woman. In addition, the women are sometimes used as a 'mules', unwitting drug couriers. Often they are first married off to a German man in order to acquire legal status.

More than three-quarters of all prostitutes in Germany are foreigners; many in Frankfurt, for example, coming from the Dominican Republic. Before the Schengen Convention was signed in March 1995, it was relatively easy to enter Germany through the Netherlands with a tourist visa. Since then, however, it has become more difficult and above all more expensive, because women come by more complicated routes and through narrower gaps in the fence. At the 'Eros centres' near Frankfurt's main station, they try to earn as much as they can in the shortest possible time, knowing that they will be deported at the latest when the police carry out a second check. This explains why the scene fluctuates so much. Around the core of prostitution, an economic field is organized between legality and illegality, and those who profit from it are mainly men.

Sociologist Ulrich Koch, who has made a study of Frankfurt's station district, uses the term 'branches of the Third World' to describe these international subcultures which have sprung up in the cities of the industrialized societies. They are products of globalization, which 'brings into direct contact with each other, societies at different levels of modernization and with different cultural characteristics'.[44]

The new communications technologies have helped to expand these body markets and to give them further commercial dimensions. The Internet is one floodgate controlling the supply of women and children for sex tourism and marriage: electronic sex markets. In the comfort of one's own living room, it is possible not only to book a flight and hotel but to choose a holiday playmate according to sexual predilection or to search for a possible wife. E-mail also provides access to organizations that trade in women and children, as well as networking like-minded people with one another. Information superhighways offer performances of rape in addition to published pornography – the former to entice leisure-time surfers, the latter complete with a mailbox service. It has been estimated that there are 10,000 pornographic web sites on the Internet, where men can exchange information and work off their cravings for sex and violence. Either they play interactively with virtual shapes, or they order real women in front of a video camera to undress and behave in certain ways, for $6 a minute. Digitizers also make it possible to produce interactive CD-Rom games out of prerecorded videos. Thus, recordings have appeared on the Internet of mass rapes in the former Yugoslavia – an endlessly repeated humiliation for the women concerned.

Monika Gerstendörfer, a computer scientist and analyst of Internet porn and violence, is strongly opposed to its trivialization as 'digital filth'.[45] Consumption in the private domain reduces inhibition levels, so that men become more ready to seek a prospective wife, to watch violent porn films and to abuse women and children interactively. Internet cybersex has long been taking place in a realm partly free of legislation, in which the torture, rape and sometimes even murder of women and children are graphically depicted.

Whereas politicians have not yet tackled the issue of international legislation to cover the Internet, the legal committee of the Council of Europe is drafting a convention against the trade in women. This will provide for fixed-term residence permits for those who have entered an EU country illegally, so that women can feel free to speak out against the immigration racketeers and modern slavetraders. Lea Ackermann, however, whose organization 'Solwodi' looks after victims of the trade in human beings, complains that it is still current practice in Germany to deport women immediately after interrogation, which means that they are no longer in the country when the main proceedings take place. She therefore calls for a real improvement in the rights of witnesses, and for a more effective agreement on mutual law enforcement between the women's country of origin and the host country. Women's groups such as Terre des Femmes also demand that more liaison officers should be sent from the Federal Crime Bureau to back up the prosecution of dealers in prostitution and to safeguard various forms of evidence in the countries concerned.

The sealing of the EU against immigrant workers has not stopped the trade in women; on the contrary, it has made their legal position more precarious and their exploitation more intense. This means that marriage to a European man – or a Japanese or North American – has become even more attractive as a way of supposedly gaining security and protection. The Internet has taken over from the picture catalogue as the principal means of communication on the commercial marriage market. East–West and North–South arranged marriages are a profitable business, linking women's longings and maintenance interests with men's wishes for a sub-missive and undemanding wife. According to the German penal code, trading in women is defined as criminal traffic in human beings only when the context is one of prostitution, so that trading for the purposes of marriage or exploitative labour is not liable to prosecution. Moreover,

Section 19 of the Aliens Act allows the husband to 'return the goods' within three years, since women do not have an independent right of residence during that period. In such cases, if a man testifies before a divorce court that his wife has been a prostitute, she will be deported immediately after the divorce is granted.

In the industrialized countries, women from the South have to face everyday racism. Neither pity for the stereotyped victim nor stigmatization of the 'bought woman' or prostitute recognizes individuals as subjects with different desires, hopes and plans. It is not accepted that women pursue on the global market not only their economic interests but also their longing for love and happiness. The fact that they do this in an exploitative global system, which constantly subjects them to sexist and racist humiliation, is in no way their fault or in their interests; it is simply one of the laws of the market.

Notes

1. Altvater and Mahnkopf (1997), p. 281; Birgit Mahnkopf, 'Deformalisierung der Arbeit', in DGB (1995a), pp. 21–30.

2. Susan Joekes, 'Does Trade Liberalization Carry a Gender Price Tag?', in Oxfam (1996b), p. 27.

3. Ulrich Menzel, 'Die neue Weltwirtschaft. Entstofflichung und Entgrenzung im Zeichen der Postmoderne', *Peripherie* 59/60, pp. 30–45; Altvater and Mahnkopf (1997), pp. 276ff.

4. Europäische Kommission (1997), *Chancengleichheit für Frauen und Männer in der Europäische Union: Jahresbericht 1996*, Luxembourg, p. 31.

5. DGB (1995b), pp. 8ff.

6. *Der Spiegel* 17, 1997; Michael Hahn (1997), 'Die McJob-Maschine. Das Beschäftigungswunder in den USA', *iz3w* 223, August, pp. 23–6.

7. IBFG (1996), p. 13; Carola Möller (1991), 'Über das Brot, das euch in der Küche fehlt, wird nicht in der Küche entschieden', *beiträge zur feministischen theorie und praxis* 29, Cologne, pp. 7–25.

8. *Frankfurter Allgemeine Zeitung*, 6 November 1997.

9. Eva-Maria Thoms (1997), 'Sackgasse Teilzeit', *Die Zeit*, 24 October.

10. Sibylle Raasch, 'Das Korsett sprengen! Feministischer Umbau der Arbeitsgesellschaft?', in Bündnis 90/Die Grünen in Bayern (1997), pp. 23–32.

11. Hans-Jörg Bullinger and Stephan Zinser, 'Zukunft der Arbeit – Arbeit der Zukunft', in HVGB (1997), pp. 115–43.

12. *Le Monde Diplomatique*, May 1997; Elke Wiechmann and Leo Kißler, 'Die Modernisierung der Verwaltung schließt die Frauen aus', *Frankfurter Rundschau*, 18 July 1997.

13. Walter Ch. Zimmerli, 'Vergangenheit und Zukunft der Arbeit – Arbeit der Zukunft', in HVBG (1997), p. 152.

14. dpa (German Press Agency), 17 October 1997; *Frankfurter Rundschau*, 11 April 1996; IPS, 15 September 1997.

15. The name in question has been changed.

16. Eva Wonneberger (1997), 'Frauen und Geld', *Kofra* 83/84, pp. 36–44.

17. Ruth Pearson, 'The Case of Industrialisation and Export Promotion in Jamaica', talk to the UNRISD workshop, Technical Cooperation and Women's Lives: Integrating Gender into Development Policy, Kingston, Jamaica, 7 April 1995.

18. Ruth Pearson, 'Gender and New Technology in the Caribbean: New York for Women?', in Janet H. Momsen (ed.) (1993), *Women and Change in the Caribbean*, London, pp. 287–96; Beverley Mullings, 'Telecommunications Restructuring and the Development of Export Informational Processing Services in Jamaica', in Hopeton Dunn (1995), *Globalization, Communications and Caribbean Identity*, Kingston, Jamaica, pp. 163–85.

19. Cecilia Ng, 'The Descent of New Technology: Computerization and Employment in Malaysia', in Ng and Munro-Ka (1994), pp. 25–49.

20. Europäische Kommission (1996), *Die Informationsgesellschaft*, Brussels, pp. 4f.

21. *Soziales Europa*, special issue, 1995, p. 27.

22. Werner Zorn, 'Telearbeit: eine neue Arbeitskultur mit mehr Produktivität für die Unternehmer und mehr Selbstbestimmung für die Mitarbeiter', in HVBG (1997), pp. 73–84.

23. IBFG (1996), pp. 37f.

24. *Soziales Europa*, special issue 3, 1995, p. 22.

25. Ibid., pp. 18f.

26. Gabriele Winker (1996), 'Weibliche Arbeits- und Lebensrealitäten in der Informationsgesellschaft', *Frauenarbeit und Informatik* 14, December, pp. 45–51.

27. In Ng and Munro-Kua (1994), p. vii.

28. A. Frances Grundy, Doris Köhler, Veronika Oechtering, Ulrike Petersen (eds) (1997), *Women, Work and Computerisation*, Berlin.

29. Marianne Braig, 'Frauen in der internationalen Arbeitsteilung', in M. Braig, U. Ferdinand, M. Zapata (eds) (1997), *Begegnungen und Einmischungen*, 1997, p. 114; Cynthia Cockburn already demonstrated this in the 1980s in her classic study *Mechanics of Dominance: Women, Men and Technical Know-How*, London, 1985, with the aid of numerous examples.

30. Ulrike Erb (1996), 'Frauenperspektiven auf die Informatik', Münster, p. 198.

31. Based on research in Bangalore in January 1997. Since then, the heads of Siemens Communication Software and Deutsche Software have changed.

32. R. Narasimhan (1996), 'Walking on One Leg. India's Software Industry', *Economic and Political Weekly*, 3 August.

33. *Frankfurter Rundschau*, 12 June 1997; Eva Klippenstein, 'Haushalts- und verbrauchernahe Dienste: nur eine neue Variante der Politik des gespaltenen Arbeitsmarktes oder alternative Arbeitsmarktchance für Frauen?', in Frauenpolitischer Runder Tisch (ed.) (1996), *Arbeitsplatz Privathaushalt – die Arbeitsmarktperspektive für Frauen?*, Berlin, pp. 19–26.

34. Hans-Jörg Bullinger/Stephan Zinser, in HVGB (1997), pp. 118f.; and Walther Zimmerli, 'Vergangenheit und Zukunft der Arbeit – Arbeit der Zukunft', in HVGB (1997), p. 152.

35. Südwind e.V. (1994).

36. Brigitte Stolz-Willig and Christina Klenner, 'Arbeitsplatz Privathaushalt – Prekäre Beschäftigung oder neue Chance für Frauen?', in Frauenpolitischer Runder Tisch (ed.) (1996), *Arbeitsplatz Privathaushalt*, pp. 26–43.

37. Elvira Niesner, 'Rechtlos beschäftigt', in *Frauen in der einen Welt* (1996), pp. 87–95.

38. UN, E/CN.4/1997/47/Add. 1, 'Report of the Special Rapporteur on Violence against Women, Its Causes and Consequences', Poland, 10 December 1996.

39. UN, E/CN.4/1997/47, 'Report of the Special Rapporteur on Violence against Women, Its Causes and Consequences', 12 February 1997, pp. 19ff.

40. IPS, 28 March 1997.

41. UN, E/CN.4/1997/47, 12 February 1997, pp. 20f.

42. UN, E/CN.4/1997/47/Add. 1, 10 December 1996, p. 12.

43. Aktionsgemeinschaft Solidarische Welt, 'Mulher da vida – Frauen des Lebens', in *Traumwelten, Migration und Arbeit* (n.d.), Berlin, pp. 24ff.

44. Ulrich Koch (1996), 'Bahnhofsviertel Frankfurt', *epd-Entwicklungspolitik*, 15–16, pp. 35–42.

45. Monika Gerstendörfer (1997), 'Das Internet: Bühne und Börse für die massenhafte Verbreitung von schwersten Mißhandlungen an Kindern', *Kofra* 82, February–March, pp. 3–9.

3

Means of Living

Land for Men, Work for Women

A dozen women are sitting beneath a tree in Bungoma, Kenya. They are discussing how they can increase the yield of their kitchen gardens by digging deeper and on rich beds, and what kinds of millet, fruit and vegetables are suitable as baby food. Two men listen attentively. When asked why they are there, one of them replies: 'We have to know what the women are getting up to with our land.'

In Africa men have the land and call the shots. The masters share out some of the land for their wives to use (marriage often being polygamous). This 'kitchen garden' derives its name from the fact that women grow food crops there for the kitchen; if the crop is larger than they need for themselves, they sell the surplus at the nearest market for other people to use in their kitchens. Every such garden is a model of biological diversity. The women plant alongside each other a mix of cabbage and turnip, leaf and root vegetables, local and imported varieties. It is often mockingly called 'female agriculture'.

Less than 5 per cent of farmland in Kenya is owned by women. Fields are mainly handed down in a male line of descent, and it is not uncommon for women to lose use rights at the death of their husband. Only a small number manage to buy a piece of land for themselves. Most remain stuck in a Catch-22 situation: they are not given credit to purchase land, because they cannot put up any land as security.[1]

The greater part of the land is used by men for the growing of cash crops – mainly sugar-cane or tobacco in the west of the country. But instead of bringing in quick money, the cultivation of the sweet cane leads directly to food bottlenecks. In recent years, Bungoma district has witnessed an alarming growth in malnutrition among children. The reason for this is all the seedlings, fertilizer, pesticide and herbicide that the sugar factory supplies to the farmer at his own cost. After eighteen months, a column of workers hired by the factory returns to fell the juicy cane. But all these costs are charged to the farmer, and deducted from the price that he eventually receives for his produce. Since he first has to get through the eighteen months, he is forced to borrow money. And what is left after he has paid off this debt with compound interest is little more than a joke.

If a woman wants to expand her kitchen garden, she must ask her husband to let her use a larger plot of land. By no means all men agree to this. Many hold the view that the growing of fruit and vegetables is a waste of their valuable land and soil. They do not worry themselves about how the pot is to be filled – that is women's business.

Usually, the labour of farming women is less productive than the men's. A study for the International Food Policy Research Institute in Washington explains this by the fact that women do not have the same use of machines, technology, credits and assistance, and that the soil is often poorer in 'women's fields'. 'If women were given the same resources as men, developing countries would see significant increases in agricultural productivity,' concludes the study *Women: The Key to Food Security*.[2]

Seventy-five per cent of all agricultural labour in Africa is performed by women. This over-representation is in blatant contradiction to the fact that women own less land and find it much more difficult to get advice or loans. Besides, only 7 per cent of agricultural advisers are female, and the advice usually given is that medium-sized farms (owned by men) should specialize in cash crops. As to loans, women in Africa receive barely a tenth of what is handed out to male small farmers, and a mere 1 per cent of total agricultural credits.[3]

This picture is changing only very slowly, even though in the 1980s Africa experienced a far-reaching structural transformation of small-farm agriculture. In the west, east and south of the continent, men became a rare sight in the fields as they migrated in search of work in the cities, coastal regions or neighbouring countries. For at least a large part of the year, women are left alone to cope with fields and livestock, house and yard, children and old people. And when the men stay away for a long time, as they do in West Africa, this results in a shrinking of the land available for agriculture, since the women alone are capable of tilling only the smaller fields.

The International Labor Organization (ILO) has established that, in some parts of Kenya and Zambia, three-quarters of small farms are run by women. The men are at most part-time or seasonal farmers. This tendency, known as the 'feminization of small-farm agriculture', weakens the old gender division of labour whereby men were responsible for market produce and women for food consumed by the family. Nowadays, women also do most of the work in the 'men's fields', and in their own they also plant market produce from coffee, sunflowers and pyrethrum to cut flowers and vegetables for export to Europe. Whereas they used to look after only small farm animals, now they are also responsible for the cattle that have started to be kept in farmyard stalls.[4]

Mama Miriam lives in the Kitui district of Kenya, a semi-arid region with fertile soil which, because of drought, can be farmed only in the proximity of the river. Until now Mama Miriam has grown a mixture of maize, manioc, beans, bananas and a few other crops. But an Italian agri-business has appeared on the scene and has talked the men and women farmers into growing fruit and vegetables for the export market. The firm supplies seed, fertilizer and pesticide, as well as cardboard packaging, and it picks up the produce from Mama Miriam's garden gate. Foreign-funded development projects also often help out with the conversion from sub-sistence to export: small loans are available only for cash crops, seed hybrids and the recommended fertilizer, herbicide and pesticide.

Mama Miriam has now been integrated into the world market and has stopped growing produce for herself and local consumers. Income from cash crops is supposed to provide her with food. Mama Miriam is proud that she earns more money than ever before, but this does not alter the fact that her farmland and soil belong not to her but to her husband. When he comes home from Nairobi, he will still make all the major decisions about how her earnings should be spent.

Mama Miriam soon understood that imported varieties are much more susceptible to disease, pest attack and drought, and she suspects that she is now dependent on more things than just the weather and vermin. Demand in Italy, international price fluctuations and competition from other cheap suppliers are risks over which local people can have no in-fluence.

After the huge drop in coffee prices, every Kenyan farmer knows that the ground rules of the world economy hold many risks for individual producers. In 1989, when the International Coffee Organization put an end to a quota system that had stabilized price levels on the world market, coffee prices fell through the floor. It was a catastrophe for producers in Africa – a result of what is known as the 'cash crop trap'. At the same time, production costs increased because certain pests had begun to develop high levels of resistance to pesticide. The whole business was no longer worthwhile. Many farmers therefore switched to other export products that would make them some money.

Since the collapse of coffee and cocoa prices, agricultural policies every-where in Africa have been geared to diversification and 'non-traditional export goods'. In Kenya, it is especially horticultural products and cut flowers that offer the prospect of quick money. In Mozambique, tobacco is held up as the means of churning out foreign currency. In Uganda, the World Bank is pushing for more export production and vanilla cultivation.

Roses and carnations, beans and avocados are taking the best soil away from cereals and vegetables grown for local consumption. The market is occupying the most fertile land, as subsistence production moves out to the margins. Women are forced to take an axe to bushland or steep slopes, to use up the soil without care or consideration, and to open the way for further erosion. The ecological consequences are truly disastrous, for results that are meagre at best. Less and less of agriculture serves to feed the local people themselves.

David Gray, director of Sulmac, Africa's largest flower exporter, has himself warned that the market is 'extremely temperamental and hard to predict'. But Sulmac – a subsidiary of the tea giant Brooke Bond, which is in turn owned by the Unilever family – is well protected by its various economic connections. Kenyaflowers at Kelsterbach near Frankfurt, for example, the German subsidiary of the world flower-market leader Florimax, provides Sulmac with additional access to the most important European market: Germany.

On Sulmac's plantations and means of transport, everything is planned down to a fine art. Nimble women's hands pick, sort and pack the flowers on the shores of Lake Naivasha, from open carnation beds that are by far the largest in the world. They manage 2600 stems a day, for a wage of not even $1.50. Then begins the cool journey: from the storage room beside the sorting hall, on the refrigerated lorry to Nairobi airport and the firm's own cold storage rooms, and finally on the cooled air freight compartments to Holland or Frankfurt. The next day, they turn up as fresh luxury petals in German shops, running time altogether: five days. In 1990 Kenya exported cut flowers to the EU to a value of US$40 million. By 1994 the figure had climbed to $150 million. So long as world market forces allow!

In the cases of maize, wheat and sugar, Kenya has already come to feel the laws of a world market freed from import and export restrictions. Until the end of the 1980s, the country was self-sufficient in basic food-stuffs. In 1992 19 per cent of national grain requirements were imported, and in 1993–94 a drought actually led to a large deficit in foodstuffs. The resulting deprivation was then cynically used to open the door wide for international agribusiness. Maize imports rose two-and-a-half-fold, wheat imports by more than half, and even sugar requirements were covered by imports to the tune of 40 per cent. It was mainly a question of highly subsidized agricultural produce from the EU and the USA.[5]

Although Kenya notched up a record harvest the following year, imports continued to flood the internal market. A revaluation of the Kenyan shilling made local products more expensive in relation to foreign goods, and in 1994 special duty-exemptions for agribusiness (in which politicians were directly implicated) widened the price differentials. For Kenyan suppliers, maize and wheat prices fell by half to well below their costs of production.

While its markets were forced open for subsidized farm produce from the industrialized countries, Kenya's own fertilizer subsidies were abolished and government advice and support for small farmers was wound down. As a result, surpluses from the industrialized countries undercut Kenyan produce and drove local farmers to the brink. The cultivation of maize as a basic foodstuff has become a loss-making business for which there is no incentive; food security no longer enters into the picture.

Eating habits have also changed in Kenya. Colonial influences, food aid, development projects and cheap new imports have served to alter people's tastes: cabbage and tomatoes instead of wild leaf vegetables, white bread instead of cassava bread, Maggi powders instead of local spices. Traditional, ecologically sound foods such as tubers, roots and drought-resistant millet have been all but abandoned. Tastes have switched to locally unsuitable produce and thus made the food supply dependent upon two uncontrollable conditions: heavenly grace (in the form of rainfall), and market grace (in the form of favourable prices).

In 1996–97, when the price of maize in Kenya doubled as a result of a new drought plus currency-rate changes, it was not only in Bungoma that women were forced to reconsider plans to expand their kitchen gardens. In the towns too, where such forms of agriculture had also recently been expanding, green roadside strips, front gardens and wasteland sites were immediately occupied with maize plants and *sukuma wiki*, the most popular type of cabbage. Domestic servants, nightwatchmen and sales assistants, who could not feed their children on what they earned, planted every free square metre in the towns of Kenya and other African countries. There were onions and papaya trees instead of flower-borders in front of the housing estates of underpaid civil servants in Dar-es-Salaam; chickens and banana plants in the backyards of Lusaka; vegetables on the wide central reservations of the arterial roads of Kampala, and especially of Kinshasa, where the food supply system had largely collapsed. That is self-provision through self-help. Illegal garden plots, though often no wider than a towel, make an important contribution to survival in the big population centres – so long as speculators have not grabbed and concreted over the last patch of green land, and so long as the city elders are willing to turn a blind eye. Urban agriculture is nearly everywhere prohibited on health grounds and condemned as an eyesore. Yet a quarter of people living in Africa's capital cities state that they would not be able to survive without it.[6]

The urban farmers are mainly women from the lower classes. When they plant cabbage and sweet potato, they first burn the refuse of better-off local residents to use as fertilizer and fetch water from the nearest leaking drainpipe. It is not without health dangers – nor, for that matter, is the growing of food in the polluted air of traffic-clogged roads. But it is a question of life and death. One ecological plus is that organic waste is used as compost and that transport is not used to bring food from country to town: a chain of cold storage units is not necessary here. So, in effect, two supply systems exist alongside each other in Nairobi and many other African cities: an expensive, modern transport-dependent system controlled by big traders, and an informal, short-distance, direct-marketing system from mini-field to cooking pot, which has no need of lorries, covered markets and supermarkets. The second of these, according to agrarian expert Jac Smit, 'has long been overlooked, underestimated and under-valued', but it is becoming more important for city life, because not only the urban population but also poverty are on the increase.

Women are developing new strategies of self-provision within the liberalized global agri-market, as a way of securing their own needs in a space between cash crop exports and subsidized imports. But the central importance of women in both rural and urban agriculture has nowhere been properly understood as pivotal to a political strategy to secure the food supply. Nor is it ever recognized that the genuine female principle of an economy centred on needs and caring – what we might call cooking-pot economics – is the most reliable guarantee of food security.

Proteins for the Well-fed

Shrimps in the salad. Over the last decade, the menus and lunch tables of Germany have seen a miraculous multiplication of shrimps and prawns. It is a miracle not so much of nature as of aquaculture. Since the oceans have been overfished by ever larger fleets, and since the demand for deli-cacies has kept growing in the industrialized countries, it seems reasonable to suppose that the rearing of shellfish can no longer be entrusted to nature alone. Now they can be boosted with the help of hormones, pesticides and high-protein feed, so that they arrive faster and plumper on the world market.

Since the mid-1980s, the UN Food and Agriculture Organization (FAO) has recorded an 'unstoppable worldwide expansion' of aquaculture as part of the 'blue revolution', the technological revolution in the fishing industry. This has been hailed by the FAO itself as a kind of protein machine for food security, and millions have been poured into it by international development agencies such as the World Bank. After Thailand and Taiwan, more and more countries have jumped on to the currency-and-profits bandwagon since the beginning of the 1990s: India and Bangladesh among others in Asia; Ecuador, Mexico and a growing list elsewhere in the world. In the coastal regions of Asia alone, it is estimated that 10,000 square kilometres are now covered with prawn farms. Thailand is the top exporter with 220,000 tonnes, more than a quarter of annual world production. In 1995 Germany imported 17,900 tonnes of prawn and shrimp from Asia. And the international fishing trade hopes for a 50 per cent rise in sales by the year 2000.[7]

The 'unstoppable expansion' takes no heed of losses: that is, of local populations and the environment. When, for example, the farmers of Kerpan in Malaysia's Kedah province refused to make their rice fields available for a 250-hectare prawn farm, they were expropriated without further ado by the provincial government, itself a co-owner of the 'Samak' aquaculture firm, on the grounds that the project would bring economic benefits to the country as a whole. In Bangladesh, businessmen bulging with capital pressure small farmers into making over the rights to their land. Then they cut through the dykes and flood the fields, or send in shock troops to intimidate the farmers and drive out any tenants. Where rice and jute have grown until now, prawns jostle one another in brackish water. Kushi Kabir from the non-governmental organization Njira Khori reports that, because of the salty water and the use of chemicals, the rice yield on nearby fields has fallen by 30 per cent, the harvest has been only half as good as before for coconut and mango and even worse for vegetables, and chickens and ducks have been dying off. In November 1992, when cheated farming families marched in protest at the plundering of nature and of their own means of life, Karunoyami, the woman leading the march, was killed by hired assassins.

Huge numbers of shrimp brood are needed for aquaculture to prosper. On the coasts of Bangladesh, this is one way in which the very poor and landless can earn some money. Men draw simple nets through the breakers in which the shrimp brood are carried by the tide; women and children then sort through the landed booty. At the most, 5 per cent of the catch are the sought-after brood – black threads one centimetre long. The rest is 'waste': little fishes and the brood of other sea creatures, which the women throw back into the water. Often they do not survive the proceedings.

During the high season in April and May, a family may catch as many as 2000 shrimp mites a day. Traders pay 20 US cents per hundred and sell them in turn to shrimp farms at a 100 per cent profit. These then raise the creatures in three months and make a 100 per cent profit for themselves by selling them to exporters. The costs of a shrimp farm installation can thus be amortized in the second year – truly a profit machine.

The most a beach family can make is $4 a day, but low-season earnings are not even half that. Forty thousand people are occupied in gathering shrimps off the coast of Cox's Bazar in Bangladesh. There are three times as many in the Sundarbans Delta, where sea prawns lay their eggs on the roots of mangrove trees. Local people fish up the larvae with fine-meshed nets, often damaging the mangrove roots in the process. Mangroves are of immeasurable value for the coastal ecology, both as a barrier against floods and storms, and as a habitat for the 'upbringing' of ocean species. Nevertheless, in Bangladesh as well as in Thailand, the Philippines, Indonesia and Vietnam, whole mangrove forests have been made to give way to shrimp farms.[8]

Since 1992 India too has been caught up in the global shrimp and prawn fever, often with the involvement of local politicians. Indian entrepreneurs and firms from Thailand and Taiwan make huge profits from export of the little delicacies to Japan, Europe and the USA. In the South Indian state of Tamil Nadu alone, there are fifty-four breeding farms and 910 aquacultural installations over a surface of 6224 hectares. Scarcely one of the shrimp barons has an official licence.

The Cauvery Delta has always been considered key to Tamil Nadu's rice production, with three harvests a year thanks to fertile soil and regular irrigation. Now tiger prawns crawl on the rice fields in a mixture of sweet and salty water. The landowners were tempted by quick money and sold or leased their land to aquaindustrialists, thereby causing thousands upon thousands of agricultural families to lose their whole livelihood. There are hardly any replacement jobs: seventy-five people per hectare used to be employed in the harvest season, but now a five-hectare prawn farm can be run with a workforce of three. In the neighbouring state of Andhra Pradesh, 10,000 tonnes less rice a year – enough to feed 10,000 families – are produced as a result of aquaculture.

With dykes and barbed-wire fencing all around, with watchtowers at every corner, lucrative giant prawns grow up in Pudukuppan in farms that are more like a prohibited military area – forty-eight ponds spread over 100 hectares as far as the eye can see, right up to the fringe of the coconut palms. Like battery chickens, the pond prawns are highly prone to disease, and so the breeders try to prevent epidemics through the use of pesticides and antibiotics. This, together with the feed and excreta, soon turns the ponds into a stinking poisonous brew. The water has to be changed at frequent intervals.

Men and women in the fishing village of Pudukuppan (population 500) talk themselves into a rage. Strong pumps force salt water from the sea into the ponds and pump back the waste. 'We can no longer fish near the beaches,' they say. 'The water stinks to high heaven.' The drainage pipes have also damaged their catamarans and torn their nets. It has become impossible to pull the nets ashore after a catch. And it is not only the coastal waters that are poisoned. The women complain that the drinking water has acquired a salty taste, and that they have to travel three kilometres a day to fetch clean supplies. Feed for small farm animals, as well as domestic fuel, also has to be dragged a long way or else bought. Due to salination of the soil, trees die or topple over, clay houses crumble at the foundations. The men's income has fallen, and the women's work burden has risen.

Fishing families have joined the angry protests of farmworkers' families along the coast of south-east India. Together they have faced up to bulldozers trying to excavate new ponds, occupied prawn farms, damaged pipes and pumps, submitted petitions and drawn up a complaint in the form of a 'People's Report'. The well-known environmental activist Vandana Shiva calls the anti-prawn campaign 'a new independence struggle of the Indian people'.

According to an economic cost-benefit analysis made by the NEERI research institute, income from prawn-farming in Tamil Nadu in 1995 came to a total of 2.8 billion rupees, while the demonstrable ecological damage and economic losses were estimated at 4.2 billion rupees. In Andhra Pradesh, the costs were as much as four times greater than the economic benefits.[9]

In December 1996, the anti-prawn campaign scored a great success when the Supreme Court banned intensive farming within 500 metres of the coasts and held the industry liable for the ecological damage. But the economic and political powers of this world cannot be dislodged so easily. More than two hundred objections were raised and alternative draft legislation submitted. The FAO and the World Bank condemned the Supreme Court ruling. Jesu Rethinam, a legal expert and spokeswoman for the campaign, joked: 'Now they'll promise a "clean prawn industry". How is that supposed to work?'

Less land, less rice, less clean water and less employment – for the poor it is certainly a negative balance-sheet. In fact, aquaculture functions as a protein and calorie transfer from the South to the North. Even the FAO now admits that the availability of fish, 'particularly for low-income consumers in Asia, is being reduced as a result of competition from aquaculture feed demands'.[10] Particularly absurd is the fact that intensive farming uses two kilos of feed concentrate – often flour from less valuable species of fish – for one kilo of prawn. India imports nearly half of the feed concentrate in question from Chile and Peru.

These massive holdings last an average of eight years, by which time the ground is so contaminated that the ponds have to be abandoned. Hit and run is the name of the game. The shrimp industry simply moves on, leaving behind poisoned land that will not be available again for agriculture for decades to come.

So is the answer to stick to North Sea prawns, especially as they are fresh? But what does fresh mean here? Between catch and restaurant plate, there is usually a journey of three weeks and (often enough) more than 6000 kilometres. The Heiploeg company of Groningen in the Netherlands ships 40 per cent of its North Sea prawns at -3°C to be shelled in the Tetouan industrial zone in Morocco.[11] For generations this work used to be done at home by North Sea fishermen's wives, but today that is no longer permitted for hygienic reasons. If the shelling took place in an approved plant in the Netherlands or Germany, the wage costs would be ten times higher than in Tetouan.

A thousand women work there, paid roughly $175 a month on piece-rates to remove heads and armour from the prized shellfish. The daily norm is three kilos of finished product per worker. The women, most of them illiterate, initially spend four weeks being trained; the company lays on buses to take them to the sterile plant and even provides childcare facilities. It is a highly sought-after job.

After shelling, the prawn meat is again chilled and sent back on its 3000-kilometre journey across Europe to Groningen, aboard a refrigerated lorry that consumes 2000 litres of diesel a day. Other supplies are shipped to Poland or Russia for similar treatment, and again three weeks may well pass before their final consumption as 'fresh North Sea prawns'.

Whether the shellfish come from the North Sea, South Asia, Latin America or the coastal waters off Senegal, whether they are caught wild or bred through aquaculture, they must always be savoured with care and attention. Njira Khori in Bangladesh breeds shrimps and prawns on an ecologically sound basis, and many small family businesses also catch or breed the delicacies without causing social and ecological damage. But since no one is under any obligation to reveal the details, consumers have no way of identifying prawns that have or have not been put through extreme processes of industrial production. Precise information about origin, age and production methods is thus an indispensable requirement for consumer protection. Otherwise, consumers cannot use a shopping boycott to take political action against a socially and ecologically crazy mode of production.[12]

Hunger and Trade

In 1995, after several good harvests, the storehouses in India were well stocked. The government triumphantly declared that India no longer suffered from starvation but had become a food-exporting country. Nevertheless, some 200 million people there are still thought to be chronically undernourished. Countless thousands of small farming families have had to sell their land because the government stopped subsidizing seed and fertilizer.

These facts illustrate the difference between food security at a national level and food security at the level of individual households. For a long time now, the presence of enough food in a country has no longer meant that everyone there eats their fill of healthy food. The distribution of supplies takes place through the operation of certain economic, social and cultural filters: purchasing-power and social class or caste between households, and gender within the household. Statistics about per capita food production, or even per capita calorie intake, do not tell us anything about the actual nutrition of individual people.

Most of the 790 million people in the world who, according to the FAO, do not have enough to eat belong to one of the following three groups: children below five years of age, especially girls; women of child-bearing age, especially pregnant and nursing mothers; and low-income households, especially ones with a female head.[13]

It is above all in Asia that cultural taboos and everyday practices put women and girls at a disadvantage in terms of food. The men eat first, then the children, and in poor households women get only what is left over. In rural areas of Bangladesh, the risk of dying from the effects of malnutrition is more than twice as great for girls as it is for boys; in poor households in North India, 21 per cent of girls but only 3 per cent of boys are severely undernourished. Again it is mostly women and girls who have deficiencies in Vitamin A, iron and iodine and who fall ill as a consequence. Eighty per cent of pregnant women in Asia are anaemic, and of course their nutrition is an important factor in a baby's weight at birth and susceptibility to illness. If the mother is infected with HIV, then malnutrition increases the risk that the virus will be transmitted to the child.[14]

Household studies show that mothers tend to act as shock absorbers for their children. If the daily bread runs short, the children's food situation at first remains the same, whereas the mother's immediately worsens. Whether or not women themselves till the fields or decide on income expenditure, the provision of food is their main priority. Whereas men particularly like buying consumer durables, the family food situation improves considerably when women have more money available. They are the food securers *par excellence*.[15]

At the World Food Summit held in Rome in November 1996, which affirmed the human right to adequate nourishment, the assembled governments undertook to bring about food security and to wage war on hunger; trade was to be the strategy, the world market the battlefield; each country's 'comparative advantage' would act as the neoliberal spur for the feeding of everyone around the world. The idea, then, was that every location would concentrate on growing what best suited it geographically and climatically – not what people needed there, but what could be sold at a good price on the world market. During the GATT Uruguay Round talks in 1994,[16] governments had agreed on a liberalization of agriculture, and in particular on the opening of markets to imports and the removal of protective barriers for national producers.

The Philippines government of former president Ramos promised to permit increasingly larger quantities of two basic foodstuffs, rice and maize, to be imported, and to lower import duties on them by successive amounts. This chimed in well with the orientation of the country's agricultural policy towards the world market and the earning of foreign currency. The aim was to reduce the five million hectares of land under rice and maize to no more than two million hectares; the other three million would be divided equally between export cash crops and livestock breeding. A law enacted in 1995 further allowed foreign companies to prospect and mine for raw materials such as ore, copper and gold over a couple of million hectares for a period of seventy-five years. Large areas of cultivable land will certainly be destroyed as a result.

Since the productivity of maize cultivation is relatively low in the Philippines, highly subsidized imports from the USA are considerably cheaper there than local supplies. Oxfam has calculated that every farmer in the USA is subsidized annually to the tune of $29,000 – almost a hundred times more than the $300 which the 1.2 million farming families on the Philippine island of Mindanao earn each year from their maize. The competition is extremely unequal, then. Oxfam predicts that maize imports will take away the livelihood of half a million people in Mindanao.[17]

The rural women's federation Amihan further estimates that the annual import quota of 239,000 tonnes of rice until the year 2005, which was allocated by the GATT Round, will gradually destroy the livelihood of 750,000 rice farmers, most of them women. The government recommends that small farms should prepare themselves by going over to the cultivation of flowers, asparagus and broccoli for the world market.[18]

In Mexico, too, the United States has captured markets for its maize surplus. Under the terms of the NAFTA Agreement, the Mexican government is supposed to phase out its policy of guaranteed minimum prices for cereals that has been practised since the Revolution of 1910, and to increase its duty-free import quotas for maize; while the United States has promised gradually to abandon its own import restrictions on Mexican agricultural products. Soon afterwards, the upper limits on land ownership in Mexico were raised in an open invitation for agribusiness to move in.

The losers will be the estimated 2.4 million producers whose maize is unable to compete with the cheap imports.[19]

In the GATT negotiations of 1994, the industrialized countries undertook to pay compensation to poorer cereal-importing countries if the price of basic foods increased as a result of liberalization. But although cereal prices rose sharply between 1994 and 1996, no such payments have been made.

The EU is currently offloading tomato puree at dumping prices on to the African market, as well as shipping powdered milk to Senegal and beef to South Africa (with a 56 per cent subsidy, and in direct competition with cattle-breeders in South Africa and Namibia). The estimated damages for South Africa are roughly equivalent to the total development aid that it receives from the EU: DM200 million.[20]

Whereas governments of developing countries have for years been compelled under IMF and World Bank restructuring programmes to end food subsidies for poorer sections of the population, the Uruguay Round agreed on only a small limitation of export subsidies by the year 2000 for the industrialized countries: 21 per cent by quantity and 36 per cent by financial volume. The head of the US negotiating team was a representative of the Cargill Corporation, the world's largest cereal producer and food trader.[21]

Agricultural subsidies total US$19 billion in Germany and $47 billion in the EU. Agricultural policy thus consumes nearly two-thirds of the EU budget, and so far there has been no reduction in the subsidy level. Before the EU's agricultural reform, 60 per cent of subsidies went into high levels of stock maintenance, the processing industry and the export trade. As the subsidies to farmers varied according to output and acreage, 20 per cent of farms – that is, the big capitalist ones – received 80 per cent of the total. Thus the industrialization of agriculture and production of surpluses, on the one hand, and the elimination of small family farms on the other, were positively promoted by EU policy. Although the agricultural reform was supposed to bring about restrictions on output and the area under cultivation, the European butter and meat mountains and milk and wine lakes continued to grow. In Germany, 20 per cent more wheat was produced in 1996 than was consumed. The surplus was 40 per cent in the case of sugar, and 14 per cent in that of beef and veal.[22] Ten per cent of the fruit harvest is destroyed by the EU, while at the same time fruit and vegetables are imported from other continents.

The industrialization of agriculture means fewer jobs, major ecological damage and the death of small farms. In the first half of the 1990s, more than fifty small farms went to the wall each day in Germany – an annual loss of roughly 20,000 full-time jobs, or close to half a million at a

European level. This trend is a deliberate result of economic policy, for small farmers produce at too high cost. In July 1997 the price of a hundredweight of wheat on the Chicago Exchange was $13, while a farmer in the Eifel region had to make well over $18 to cover his costs. The competition is even fiercer in the cases of milk and beef.[23] Nor are nutrition and soil quality a criterion in the planning of how space is to be used. Thus the area west of Cologne, which has some of the best land in Germany, has in recent years been concreted over with shopping centres and deprived of its capacity to feed the local population.

Owing to the conditions resulting from unification, 700,000 of the 915,000 well-educated land and forestry workers in Eastern Germany lost their jobs. At the same time, agriculture has become more male dominated, with women falling from 60 per cent to 53 per cent of agricultural employees, many of them being retrained as landscape gardeners.[24] Many small family farms in both East and West are able to survive only because they have made the provision of holiday board and lodging their main source of income.

More and more countries, more and more people, are supposed to eat their fill from the world market instead of their own fields. At the same time, experts are warning with increasing urgency that the rise in agricultural productivity will not continue. World supplies of wheat, maize and oil-seed are tight, and prices are growing accordingly. The renowned Worldwatch Institute in Washington has pointed out that US farm crops – on whose export more than a hundred countries now live – are dependent upon the weather to a disturbing degree.[25]

In India the productivity growth of recent years has already been reversed. Both the growth and the subsequent shortages have the same cause: the Green Revolution. For the massive use of chemicals in intensive farming has exhausted the soil and destroyed its organic nutrients, while artificial irrigation has led to excessive levels of salt. As yields fall, farmers give up rice and wheat and turn to cash crops such as tomatoes, flowers, coffee and rubber.[26]

In Vietnam, which has become the world's third largest rice exporter since the turn to a market economy in 1989, monoculture involving huge doses of fertilizer and chemicals has had a catastrophic effect upon the environment. The use of chemicals soared from 7600 tonnes in 1989 to 20,000 tonnes in 1991. And according to FAO data, farmers in the Mekong Delta spent an average of $40 dollars in 1992 on chemical pesticides, compared with $26 in the Philippines and $3.7 in Indonesia. Since they have to spray more and more to maintain output levels, they go for the cheapest ones on the market. But the cheapest are also among the most dangerous – DDT, for example.[27]

For years it was assumed that the handling of agricultural toxic sub-stances was men's work. In the last few years, however, a number of studies by the Pesticide Action Network have shown that women also come into contact with them on a daily basis, in soil preparation and the sowing or harvesting of crops. In Malaysia and the Philippines, they themselves either spray or prepare chemical cocktails, sometimes with bare hands. They also have to wash pesticide-soaked clothing, as well as rinsing out containers and using them to fetch water. Even in an advanced state of pregnancy, they cannot escape when aircraft spray chemicals from the sky, as they do in Costa Rica over banana plantations. The consequences are illnesses of the respiratory tract, the skin and the reproductive organs, and a dispro-portionately high number of deformed children, especially as few women are able to read instruction leaflets warning of risks to the health.[28]

Meanwhile, the international seed and chemical giants – ten corporations controlling 74 per cent of the world pesticide trade – present themselves as pro-woman and environmentally friendly. The British corporation ICI uses adverts of scantily-clad blondes with a pesticide flask on their back, who beam as they casually spray the toxins around as if they were health-giving balsam. And the Anglo–Dutch oil multinational Shell hired a well-known actress to dance with one of its products poised in her hand.

It is not so much the growing population as the growing appetite of the well-fed that threatens the world's food supply. For wherever the middle classes multiply, as in China, the hunger for meat also sharply rises; proteins are prestige. A diet high in meat and milk, however, requires a large supply of cereals as animal feed. Naturally, attempts are made to reduce the costs of livestock production – for example, through the use of steroids to shorten the fattening period. BSE in Britain is a result of cost-cutting through adding matter from dead animals to the feed.

World market competition is the engine driving further industrialization of agriculture and livestock farming. Thus, governments and development agencies set so much store by raising productivity that they will grant loans for seed only if artificial fertilizer is purchased at the same time. Development aid also helps to open up new markets: the Japanese foreign ministry donated tonnes of chemicals to Cambodia in 1993. Labour-intensive small farms less geared to the use of technology and chemicals, which work to cover local or national requirements, are therefore neglected in the formation of agrarian policies. At the World Food Summit in Rome, for example, small farmers from the South complained about something long familiar in Europe: 'We are a dying species.'

The price that people all over the world pay for the gradual extinction of small-scale farming is a loss of food security. To achieve food security through the world market is extremely problematic, both quantitatively and qualitatively. To use world trade as a means of combating hunger and guaranteeing the human right to food is a risky game indeed, a gamble on the future that may fail for any number of reasons. It certainly does not feed many poor people; however, it brings the agri-multinationals fat profits.

Fast Food, Junk Food, Novelty Food – or the Lost Power of the Cook

When McDonald's opened its first Moscow branch in 1991, people knew that the change had really begun to a Western-style market economy. In the informal market, too, traders soon adapted to the new tastes: hot dogs appeared all over the capital as 'local' fast food, at mobile stands and street kiosks. Moscow's mayor, a capable businessman, countered this with a 'Rossiya' chain of bistros selling pirogi, borshch and kvass instead of hamburgers and coke. But the crowds at McDonald's are still larger.

The fast-food empire is expanding into the last blank spots of the gastronomic world map, as the multinationals buy and fight their way into newly liberalized markets. In India Coca-Cola has taken over Parle, the country's largest soft-drinks producer, and British American Tobacco is trying to swallow up the Indian Tobacco Company, the local market-leader.

Kentucky Fried Chicken has become India's hotly contested heraldic beast of liberalization. Its first branches in Delhi and Bangalore were closed down when Hindu nationalists claimed that a couple of flies had been served as a 'side-dish'. But the Supreme Court eventually ruled that this was against the law, and the corporation can now make a killing from its industrially produced poultry.

Pepsi-Cola, on the other hand, attempts to pinch recipes for local delicacies – *bikaneri bhujia*, for example, the snack much loved all over India which has mainly been produced by women at home or in small businesses and sold by street-traders. Recently, Pepsi-Cola built a high-tech factory on the outskirts of New Delhi which churns out 50 tonnes of *bhujias* a day – as much as 80,000 people produce by hand in Bikaner, the old *bhujia* centre. Everywhere the market for snacks between meals has been an important source of women's income, but now it is becoming keenly contested. Pepsi has mounted a racy advertising campaign to win away their customers, which emphasizes its own high-tech and supposedly hygienic methods of producing the traditional recipe of the women of Bikaner. 'We can't let a handful of people hold up industrial modernization,' is how Pepsi's Indian boss meets the objections of local producers. And the firm has already started to extend its range to other ethno-snacks.[29]

The McDonaldization of catering and the capture of markets by the multinationals have two grave consequences: a process of economic concentration that often ousts women from the processing and selling of food; and a forced industrialization that turns ingredients into a commercial secret and leads to a standardization of eating habits. Tastes are no longer supposed to differ; they are 'brought into line'. In a McDonald's advert that illustrates this cultural levelling to perfection, a group of burger-eating Tibetan monks change their mantra from 'Om' to a simpler 'mmmmmmmm'. Junk food with identical added tastes and with a low nutritional value, stored in cans or a deep freeze, is thus raised in an act of technological arrogance above the cycles of nature, above time and space themselves. Christmas strawberries and asparagus, New Zealand lamb, Senegalese shellfish and Chilean mangoes – everything is always in season in the supermarkets and canteens, and increasingly in private homes too. What women serve up at midday, or what is on the restaurant and canteen menus, has been to a large extent internationalized, bought on the global market and prepared by a global industry, with their thousands of miles of transport routes, their energy costs and environmental damage. More and more, it is multinational corporations rather than women in control of pots and pans which decide what is dished up on the table. Seventy per cent of the European food and drinks market is in the hands of eight companies, with Nestlé, Cadbury and Schweppes at the top. They supply everything that humans and animals take into their digestive tract – from baby food to dogs' meals.

The catering giants that supply workplace meals also contribute to the formation of taste by the private-sector economy. In Germany it is a market worth US$11 billion a year, which, since the preparation of meals was taken away from the canteens themselves, has been keenly disputed by firms such as Sodexho, Appetito, Eurest and Hansa. The unit costs (regardless of season) of the canteen chains mainly consist of salads, pasta and light poultry or fish dishes for 7.2 million employees.[30] Fear of excess kilos means that more fish and salad oil have to be imported.

There is an easy transition from this industrial mass production to the phenomenon of novelty food. Ten thousand new products come on to the market every year, mainly the easy-to-prepare 'convenience foods'. Pharmaceutical and chemical corporations are racing one another to come up with new synthetic foods following the success of cola and energy drinks, diet margarines and artificial fats. Food engineering has now moved on to powdered salads and vegetables, vitamin biscuits and cakes, and new types of artificial fat. All these pseudo-foods have a 'light' image – long-life, attractive-looking and nice-smelling.[31]

Instant and frozen meals, designed in the Petri dish and centrifuge, often with genetically modified components, are replacing the recipe book in mother's kitchen. It is no longer thinkable to produce food without the addition of enzymes, vitamins, sweeteners and micro-organisms. It has to be aromatized and coloured, sweetened and soured, stabilized and pre-served. Emulsifiers, fillings and gelling agents bind water into an edible and palatable form. Quick-acting yeast speeds up the rising of pizzas or the fermenting of beer. The world enzyme market, worth nearly $1 billion a year, is dominated by the Danish firm Novo Nordisk, whose industrial products ensure that dough can be frozen and then microwaved without loss of taste or visual appeal.

It is hardly ever checked – and is anyway hard to detect – whether imported prawns have been farmed with the use of growth hormones, oestrogen or the anti-salmonella antibiotic chloramphenicol (which is banned in the EU). Nor are there systematic tests to establish whether the titbits used in pizzas or paellas have been given the radiation treatment.

The EU prohibits both the use of steroids in cattle feed and the import of US beef containing hormones. But a complaint lodged by the United States with the WTO is putting the EU under pressure to lift this ban. So who decides what we eat? Certainly not the women who do the shopping and cooking. They know less and less what they actually handle; their cooking power has been broken. Now it is a slick advertising clip, rather than any knowledge about food or nutrition, which allows women to rest easy that they have prepared a nourishing meal for their children. Our food has become a kind of mystery: we do not know what is inside, taking the power of self-determination away at great speed.

Whose Seed is It?

From time immemorial, farming women have been in charge of the seeds that are a key to food security. After the harvest, they put the best aside for the next sowing. Experience has taught them to judge how long the seed will last and how it will taste, as well as to assess its suitability for certain soils and its resistance to disease, dryness or humidity. They swap seeds with their neighbours, and take the best varieties as a gift when they visit their sisters.

The safeguarding of grain-seed, and knowledge about the different strains, are a female power resource which is being lost through com-mercialization. Once there used to be 30,000 varieties of rice in India; now there are just a couple of dozen. At the beginning of the 1990s, half of wheat-growing and 60 per cent of rice cultivation in the countries of the South consisted of hybrid strains incapable of germination that have to be bought again every year.

Thirty years ago the Green Revolution, with its techno-package of hybrid strains, field chemicals and artificial irrigation, unleashed the great commercial run on seeds. But it also continued the South–North genetic transfer initiated by the colonial rulers. Ostensibly as part of the fight against world hunger, a large number of species from the South were collected for the gene banks of the Washington-based Consultative Group on International Agricultural Research and the seed industry – a colonization of resources that the Indian physicist Vandana Shiva calls 'biopiracy'. The faster that species die out, the greater is the research fever to step up 'bioprospecting', that is, systematic classification of the genetic material of plants and animals. Gene-hunters have become 'biodiversity brokers' trading in green gold. Nearly three-quarters of world research in genetic engineering is being carried out by the private sector, and any public funding is often mixed up with private capital.

Theft of genetic resources and of knowledge about them go hand in hand. The US chemicals corporation W.R. Grace turned up in India, no less, with a patent for the very neem-leaf pesticide that has been produced and utilized for many years by Indian farmers.[32] Even knowledge about the healing properties of turmeric, the key spice in curry and other Asian dishes, has been pilfered. In India itself, where it is known as *kurkuma*, women keep turmeric powder around the home to treat wounds and as a general antiseptic. But in the USA this age-old cure acquired the patent number 5,401,504, registered by the medical faculty of the University of Mississippi. Indian activists then challenged the patent on the grounds that the university had simply expropriated the 'intellectual property' from India and was trying to exclude the real owners of the knowledge from any share in the business. The complaint was upheld, and the university no longer has sole rights of use and application.[33]

And what of the gene banks, which were supposed to serve as 'trustees' for threatened species? According to the biologist Christine von Weizsäcker, they have become 'fortresses of technology under Northern administration'. After thirty years, many seeds lose their capacity to germinate if they are not planted out separately, but the means to do this are often lacking. The hope that gene banks might check the disappearance of species has proved to be illusory. An 'irreversible genetic erosion is taking place', she concludes, whereby the number of seeds is 'reduced to a core suitable for industrial exploitation'.

This material is then employed for genetic engineering. This is supposed to lead to the eradication of hunger, as the Green Revolution was in its time, but also to a high-yield, environmentally friendly agriculture that requires fewer toxic chemicals. In reality, the main emphases show that industry is not at all concerned to combat hunger: 80 per cent of agricultural research revolves around the resistance of plants to pesticides, so that the chemical corporations can sell more of their weed killers and the like. As to health matters, the main focus is on slimming aids.

The genetic manipulation of natural substances is the logical consequence of the industrialization of agriculture. The GM soya produced by the US corporation Monsanto has been immunized against the chemical weedkiller Roundup. Monsanto thus makes a double profit by selling to farmers a 'Roundup-Ready' pack containing both the new seed and the matching toxin. For a long time now, says Kerstin Lanje of the German NGO BUKO, the soya food plant from China has been a 'world economy plant', an industrial raw material. Half of the world's soya crop now comes from the United States, and in the form of lecithin, oil or meal it finds its way not only into powdered coffee, puddings and medicines, but also into adhesives and paints, plywood and plastic. In Brazil, in the last fifteen years, the forest has been cleared, species destroyed and landholdings concentrated in order to produce soya fodder (some of it already genetically modified) in huge monocultures for the fattening of cows in Europe. In the north-east of the country, twenty times more land was given over to export soya in 1995 than in 1991.[34]

What the genetic engineers 'purée' (as von Weizsäcker puts it) is then patented as the 'intellectual property' of the agribusiness and food industry. Since the conclusion of the Uruguay Round in 1994, when such TRIPS or 'trade-related intellectual property rights' came under the GATT agreement, it has been possible to patent living organisms, genetic technology functioning as an instrument of the privatization of biological resources. Gene banks, research laboratories and patent offices have ensured that the commonly owned seeds once kept by women in huts and villages are now a company product that women have to buy. A licence is now compulsory if you want to grow them yourself. And the whole mechanism of global expropriation is placed under the banner of free trade and the war on hunger.

Monsanto's EU-awarded patent for its 'Roundup-resistant seed' means that it will control all generations of gene-soya for the next fifteen years. Monsanto's gene-soya, like Novartis's insect-resistant gene-maize, was released for marketing by the novelty food directive of the European Union, which came into effect on 15 May 1997 and stipulates that products must be labelled 'if a novel type of food is no longer equivalent to an existing one'. If it can no longer be demonstrated by measurement technology that an alien gene is present in a product, although it may actually be present, then it does not have to be declared. The Green MEP Hiltrud Breyer, who sees this as a licence for 'deceptive packaging', fears that 80 per cent of genetically modified food might go undeclared and unrecognized on the supermarket shelves. Environmental groups are therefore calling for a seal of guarantee that a product is 'free of genetic technology'. To refuse this is tantamount, in the view of Greenpeace, to 'forced consumption' of genetically modified food. And the Cologne-based ecofeminist Maria Mies sees it as an abolition of the basic democratic right to information.

Hard on the heels of FlavrSavr, the eternally youthful, non-softening tomato, we now have melons, pumpkins and other fruits without an eat-by date. Virus-resistant potatoes and sugar beet, cocoa beans already containing a sweetener, cows turned into veritable milk-fountains by the BST growth hormone, rice with sealed-in Vitamin A, frost-resistant salmon that can spread into colder waters and whose eggs are treated in such a way that only the (plumper) females develop – the range of transgenic food is growing broader all the time. Cooperation between industry and governments or universities is paving the way for more and more field-tests of genetically modified plants in the countries of the South. Transgenic cotton and tobacco have been planted in Zimbabwe, for example, and cold-resistant potatoes in the Andes. So far, the most widespread use of transgenic maize has been in the Caribbean and Latin America. In China, GM euphoria has led to the rapid release of new strains of tomato and tobacco. In Brazil, a US tobacco company has for years been growing transgenic crops with double the usual nicotine content.[35]

The genetic engineering industry has been working under great pressure to develop substitutes for produce exported by the South. Thus gene-rape may in future replace imports of coconut or palm oil, with which it shares essential properties. In the early 1960s, 80 per cent of world palm-oil production came from Africa – much of it from land worked by farming women. Like the producers of ground nuts, however, they have been pushed out by male-run monocultural plantations in Africa, and by new world-market suppliers in Malaysia, the Philippines and elsewhere. Gene-rape from northern latitudes will deprive countries in the South of foreign currency and small farmers of a major source of income. Already an application has been made to the EU in Brussels for approval of rapeseed oil produced by the Hoechst/Schering subsidiary AgrEvo.[36]

Even cocoa butter, a traditionally expensive product, could be replaced by enzyme technology using cheaper vegetable oils; farms in the North or huge plantations in developing countries would then put still more small family farms in West Africa out of business. Nestlé is already experimenting with cocoa-producing cell cultures. And in the United States, laboratory vanilla 'identical in nature' but costing a mere fifth of what is obtained from vanilla orchids could make thousands upon thousands of small producers redundant in Madagascar.

For farming women in the South, then, genetic technology is both devaluing their knowledge and expropriating their role as guardians of the rich variety of species and seeds. The use of GM seeds on giant mono-cultural plantations will displace more and more family farms, as price cuts make them incapable of withstanding competition. Laboratory products can quite simply replace their traditional forms of cultivation.

Amid the feverish discussion about competitive business locations, politicians continually argue that genetic technology will provide new jobs. The Prognos research institute, however, thinks that such expectations are far too high: not 2.8 million but 40,000 new jobs will result in Germany, for example.[37] Women are quite strongly represented as micro-biologists and genetic technologists on this new jobs market, accounting for as much as 80 per cent in the Philippines. Perhaps the reason for this is that the work calls for the so-called female virtues of patience and persistence.

A majority of European consumers (80 per cent in Germany) reject genetically modified food because of its possible consequences for the environment and the food chain, with attendant health risks such as the growth of allergies. Mae-Wan Ho, who herself worked for many years in biotechnology in Britain, is seriously concerned about the effects that transgenic organisms may have on the environment. An uncontrollable horizontal transfer takes place as genes migrate between unrelated species and completely new DNA superhighways come into being. Genes with the antibiotic resistance of transgenic plants have been found after release in field mushrooms and bacteria, which means that they have spread and combined with other genes. Bacteria and viruses 'stunted' through genetic modification in the laboratory nevertheless manage to replicate in the wild and to lock into other DNA chains. Many may lie dormant for a generation, before fusing with other genes and triggering genetic disturbances.[38]

What happens to genetic laboratory waste and to material released in the open? What happened to the 270 attempted clones before Dolly came into being? Is it true that in Switzerland human foetuses are processed into pigswill? BSE and new variant Creutzfeld-Jacob syndrome might be the harbingers of disastrous genetic turbulence. It is even suspected that the comeback of diseases such as cholera, malaria, tuberculosis and diphtheria, which the WHO long considered to be at least tamed, is due in part to new genetic linkages. Salmonella infections have dramatically increased, and new diseases such as ebola and hepatitis C are also on the rise. Excessive use of antibiotics in agriculture and livestock breeding may be causing the growing human resistance to antibiotics that has been noted by the WHO.

The genetic engineering industry has been waging a major publicity campaign, and it is optimistic that public opposition on the food front will crumble once doubts about medical applications have been overcome.[39]

The convention on biodiversity agreed at the Rio Earth Summit in 1992 calls for the protection of 'indigenous knowledge'. Farmers' organizations insist on 'farmers' rights', and on the right of local communities to enjoy and control genetic resources they have preserved and developed down the ages. They demand fair compensation, as well as local participation in the commercial use of such resources. At the UN conference on genetic plant resources held in Leipzig in June 1996 they also totally rejected the patenting of organisms:

> The pulling down of the Berlin Wall is a symbol of people's power against totalitarianism. New walls are now being built in the shape of intellectual property rights over genetic resources and the patenting of various forms of life. These are undermining the rights of farmers to biodiversity. Farming women play a central role in the preservation of diversity. We shall tear down the new Berlin walls.[40]

A number of states still do not have laws providing for private ownership of parts of plants, animals or humans. The United States is trying, on pain of trade sanctions, to force Thailand, India and other countries to adjust their legislation in the required way. In the new negotiations on intellectual property rights the World Trade Organization plans to hold, farming women and men will again be insisting on their demands and resisting patent rights over living organisms.

A Step Further: the Human Cell Economy

In July 1997, after eight years of disputes, the European Parliament reversed its previous position and passed a directive on 'legal protection of biotechnological inventions'. This directive defines the discovery of a gene as an 'invention' – the basis on which patents have already been issued in the United States.

The European Patents Office in Munich has granted to the US firm Biocyte a patent on blood cells of the umbilical cord, and hence the right to make any use it likes of these cells for medicinal purposes. Myriad Genetics, also from the United States, has applied for a European patent on the breast cancer gene BRCAI and any resulting therapeutic–diagnostic uses. Private companies are thus acquiring property rights over human body cells.

The EU's directive was a victory for the European pharmaceuticals and biotech industry. With the slogan 'No patents, no medicines', it put pressure on public opinion to accept genetic engineering in medicine. Patents would save lives, it was suggested, and who doesn't want that? The Corner House, a monitoring project on genetic engineering in Britain, doubts that the industry has any humanitarian motives and considers that the main point of patenting is to secure markets and licences.[41] It was precisely this market logic – namely, that research and jobs would otherwise move to the USA – which made many MEPs cave in.

The EU directive sets out the legal ground for a new stage in the commercialization of the human body. It turns people into a kind of biological arsenal of raw materials, whose parts can be privatized and patented for exploitation as commodities. A first stage on the road to exchangeability of human body parts is the lucrative international trade in organs for transplant, where competitive undercutting is more prevalent than on any other market. Who will offer the cheapest kidneys? Who will accept less than Indian donors do? As the market is undersupplied, more and more cases are reported from the Indian subcontinent in which people are drugged and robbed of their organs.[42] Fresh supplies of foetuses are mainly provided by countries of the former Soviet Union.

Foetuses are a special kind of spare part. Their brain cells are used to treat Parkinson's disease, their pancreas to control diabetes, their liver cells to combat disorders of the metabolism and immune system, and their ovum cells (in the case of female foetuses) to experiment with artificial gestation and fertilization.[43] At one women's public clinic in Moscow, patients do not have to pay for an abortion in the second third of a pregnancy, so long as they are willing to hand over all rights to the foetus. The foetal tissue is then exported for further research and applications in places such as California.[44] But the women themselves, who supply the raw materials for the biomedical world market, do not have any share in the profits.

For a long time now, ovum cells and sperm have been commodities on lucrative global markets where transnational corporations build and run chains of clinics. Along with spare body parts, fertilization is another booming sector. Just as genetic engineering is legitimated in agriculture by reference to the fight against hunger, reproductive technology is promoted under the banner of a cure for infertility. From egg or sperm donation to in vitro fertilization, from prenatal sex determination to surrogate motherhood, the industry operates across frontiers on an ever greater scale. The Australian IVF corporation has sold foreign use rights for reproductive technology and is quoted on the stock exchange. German women eager to bear children are driven to fertility tourism in Hungary, while Italy is a mecca for women already on a pension who want to have a child.[45]

The overcoming of spatial and temporal limits, which is such a characteristic feature of the latest phase of globalization, also strongly marks the new reproductive technologies. Pregnancy at an age more normal for grandmotherhood turns back the biological clock, while the artificial maturing of foetal cells pushes it forward. Frozen ovum cells, semen and foetuses are able to travel around the world or to leap across a few generations.

With artificial fertilization outside the womb, and with the isolation and marketing of raw materials from the human body, procreative power is being transferred to medical experts and the biomedical market. Women are reduced to fields for the growing of raw material. Biomedical research prepares the ground on which the logic of capitalist exploitation and universal exchange can force its way into the innermost core of society: the creation of human life. The test-tube baby would spell the end of women as biological mothers.

Genetic determinism, currently a major theme of public debate, is being used to create the legitimacy for human eugenics. Genes are increasingly held responsible for illnesses and even for social behaviour such as homosexuality or aggression. An international Human Genetic Diversity Project, initiated in the United States with an estimated budget of $5 to $7 billion, aims to decode the whole hereditary genetic make-up of humanity.[46] In 1993 it was announced that geneticists, anthropologists and molecular biologists were trying to record as quickly as possible the genetic diversity of 500 indigenous peoples threatened with extinction. Researchers, biotech firms and pharmaceutical corporations are dividing up the last *terra incognita*, the human body, for genetic decoding and patenting, and subjecting it to the laws of the market. The occupation and settlement of land is being followed by the occupation and settlement of human beings. In Europe alone, more than 1000 patents on human genes have already been granted.

Indigenous peoples are demanding a moratorium on the project and strongly protesting against the appropriation of their genetic make-up. A Declaration by Indigenous Women at the Fourth World Conference on the Status of Women in Beijing stated: 'Their ambition to patent forms of life is the ultimate colonization and commercialization of everything we hold sacred. It is no longer important that we are being wiped out, because we will be "immortalized" as "isolated components of historical interest".' In October 1997, the National Research Council of the United States agreed with them and declared that it was 'unethical' and 'scientifically unjustifiable' to collect blood and hair samples from 'endangered ethnic groups'.[47]

When genes are identified as pathogenic or degrading, the obvious next step in the technocratic feasibility madness is to modify them at an early stage of development of the human organism – for example, to prevent obesity and cancer or even lesbianism and homosexuality. This would permit a truly industrial optimization of human beings. Prenatal diagnostics has paved the way for this; the next stage will be prenatal surgery to correct the foetus. Quality protection seems to become more important, the more the competitive struggle rages in society at large.

Genetic modification of human ova, sperm and embryos has not so far been permitted, nor has the cloning of embryos. For interference with genetic make-up is necessarily selective: it involves 'quality control', the enforcement of eugenic norms. But the European convention on bioethics, as well as the UNESCO declaration on bioethics that established worldwide standards in 1998, no longer envisage a ban on embryonic modification. In the German research community, too, demands are already being made for the repeal of laws protecting live embryos, so that they can in future be made available for research.[48] Brave new worlds are looming ahead.

For a long time both the quality and the quantity of human beings have been regulated. Infertility is fought by childless women, fertility by those with children. Whereas demographic experts and politicians in Germany, France and other industrialized countries have for years been worrying that reproduction will fall below the 'replacement level', family planning programmes in countries of the South have been aiming over four decades to bring about a decline in birth rates. Mass campaigns, sometimes using coercion and carrot-and-stick methods, have managed within a context of rising consumerism to popularize the norm of two children per family. Birth rates in the South have been falling faster than expected – with the exception of sub-Saharan Africa – and in countries such as Thailand and Indonesia a democratic shift from high to low fertility has been effected within the space of two decades.

Population control has been inserted into global theoretical frameworks. It is argued, for example, that demographic growth in the South will lead to environmental destruction and resource shortages of a character threatening to global survival. Since the World Population Conference held in Cairo in 1994, demands have also been officially raised for the protection of women's reproductive rights, for their freedom of choice and autonomy. Studies on how this can be achieved, however, focus not on women's needs but on the maxim of technical efficiency. The most favoured methods of contraception are hormonal sprays, coils, hormone implants and immunological agents such as the anti-pregnancy vaccine – all unlike the pill in that they work independently of the user and leave her no control over whether to continue with them or not. The health side effects are also ignored in all these methods. The danger of abuse involved in such 'involuntary' methods is especially great in the case of vaccines, but is also evident in non-surgical sterilization with the malarial agent quinacrine that has been widely tested in Vietnam.

Universal norms of quality and quantity are being imposed without any distinction between cultures or local gender relations. The formation of human beings is increasingly subordinate to technologized commercial intervention in women's bodies, and a new world order of reproduction is taking shape right across a global market.[49]

Notes

1. Rekha Mehra (1995), 'Women, Land and Sustainable Development', ICRW Working Paper no. 1, Washington DC.

2. IFPRI (1945), *Women: The Key to Food Security*, Washington DC.

3. FAO (n.d.), *Gender and Food Security Work. Synthesis Report of Regional Documents*, Rome, p. 15.

4. Constantina Safilios-Rothschild, 'Agricultural Policies and Women Producers', in Aderanti Adepoju and Christine Oppong (eds) (1994), *Gender, Work and Population in Sub-Saharan Africa*, ILO, London, pp. 54–64; Katrine A. Saito (1994), 'Raising Productivity of Women Farmers in Sub-Saharan Africa', World Bank Discussion Paper no. 230, Washington DC.

5. Bernhard Walter, 'Auswirkungen der deutschen und europäischen Subventionspolitik auf die Entwicklungsländer im Agrarsektor', in Deutsche Welthungerhilfe/terre des hommes (1997), *Die Wirklichkeit der Entwicklungshilfe*, Bonn, pp. 26ff.

6. International Development Research Center (1994), *Cities Feeding People*, Ottawa.

7. Bob Rosenberry (1996), 'Shrimps weltweit', *FischMagazin* 1–2.

8. Gerrit Harms (1997), 'Untergang der Mangroven', *Robin Wood Magazin* 52, January.

9. Shiva (1995), p. 16.

10. FAO (1993), *Agriculture Towards 2010*, Rome, p. 182.

11. Report 'Krabben auf Achse' by Thomas Seekamp and Jens Fintelmann, North German Radio, 1996.

12. ASW (1997), *Fragwürdige Leckerbissen*, Berlin.

13. FAO (1996), 'Food Security and Nutrition', WFS 96/Tech/9, Rome.

14. Ibid., p. 9.

15. IFPRI, *Women*, pp. 9ff.

16. Negotiations within the framework of the General Agreement on Tariffs and Trade began in 1986 in Uruguay (hence the name the Uruguay Round) and ended in 1994 in Marrakesh with the foundation of the World Trade Organization.

17. UNDP (1997), p. 104.

18. Liza Maza (1996), 'Trade and Gender from a Southern Perspective', *WIDE Bulletin*, p. 24.

19. Kevin Watkins, 'Markets and Modernization: Maize Crises in Mexico and the Philippines', in Oxfam (1996b), p. 6.

20. Walter, 'Auswirkungen ...', p. 25.

21. WEDO (1996), *How Secure is Our Food? Food Security and Agriculture under the New GATT and World Trade Organization*, WEDO Primer no. 4, New York, pp. 6f.

22. Walter, 'Auswirkungen ...', p. 23.

23. *Die Zeit*, 5 September 1997; *Tageszeitung*, 16 January 1998.

24. Christel Panzig (1997), 'Frauenerwerbstätigkeit – die "Wende" auf dem Lande',

in Zentrum für interdisziplinäre Frauenforschung, *Rurale Frauenforschung, Bulletin 15*, Berlin, pp. 71–85.

25. IPS, 6 May 1997.

26. IPS, 13 October 1996.

27. IPS, 9 March 1996.

28. Pesticide Action Network (1994), *Planting the Future. Women in Agriculture*, Penang; and (1994), *Annual Report 1994: Asia and the Pacific*, Penang.

29. IPS, 13 January 1996.

30. *Tageszeitung*, 17–18 May 1997.

31. *Tageszeitung*, 10 June 1997.

32. Shiva (1995), pp. 24ff. For this whole section, see also Sprenger et al. (1996).

33. IPS, 21 September 1996.

34. BUKO (1996), *Agrar Info* 57, October–November.

35. Die Verbraucher Initiative (1995), *Info: Das globale Geschäft beginnt. Gentechnik bei Nutzpflanzen*, Bonn; Gerd Spelsberg, 'Das Testgelände des Nordens', in Sprenger et al. (1996), pp. 93–106.

36. BUKO, *Agrar Info*.

37. Ibid.

38. Mae Wan-Ho (1997), 'The Unholy Alliance', *Ecologist* 27/4, July–August, pp. 152–9.

39. Wolfgang Löhr, writing in *Kölner Stadtanzeiger*, 5–6 July 1997; Conference of the VDL-Bundesverband, *Agrar, Ernährung, Umwelt*, Bonn, 21 November 1997.

40. 'NGO Resolution on Farmers' Rights', Leipzig, 16 June 1996.

41. Corner House (1997), *No Patents on Life!*, Dorset, September.

42. Siegfried Pater and Ashwin Raman (1991), *Organhandel – Ersatzteile aus der Dritten Welt*, Göttingen.

43. Ingrid Schneider, 'Fötal Gewe(r)be: Der Traum von der technisch produzierten Unsterblichkeit', in Sprenger et al. (1996), pp. 176–92.

44. Ibid., pp. 186f.

45. Ingrid Schneider, 'Befruchtungs-Märkte – Frauen als Lieferantinnen und Konsumentinnen der Fortpflanzungsindustrie', in Christa Wichterich (ed.) (1994), *Menschen nach Maß*, Göttingen, pp. 39–67.

46. On EU policy see Elisabeth Gerhard (1994), 'Europa und die neue Biotechnologie', *Beiträge zur feministischen theorie und praxis* 38, pp. 23–39.

47. IPS, 28 October 1997; cf. Ute Sprenger, 'Aufruhr im Genomic Park', in Sprenger et al. (1996), p. 210.

48. Ursula Aurien (1994), 'Alles unter Kontrolle? Auf dem Weg ins Bio-Paradies', *Beiträge zur feministischen theorie und praxis* 38, pp. 23–39; Gen-ethisches Netzwerk e.V. (1997) *Die Gene des Menschen sind unantastbar!*, September.

49. Christa Wichterich, 'Menschen nach Maß – Bevölkerung nach Plan: Die neue Weltordnung der Fortpflanzung', in Wichterich (ed.) (1994), *Menschen nach Maß*, pp. 9–39.

4

The Sweeper Women of Structural Adjustment, or the Feminization of Social Security

Unpayable Labour

For years economists, ergonomists and publicists have been predicting that we will soon run out of work – even as a jobs miracle is celebrated in the USA or Holland. Far from being accidental, it makes theoretical and practical sense that it should be men who are striking up the requiem for the work society. When Jeremy Rifkin speaks of a coming 'world without work',[1] he closes his eyes to the fact that nearly 70 per cent of work performed on this planet is unpaid: work, that is, in personal care and relationships, child-rearing and education, in homes, gardens and fields. This blindness to everything outside the market and money is the reflex of a totally earnings-centred economy.

The paid labour about which gentlemen speak, and which is treated in classical economics as the only productive and valuable form of work, is for women only part of a larger whole. For only a third of the work performed by women is paid; two-thirds is unpaid and left out of the economic statistics. In the case of men, the proportion is almost exactly the reverse. It is the merit of the United Nations Development Programme to have globally quantified unpaid female labour for the first time, in both time and money. It is estimated at $11 billion a year – nearly half the total of world production, which is thought to be around $23 billion a year.[2]

These findings are confirmed by a time-budgeting study conducted by the German Statistical Office for the constituent states of the old Federal Republic. In 1992, it concluded, 77 billion hours of work were unpaid and only 47 billion paid. If every hour of housework had attracted DM11.70, a total of nearly DM900 billion marks would have had to be paid out. Inge Rowhani-Ennemoser has calculated for Austria that, if all housekeeping and child-rearing work were converted into salaried positions, it would create more than the existing total of jobs held by women on the formal labour market.[3]

The Platform of Action adopted by governments in 1995 in Beijing, at the Fourth World Conference on the Status of Women, recommended that unpaid labour should be calculated in parallel to gross national product, so that its true extent could be made known and economically evaluated. The Women's Ministry in Bonn immediately stated that the money was lacking for another time-budgeting study.

The bulk of unpaid labour is assigned to women as if there were a natural law which said that it should be so. The economist Ingrid Palmer calls this the 'reproductive tax' that societies impose upon women.[4] The market economy externalizes the costs of its own reproduction by entrusting this to women as a labour of pure love. With their free labour, usually without Sundays or holidays off, women subsidize a market economy which itself operates according to quite different principles. For their 'care economy' is geared not to turnover, profits and growth, but to well-being and social security, living and survival. As the sociologists Veronika Bennholdt-Thomsen, Maria Mies and Claudia von Werlhof have argued, it is literally life-creating and life-preserving and oriented to subsistence. The market economy is bolstered and nurtured by the altruistic principles of this 'love economy' (Hazel Henderson) in which it is embedded.[5]

For decades, two tendencies seemed to be reducing the amount of unpaid female labour: the introduction of technology into the home, especially in the industrialized countries; and the public assumption of socially necessary tasks, both by the Western welfare state and by the socialist state in the planned regimes. The care-work thus transferred from private households was integrated into the labour market: unpaid labour was transformed into paid work.

Now this trend is being reversed. Rationalization is converting paid labour into unpaid labour. In the service sector, 'prosumption' work, i.e. consumption-related work, increases: supermarket customers weigh their own vegetables and begin to scan the prices of their goods, bank customers take money from their account via automatic machines. New activities tend to cancel out the time saved through household appliances: parents are expected to help children more with their homework, and mothers to chauffeur them around between tennis clubs, piano lessons and visits to friends. The Freiburg Ecology Institute calculates that, despite the technological revolution in washing, no less time is spent on it today in German homes than in the 1950s – simply because there is far more washing to be done. Societies are falling back on unpaid work as on a natural raw material that can be appropriated free of charge.

The advances that women made towards equality in the former GDR and other 'actually existing socialist countries' mainly rested upon the extensive daytime facilities provided for children by the state. If 90 per cent of women could go out to work, this was only because workplace crèches and day-centres socialized childcare and released women for paid employment. The great difficulty of combining a job and a family is something new for women in Eastern Germany and elsewhere in Eastern Europe. When day-nurseries that used to be virtually free now cost DM500 a month and private lessons or holidays for children are also expensive, childcare inevitably wends its way back into the home. This, together with the waves of redundancies, is forcing many East German women into becoming full-time mothers and housewives. Their 'propensity to outside employment' has not changed – indeed, a mere 4 per cent consider a life only as mother and housewife to be desirable. Abstinence from child-bearing was the first reaction of women in the new states of the Federal Republic to this female variant of the 'unification shock', birth rates falling by almost two-thirds. It was not that they had ceased to want children, only that they considered living conditions with children to have become much more difficult.[6]

The number of European women in paid work is highest in the countries where public childcare support is best: that is, in Scandinavia. In Denmark, where the government provides the most facilities for mothers and children, the proportion of childless women in paid work is almost as high as that of mothers with several children: 79 per cent.[7]

The state is 'a girl's best friend', more dependable than diamonds and men. That, anyway, is what women thought for a few decades in the welfare systems of Scandinavia. Pre-school nurseries as well as midday meals for children of school age really made it possible for women to choose between staying at home and going out to work. As a result, Swedish and Finnish women could afford to have the highest birth rates in Europe.

Sweden is the only country in the world which takes the idea of equality so seriously that it tries to get fathers to spend a month full-time looking after their child. This month of childcare 'leave' can be taken only by the father, not the mother – otherwise the entitlement lapses.

The German concept of childcare 'leave' for pocket-money of DM600 a month effectively removes any burden from the father and drives the mother out of the jobs market. The father's prospects of career advancement and higher income, as well as the still widespread acceptance of gender roles, mean that 99 per cent of those taking childcare leave are women and only a derisory 1 per cent are men, and that even these often have to pay the price of employers' ill-will and career sanctions. This is in keeping with an economy that still operates under the model of one breadwinner and one supporting income. The woman's work at home among the family ensures that the husband is not troubled by anything other than his paid employment.

The financial crisis facing local authorities in Germany has so far prevented all parents from taking up their legal right to nursery provision.

And now the tighter labour market makes it more difficult for mothers to return to work after a break of a number of years. Every child is a 'labour market risk' unevenly distributed between mother and father.[8] It reduces the opportunities for women to get out of their full-time activity as unpaid reproductive workers. The gender division of labour remains in place.

Honour Where Honour is Due

The futurological visions to which we referred at the beginning of this chapter have one striking feature in common. Starting from the fact that there will never again be full employment for all, the experts turn their eyes on the unpaid labour they never previously noticed and call for a new distribution of paid and unpaid activities.

The Olympian 'Club of Rome', for example, in its report 'The Employment Dilemma and the Future of Work', proposes the division of work into three spheres: one provided and subsidized by the state; one comprising a private market completely free of government regulation; and one located within an unpaid non-profit-making sector. Each and every one of us would be expected to take part in 'voluntary' activities, but the examples given by the Club of Rome are all of typically female tasks. In order to reduce hospital expenditure, relatives or friends of patients would take responsibility for tasks that have up to now carried a monetary remuneration. Similarly, 'grandparents' would be expected to step in and help out with childcare.[9]

Jeremy Rifkin imagines that, alongside the public and private sectors, both the unemployed and people on reduced working hours could fit into a 'third sector' of useful and publicly minded voluntary work. This emphasis on the value of unpaid work in the community, as well as on the associated redistribution of tasks, takes up a key feminist demand that has been around for several decades. What male futurologists leave out of account, however, is the whole issue of power between the sexes. Feminist theorists have constantly criticized the gender division between paid employment and the work of caring for the home and other people, and have seen a fairer distribution of paid and unpaid work between men and women as a way of overcoming inequalities of power.

As the communitarian eulogization of family and civil duties gained popularity in the United States, the conservative parties in Germany again put personal responsibility and public spirit at the centre of moral–political debate, at the precise moment when the state was abandoning the public interest and eroding the principles of the social-welfare state. Claudia Nolte, formerly the Christian Democrat minister for family and women's issues, rejoiced that more and more people in Germany – 17 per cent of the total population – were willing to engage in some kind of voluntary work. In July 1997 she even brought to life a so-called Citizens for Citizens Foundation, whose use of the male form Bürger für Bürger in German ignored the fact that women make up two-thirds of 'volunteers' in the sphere of welfare activity and the churches, in homes and community care for the elderly, in hospices for the dying, in self-managed women's projects and cafés, and in self-run crèches.

To make voluntary work more visible and presentable, the Catholic Women's Community of Germany has introduced a certification booklet. Women can be found giving words of comfort or doing shopping for sick people in clinics, saving an old neighbour a trip to the city council or collecting fruit and vegetables and distributing them to homeless people after the supermarkets shut on Saturday. Whereas the women doing voluntary activity used to be mainly in the forty to sixty age group, more and more are now still at an age when they have young children to look after. 'Volunteers' step in and help out when local councils try to economize by reducing library staff, or when public baths are threatened with closure. The traditional male volunteers have been in the fire brigade, sports clubs and local community activities.

The media and education, as well as research, science and culture, are greatly subsidized by unpaid work. Many authors never see a penny for articles they publish in magazines and books. Numerous seminars, lectures and cultural performances depend upon work that is done for nothing or the merest pittance. Academics sometimes run teaching programmes without payment, for the sake of their reputation and for something to show on their c.v.

Many women do a spell of voluntary work on a project, then are given a job for a couple of years under some job-creation programme, and end up again doing unpaid work on it when the job-creation funding runs out. Such practices are widely regarded as a necessary preparation for a proper job or contract. In hospitals, for example, young doctors work a huge amount of unpaid overtime in order to obtain their specialist qualification.

An especially precarious field is the care of the elderly and chronically sick. In Germany, 1,125,000 people come under this category in private homes, and more than a million of them are looked after by friends or relatives – women providing the main care in 83 per cent of cases. A report by the Ministry for Family and Senior Citizen Affairs in 1992 showed that most carers of this kind did not have formal employment, 27 per cent had given up their job, and another 12 per cent had limited the number of hours they worked.

Public nursing insurance is far from being sufficient to cover the costs and relies upon family members or volunteers to fill the gaps, as Gerhild

Frasch of Evangelical Women's Aid critically points out. For grade three of care need, assessed at DM1300 a month, all a carer can obtain from monthly pension entitlements is DM34. Clearly we are not talking, then, either of wage compensation or of adequate old age insurance. Moreover, those who have to look after somebody for a long period often suffer from intense psychological pressure, social isolation and even psychosomatic disorders. Many women, Frasch remarks, have a whole 'life's history of care': first they bring up their children, then they care for their parents and parents-in-law and finally for their husband. All the time they are unable to save enough money to pay for care when their own health finally gives out.[10]

When the social system supposedly grows too expensive for the state, calls are heard for it to be 'democratized'. All parties aim to mobilize the hidden labour reserves of civil society in order to guarantee peace and order. The more holes appear in the social safety-net, the more volunteers (mostly women) are brought in as a stopgap to manage the crisis. 'Less state, more market' – the two pillars of neoliberalism – are supplemented with 'more work on one's own account' as a way of dampening potential causes of friction. A combination of voluntary work and cuts in social services appears as the integrated political model.

The Social State Discharges Its Children

Ronald Reagan and Margaret Thatcher must have been a dream couple for the theorists of free trade and privatization. Their programme of ridding the state of all costly ballast became the accepted credo in the industrial heartlands of the West. One government after another terminated the characteristic 'New Deal' combination of social-market economy and Keynesian welfare state. The state had proven to be an unreliable ally for women.

The Democrat Clinton completed the social reform started by the Republican Reagan. A living example of what this has meant is Martha, a seventeen-year-old black from Harlem who is pregnant for the second time, without a job, without an income and without a husband. All she has are $430 a month in welfare, two sisters, an aunt and a few friends and neighbours in a similar situation. Martha must feel really great now that, as the social reformers put it, she has been shaken out of her lethargy and freed of her dependence on the state. After two years on welfare she will have to take any job offered her – otherwise she will not get another penny. The state thus sets the limits of poverty by defining how long a person is allowed to be poor – a maximum of five years in a lifetime. When that time is up, there is no longer any right to public assistance.

Once again the United States is proving to be the land of unlimited opportunities – only this time it is opportunities for social downsizing. In the past two decades, poverty and social inequality have grown as social expenditure has been reduced. Twenty years ago, more than 80 per cent of the economically active population had a right to unemployment benefit; now it is only a quarter. This is mainly due to the transformation of stable employment into insecure employer–employee relations. But the main reason why only 30 per cent of the unemployed actually draw benefit is the state strategy of 'chumming', the systematic practice of bureaucratic discouragement and bloody-mindedness. In this way the government escapes having to bear the social costs of its policies.

Women are hit twice over by the crisis in public spending: on the one hand, they make up the majority of welfare recipients; on the other, they have fewer job opportunities as a result of the cut in social services. For the state is one of their largest employers, and social or educational activities are their main fields of employment.

Since the 1970s young single mothers – mostly blacks and chicanas – have been the thorn in the side of those carrying out forced cutbacks. Treated as a national disgrace, they are supposed to go out to work and, for heaven's sake, not to burden the state with any more children. In 1991, shortly after the five-year contraceptive implant Norplant was approved for use, it was being discussed in the media whether it could serve as a means of 'combating black poverty' and 'reducing the number of social misfits'. In the state of Maryland, where such experiments were carried out in 1993 at schools for teenage mothers, the governor proposed to link welfare payments to acceptance of the contraceptive implant.

The governor was ahead of his time in thus making welfare conditional, but since 1 July 1997 it has been common practice throughout the country. On that day the federal system of social welfare, which dated back sixty-two years to the time of Roosevelt and the New Deal, was brought to an end by an act of legislation. In its place was to be a decentralized system in which the keyword was Work. This, above all, would bring about the necessary social discipline. Anyone who wouldn't play ball would no longer get any money; at most they'd be given food coupons and a bit of poverty relief. The French sociologist Loic Wacquant calls this a turn 'from the benevolent state to the punitive state'.[11]

The responsibility for welfare has thus been transferred from the federal government to the fifty individual states. Each one receives a derisory sum from Washington and itself decides who shall be entitled to benefits. 'The result' notes the *New York Times*, 'is a system evolving from a national safety-net into a series of state trampolines: They are better equipped to lift the needy into the job market.'[12] As welfare recipients are forced to perform low-paid work, the competition in that sector is expected to become considerably fiercer and to cause a further drop in wages. More money is not planned for vocational training.

Martha is afraid that she will only be offered the most menial jobs: sweeping the streets, or 'taking some big shot's dog for a walk', or 'cleaning out their john'. For although she sat out a few years at school, she is practically illiterate. And without some educational qualifications she does not stand much of a chance. The state will take care of one thing for her: she can leave her kids at a day-centre when she finds a job. But there remains the question of health cover, which used to be provided by the Medicaid system. If she gets a job, she will hardly be able to pay for insurance out of her meagre earnings, and the employer's contribution has recently been reduced. So she and her children will join the 40 million Americans who currently have no health insurance.

In future, under-age people like Martha will be required to live with their parents on pain of having their benefit cut. But Martha has not seen her dad for more than ten years, and her mother, who does not have a grip on her own life, threw her out when she had her first child.

If Martha's children go to school in Harlem, they too will most likely end up only half-literate. For schools in the US are mainly funded out of property taxes, and whereas rich districts and regions can afford to spend a lot per child, Harlem or other poor areas of the country do not raise enough in taxes to pay teachers well and to provide a good education. Social inequality and educational differences are thus reproduced at a higher level.

The street in Harlem where Martha lives is an expanse of not only social rubble. Every third house is unoccupied and completely dilapidated, with the windows boarded or walled up. In the last two decades, public housing funds have shrunk to less than a third of what they used to be, while spending on criminal justice has risen fivefold and on prisons twelve-fold. The battle against violence and drug addiction – both of which increase with poverty and marginalization – has driven the number of prison inmates up to one-hundredth of the total population. Every third young black has been or is currently in jail, or is serving a suspended sentence on probation.

When the state has abandoned the goal of social justice and redistribution, forces in civil society are mobilized for damage limitation. Thus Bill Clinton called for an 'Alliance for Youth' and rang in a new 'era of community spirit'; two million young people are supposed to need voluntary 'mentors' to take them under their wing and stop them sliding into crime and violence.[13]

The demolition of the old social security system by the Clinton administration has been taking place alongside the deregulation of markets and the neoliberal withdrawal of the state from the economy. Both were precipitated by soaring public debt and massive pressure from capital for far-reaching liberalization. Governments loosened the reins that financial and social policy had fastened to market forces, and again disclaimed responsibility for social equality or for the creation of buffers between the strong and the weak in the highly competitive market regime. Deregulation does not mean that the global market functions without rules. Trade restrictions on goods and financial services may be overcome, but governments are introducing more and more rules to improve the free operation of business forces. This entails a long goodbye to the state's role as guarantor of social security and cohesion. More and more governments are becoming little more than backers of the private sector.

The growing power of 'global players' weakens the power of individual states for political or financial action, resulting in a general decline in the effectiveness of financial and social security policy. Huge fiscal holes appear in the coffers of the home states of transnational corporations, both because these companies transfer their profits in e-mail time to low-tax countries and because there are fewer people employed to pay income tax.[14] To make their country a more attractive location for investors, governments also offer sweetheart deals with juicy tax and subsidy breaks. Mass unemployment and rising pension payments meanwhile exert upward pressure on social transfer benefits.

Save, save, save is thus the guiding maxim of statecraft. Public assets are converted into money, public corporations are privatized, and public administrations are slimmed down. The state sheds responsibility for public welfare and wards off claims for redistribution; society is handed over to the market mechanism. As the elements of personal security are gradually privatized and commercialized, an exit from the social welfare state is presented as a necessary adjustment to altered market conditions.

In the industrialized countries, the scrapping of benefits is directed first of all against the unemployed and the elderly. For their numbers are growing as a result of mass unemployment and demographic changes respectively.

In Germany the policy of spending reductions is such that women are especially hard hit. Childcare time will no longer be covered by unemployment insurance. The long-term unemployed (70 per cent of whom are women in the new states of the Federal Republic) have to accept a three-hours travelling time to reach the workplace – an absurd proposition for mothers. At the same time, measures are being taken to ensure that women can be more easily kicked out of the labour market. There will no longer be protection against wrongful dismissal in firms with fewer than ten employees, and it is overwhelmingly women who are employed in such firms.

After the pensions 'reform', the level of pensions is due to decline proportionately, years spent in full-time education will count for less, and the retirement age for women will rise from sixty to sixty-three years. For women with a record of oscillation between family labour and outside employment, this could mean a halving of their eventual pension. In the old states of the Federal Republic, the average pension is currently DM1800 a month for men but DM1000 less for women. Only 18 per cent of women, compared with 93 per cent of men, receive a pension above social welfare level.[15] The old demands of the women's movement – that every woman needs her own protection for old age, that basic pensions should no longer be linked to time in employment, and that women's paid and unpaid labour should be taken into account – have not been given a hearing in the current pension reform.

In 1995 figures produced by the Senate of Berlin showed that nearly forty thousand people over sixty-five in the city had to live on less than DM600 a month, and that nine out of ten of these were women. Not even a fifth of them were in receipt of social assistance.[16] This is what is commonly known as bashful old-age poverty. The 'reformed' future of pensions will mean that still more women experience old age as a time of shame and need.

Ursula Sottong of the National Council of German Women's Organizations raised the alarm that the welfare cutbacks are affecting women's health three times over: as patients, as employees and as carers in the family. In rehabilitation, for example, 40,000 new breast cancer patients each year fail to be given necessary aftercare and therapy. The planned closure of 200 rehabilitation clinics now endangers 25,000 jobs, 86 per cent of them held by women. The rehabilitation work in question will be taken over, if at all, by other women in the family, mainly on an unpaid basis.[17]

In many EU countries, the convergence criteria for the Euro currency act are acting as a lever for structural adjustment. In order to plug their budget gaps, governments are further cutting spending on the elderly and the unemployed, on health and childcare; economic stability is being prioritized at the expense of social security.

In this situation, those who can afford it try to minimize their risks by all manner of individual commercial protection: from insurance for legal costs through private security services to personal pension funds. In the United States, one and a half times more is spent on private than on public security services. The massive speculation of pension funds on the stock exchange has been prototypical of the marketization of social security. They float free, instead of being part of a social contract that redistributes social costs and benefits.

Farewell to Arab Socialism

Mokattam lies at the point where the capital city has been wrested from the desert. Hoda sits with her daughters outside her front door, among heaps of bulging plastic bags. She tears open one refuse bag of the wealthy after another, and the two girls help her to sort organic from non-organic waste. It is a binary system operated without gloves or masks, amid swarms of flies. The crumbs from the tables of Cairo's middle classes stink to high heaven.

In Mokattam, 25,000 people live off the waste of a metropolis of 11 million souls. With perfect organization, 30 per cent of Cairo's household refuse is transported here on donkey carts to be sorted by women. Men collect paper into towering balls, stuff tins and boxes into sacks to be resold, and use simple machines to shred plastic into pieces that can be recycled.

This small town, which is really a transit camp for urban refuse, is part of Cairo's informal sector. Hoda and her daughters appear in statistics as 'family helpers', because the trade in refuse is in the hands of their husbands, as are the earnings from it.

There are no reliable figures for the number of women 'self-employed' or 'helping' in the informal sector. But one thing is beyond doubt. The sector is booming like no other, in every corner of Egypt.

Maisa El-Gamal, speaking for the International Centre for Economic Growth in Cairo, sees the future for women in the informal sector. 'Macro-economically, Egypt is already a near-miracle,' she enthuses in her elegant offices in Dokki, a top bourgeois district, as she refers to the country's annual growth-rate of 4.9 per cent. Then she adds with cooler objectivity, as if answering a questionnaire: 'Has the section living in poverty grown? Yes! Have many people lost their jobs? Yes! Is there hope that they will find other employment? Very little, because they don't have any qualifications.' By way of conclusion, the eloquent Harvard graduate coolly notes: 'Every problem should be multiplied with a high multiplier for women, because their starting point is much worse than that of men.'

So, in the short term, Maisa does not see any positive effects of privatization for women in Egypt. Nor in the medium term, she fears. But in the long term? Well, then the opportunities for women will improve thanks to the boom in the informal sector and small-scale industry – so long as more has been invested in 'human capital', or, in other words, so long as women are better qualified.

The farewell to Gamal Abdel Nasser's 'Arab socialism' has not been made in gung-ho fashion. President Hosni Mubarak announced a 'cautious' programme designed to avoid social injustices and harmful effects on 'people with limited incomes'. His government has been pursuing privatization and liberalization in small steps, often in a zig-zag course. One of these steps is the adjustment of labour legislation to the needs of the free market.

Two proposals currently on the table are not exactly cautious as far as women are concerned; they would mean a straightforward loss of legal protection. The first would limit maternity rights to a maximum of two children, so that a woman having a third child would not be entitled to fifty days at home on full pay. The aim of this is evidently to reduce secondary wage-costs. The second measure, involving an offer of limited redundancy payments, is supposed to make early retirement at forty-five attractive to women, and would serve to slim down the public sector workforce. The government has committed itself, under the terms of an IMF structural adjustment programme, to slash the number of public employees by 2 per cent a year through early retirement and redundancies – after many years in which there has been a freeze on new employment.

As CAPMAS, the Egyptian Statistical Bureau, tersely puts it: 'Job opportunities are becoming fewer and fewer for both men and women, but especially for women. As usually happens in times of rampant unemployment, the answer that seems to offer itself most readily is to send women back to their homes.' Already in 1992, when the jobless rate was 17 per cent, four out of five of the registered unemployed were women.[18]

Since the 1950s the state has been the largest employer of women, 43 per cent of all 'economically active' women working in public administration and services or in state-run textile, leather, food and pharmaceuticals enterprises. Now the government wants little by little to offer most of its three hundred enterprises for sale on the stock exchange.

Only 14 per cent of economically active women work in the private sector, and as everywhere else they are concentrated in low-paid labour-intensive jobs that offer no further training or chances of promotion. Private employers do not stand on ceremony: they treat maternity leave and childcare as an 'occupational hazard' that makes female labour more expensive in the end.[19] This is why, according to a recent study, only 17 per cent of job offers in the daily papers are directed at women.

In agriculture, too, less work is available for women. Traditionally they have served as stopgaps to be used in emergencies. Thus, when a lot of men emigrated to the Gulf states in the 1970s, women and children replaced their absent husbands and brothers in the fields. But when the men returned in the 1980s, female employment fell back once more. Mechanization – in cotton farming, for example – is currently the major threat to women's chances of finding work.

As Maisa baldly states, the poor section of society has grown as a result of a shrinking labour market, declining real wages and rising costs of living. There is a clear correlation between poverty and gender in female-run households: 65 per cent of their members live below the poverty threshold, compared with only half that number in male-run households.[20]

Poverty forces such women into a desperate search for ways to make ends meet. Paid labour is for them pure compulsion, not an opportunity; bitter toil, not self-fulfilment. Domestic service, street trading or outwork – that is the range of possibilities open to them in the urban informal sector.

Only every third poor household has any kind of health insurance. In the 1980s the state's per capita expenditure on health fell by a third as structural adjustment programmes demanded an end to subsidies and a move to cost-cover principles. The quality of public health care dramatically worsened, while private doctors and clinics remained beyond the reach of the poor. Much better value, sometimes even free, are the small health centres attached to the mosques.

Poor women also turn to the religious community whenever the mutual aid system in their family or neighbourhood is too weak to bear the strain of an emergency. They are helped over the hurdles of everyday life – such as the purchase of school books or kitchen utensils, clothing or wedding festivities – by the informal credit system known as *gama'iyas*. For the public safety-net does not cover them, and non-governmental organizations reach only a few.

Just when the labour market is dumping women as so much ballast, when the public sector workforce is threatened with redundancy, and when cuts in social services and ensuing impoverishment drive people into the arms of religion, the conservative Islamist leadership pushes itself to the fore. 'The first, holiest and most important task of women is to be a wife and a mother. They should not disregard this priority. Only if they have free time left over should they then take part in public activities,' says finger-wagging Zeinab El-Ghazali, founder of the Muslim Women's Union. The Islamist agitator Youssef El-Badri is of the view that Islam permits women to engage in paid labour provided they do not compete with men, who should always take precedence as the family 'breadwinners'.

A survey of female college students from the lower middle classes showed a third who believed that women should go out to work only in cases of extreme need, and 21 per cent who would in principle not like to see women employed outside the home. Many regarded their own education mainly as a preparation for their future roles as wife and mother. Male students from this social layer also spoke in favour of women's education, but against their going out to work. Clearly there is a dilemma, then, between economic compulsion and religious values. For the more that middle-class living standards are squeezed, the greater is the pressure on women to make life more secure by combining paid with unpaid labour.

Adjusting to Adjustment

The 8th of August 1990 went down in Peruvian history as the day of the 'Fuji shock'. That evening, President Alberto Fujimori officially proclaimed a tough new economic policy of structural adjustment. Overnight the price of food and kerosene tripled, and petrol became thirty times more expensive.

It is estimated that by mid-1991 as much as 83 per cent of the population was no longer getting enough calories and proteins. More than 38 per cent of children suffered from malnutrition. Every fourth child in the countryside, and every sixth in Lima, died before reaching the age of five. The proportion of poor people in the population as a whole had risen from 40 per cent to 60 per cent.[21]

Not only was health spending massively reduced; now everyone had to pay for medical care, which used to be free. Public employees, doctors, nurses and teachers all went on strike, because they were unable either to live or to die on the little that remained of their previous salary. Vaccination programmes came to a standstill for lack of funds. And in the cholera epidemic of 1992, 2000 people paid with their lives – and hundreds of thousands more with severe illness – for the government's shock therapy. Tuberculosis also took on epidemic proportions, and there was an alarming spread of both malaria and dengue fever.

What saved the impoverished masses from famine, especially in Lima, and what saved the government from an insurrection, was the people's food kitchens organized by an estimated 100,000 women. In mid-1991 there were 800 such kitchens in the poor district of Villa El Salvador alone. An average of thirty women took it in turns to shop and cook, often supplying food from their own vegetable gardens. They also organized milk distribution to ensure that children had basic nourishment.

The more the state pulls out of social services, the more community tasks are taken over by groups within civil society, especially women doing voluntary work. They collect refuse, keep their neighbourhood clean and organize basic health care. For Virginia Vargas, founder of the Flora Tristan women's group in Lima, the increased significance of NGOs in recent years is a result of the state crisis in a context of unbearable social need. She sees women's NGOs as counteracting social fragmentation through impoverishment, and as constituting the most important 'subversive force' against an undemocratic state.

In the last few years, however, more and more women from the food kitchens in Peru have been forced to hunt for some source of income in the informal sector, because men have been losing their jobs and the number of women living alone has also been on the increase. The number of group members has thus declined, individual women have had to take on heavier workloads and the costs of retail purchases have shot up. The people's kitchens movement has become noticeably thinner on the ground.

The only possible source of income for women is in the already chock-a-block informal sector. Apart from the 10 per cent unemployed, 77 per cent of the Lima population capable of work in 1993 was active in the informal sector. What they earn there is usually below the subsistence minimum. The ILO calculates that 84 per cent of the 'new jobs' created between 1990 and 1995 in Latin America and the Caribbean were informal activities – and, it must be added, not enough to provide a living.[22]

Not only mothers but children as well have to contribute their mite towards the family's upkeep, mostly within the informal sector. School attendance – no way! Many girls have been working since the age of ten as helps in middle-class homes, usually twelve hours a day for next to nothing.

UNICEF already noted in 1983 that women and children in particular were paying a huge social price for structural adjustment programmes. World Bank and IMF loans, taken up by governments when their debt-ridden economy is already in acute crisis, act as a lever for this drastic treatment. Since the early 1980s they have followed a stereotyped pattern: devaluation of the national currency plus trade deregulation plus cuts in public expenditure. This is supposed to put the state's finances in order so that it can repay its debts on time, and to promote private sector structures more compatible with the world market.

In macroeconomic terms, structural adjustment has quite often been a success. Economic growth has been given a boost, most of all in Asia and least of all in sub-Saharan Africa. Microeconomically, however, at the level of the private household, the medicine has been bitter indeed for most of the population. Women have paid for the upturn with longer and more arduous workdays, by accepting the transfer of functions from the wider economy into their unpaid subsistence-oriented economy.[23]

To meet strong criticism of these social costs, the World Bank designed a second, 1990s generation of adjustment programmes 'with a human face' and a 'social dimension'. Social funds and action programmes were supposed to pick up and relieve the most severe cases of hardship. Nevertheless, 1990s-style structural adjustment is for many still without a safety-net to soften the overnight social collapse.

For Argentinian pensioners the shock came at the beginning of 1992. In the 1980s they had enjoyed advantageous state pensions, but pressure from the World Bank, IMF and international creditors led the government of President Carlos Menem suddenly to apply the guillotine. Nearly two-thirds of the three million or more pensioners had their income cut to only $150 a month. With a cost of living roughly the same as in the United States, this meant that they could not meet even half of their monthly food and housing expenses. People who had all their lives considered themselves middle-class, as teachers, government employees but also private sector workers, suddenly found themselves in the ranks of the 'new poor'. Pensions were now equivalent to just 10 per cent of real wages. 'They were having to discover how their life's plans could go up in smoke,' commented Nélinda Redondo, an expert on the problems of old age.[24]

Paula Duarte was one of many in Buenos Aires whose life's plans were destroyed. Instead of an old age spent in security, she had to look for a job to make ends meet. Life below the subsistence threshold was a humiliation that she escaped with the help of a nylon cord; twenty-two desperate older women followed her example. The President, however, does not feel qualified to comment on the rash of suicides; he is, as he puts it, 'not a psychologist'.

Poverty, the World Bank never tires of pointing out, is a 'transitional phenomenon'. In the FAO's sober diagnosis, however, adjustment has led to the creation of a 'new class' of poor people.[25]

Meanwhile the Argentinian economy has been growing, inflation has been brought under control, and stability is attracting foreign investors to the country. The jobless rate fluctuates around 17 per cent. Labour legislation has been made more flexible, so that companies can employ for two years without any secondary wage costs (a) women in any age group, (b) workers over the age of forty, and (c) disabled people and war veterans. Today's public services employ a total of 300,000, compared with a million in 1991. Women teachers, whose income has been cut by half, declared a hunger strike in May 1997. Of the 1.3 million people who receive social benefits, 77 per cent are women. The rift between rich and poor is widening; the old middle class has been impoverished. According to a joke doing the rounds in Buenos Aires, when the magician David Copperfield came to Argentina, he was full of envy and asked President Menem to teach him how a whole middle class could be made to disappear.

The Acrobatics of Survival

In 1992 Margaret lost her secretarial job at the Ministry of Agriculture in Nairobi. She had not exactly been overworked there, and her office had not been a model of efficiency, but that was how things were run. After she had been shown the door with a small pay-off, she was unable to find another office job and had no alternative but to plunge into the informal sector as a 'self-employed' worker.

Once a month she and two friends travel to the border with Tanzania to buy a few bundles of old clothes, more expensive than the rest because they contain a high component of jeans. The three then hire a taxi and, several times on their way to Nairobi, have to grease the palms of policemen who supplement their meagre pay with a special kind of road toll. For it is illegal to bring second-hand clothing into the country, at least for small fish like these three women with their six bundles. Such laws do not apply to the son of President Daniel arap Moi, for example, who has his own fleet of lorries to carry yesterday's European fashions to the farthest corner of Kenya and into neighbouring countries.

Back in Nairobi Margaret picks out all the denim shirts, dresses and trousers and sells the less valuable remainder to women in the small markets on the outskirts of the city. She charges US$1.50 for a girl's skirt, $2 for a shirt, $4 for a pair of trousers. You have to be highly specialized, Margaret says, or else you go under. But however specialized, she will never be rich. Her customers are students who have to think twice about every shilling they spend, for a short while ago their grants were reduced yet again. The problem of selling their goods is even greater for the group of women in her neighbourhood who, with the church's help, have bought themselves a couple of sewing-machines and now stitch together children's clothing. The cheap second-hand and third-hand competition means that they hardly stand a chance.

They, like Margaret, groan under the rising cost of living. Worst of all are the soaring prices for basic foods and transport. The cost of a *matatu* or shared taxi has been rising by 50 per cent a year, and the cost of *unga* (corn meal) and sugar by 20 per cent.

The capital city, to which Margaret came ten years ago from Siaya District near the Ugandan border, has been changing at breakneck speed. Traffic in the city centre forms one continual jam in which a growing number of BMWs and Mercedes are to be seen. Office towers and shopping malls have also been shooting up all around, with high-class shops full of imported goods and restaurants boasting international cuisine. A skyline mirror-glazed by property speculators towers over poor districts peopled by street children, corruption and crime.

Sociologists use the term 'dual city' to refer to this side-by-side proximity of rich and poor, yuppies and homeless, growth and decay, all marked by both globalization and localization. Banks, shopping centres and foreign corporations occupy the inner city. But the ghettoes are also growing denser through constant inflow from the countryside. Space is the valuable commodity: street traders are driven off the pavement; 'illegal settlements' suddenly catch fire and burn down during the night; the police close off an area of land that is shortly afterwards sold to the city council; apartment blocks rise up from nowhere.

'I hate the city,' Margaret says, but there is no way back to the country. For only here can she earn the money she needs to send her two daughters to school. And the girls' education is enormously important to her.

Recently Margaret again had the hope that one of her male acquaintances might just lead the long-awaited march to the altar. Wrong message. For her friends, too, she notices that it is more and more difficult to maintain a relationship or a marriage. First the mass migration from country to town, now the permanent economic crisis, have had a corrosive effect on social and family relations. It looks as if men are more than ever roving in a network of girlfriends, which is what takes the place of polygamy in the cities. Social certainties, just as much as material ones, are constantly breaking down. In the slums of Nairobi it is an ordinary daily event for someone to 'go missing'. A husband or lover leaves the shack one morning without saying a word and never comes back. He tries to find happiness somewhere else with another woman and another casual job. Children also 'disappear' in a world full of drugs, prostitution and crime, living in street gangs and perhaps turning up again a few months later in their mother's shack. Or perhaps not.

Brutalization of relationships, decay of the social fabric, impoverishment of emotions and the psyche: these costs of the spiral pulling down more than a third of the population are never picked up in the statistics. Charities and church organizations lament the growth of domestic violence in the slums of Nairobi, the accumulated frustration with life to which it gives vent, and the ever larger number of single mothers. The more that men shirk family responsibilities through migration and multiple relationships with women, the more important for the safeguarding of society are ties among female relatives and among women in the same neighbourhood. The break-up of the social fabric goes hand in hand with a feminization of social responsibilities for provision within the family.

The idea of a neighbourhood, in which women help one another, is itself a female concept. Men also have friends, but for them the crucial bond is the drinking of alcohol together, rather than mutual aid in everyday life.

What drives Margaret to despair are the rising costs of her daughters' education. They both live with their grandmother in the Siaya District, as Nairobi is too expensive. Fees, uniforms, reading material, exercise books, school maintenance contributions: they all cost more and more since the government introduced the 'cost cover' principle into health and education in 1989. Kenya is now one of seventeen African countries where a declining percentage of children ever start school and a rising percentage leave before the end. Despite this, schools are bursting at the seams because of the high birth rate in earlier years. New teaching staff are not being taken on, nor are new equipment and teaching material being acquired.

Last year Margaret could not get the fees together, even though she has a few sources of income apart from the trade in clothing. Fortunately her mother in Siaya could make up the deficit, by supplying the headmaster with maize from her own field in lieu of cash. She also has living with her, three children of a sister who died from AIDS. The children did not know where to turn, so she took them in. As in neighbouring Uganda, it is mainly the older women who try to pick up the pieces when a sister or brother or children die a tragic death of this kind.

To fall ill in Siaya is a catastrophe. At the district hospital all that is left is a skeleton staff of doctors and nurses to handle emergencies. Anyone who can keeps well away. The laboratory equipment is ancient and ramshackle. There are hardly any drugs, and no generator to take over during the frequent power cuts. Thus, it may happen that the medical staff is thrown into darkness in the middle of an appendix operation or a complicated birth.

As real incomes and the level of education and medical care all relentlessly decline, women mobilize all their reserves to make a little extra in the informal sector, whether by cooking beans for the building workers at a nearby site or by serving them at a bar in the evening. Women also cut costs in ways that make their unpaid labour more intensive: for example, they walk instead of catching the bus, or they cook with environmentally damaging charcoal instead of the more convenient, but also more expensive, kerosene. And women cushion their hardships in neighbourhood groups, where they try to make collective savings by careful management, to cultivate their fields in common, to sell their crops and put the proceeds into a pool from which each draws in turn. Since malnutrition became more widespread among the young children of Siaya District, women's voluntary groups have been organizing twice-monthly sessions in the villages to weigh babies and to give new mothers advice about breastfeeding. More and more often, women's groups also provide assistance at burials. For AIDS means there are young people dying in every family, and other members have to bear the considerable expense of a funeral ceremony. It is well known that not even death is free.

Women's groups are the nurses of society, the Sisyphean toilers on behalf of the community – literally from cradle to grave. Their self-help and neighbourly assistance is a collective response to impoverishment that is social as much as material. Although their damage limitation and poverty management is often unprofessional enough on the ground, they remain an expression of solidarity in an age when existing social structures are being taken apart. Cooperation takes place in immediate local surroundings, but it also goes beyond the limits of geographical proximity. Women living in the city take food from their mother's field and send money back to the country. If they have themselves become middle-class, they will often form support committees for their region of origin and provide the funds for a kindergarten, a health centre or a funeral service.

This collective everyday assistance shows that the welfare of society can be achieved only through multiple strategies which combine paid and unpaid, market and communal labour, publicly and privately funded, monetary and non-monetary services.[26]

Women's groups are part of an armada of forces within civil society that are seeking to fill the gaps in care left by the failure and withdrawal of the state. These forces range from unpaid informal groupings active in villages and slums through to major NGOs and charities which receive money from foreign public or private donors and which, in some cases, carry out extensive operations in a professional manner.

Patricia McFadden, a feminist from Zimbabwe, criticizes governments for seeking to convert women's groups into a 'charitable movement' that would take some of the burden off their own shoulders. Women who have already internalized responsibility are thus called upon to invest their 'natural' capacity for welfare activity as a public resource. Florence Butegwa of the WILDAF women's rights network in Zimbabwe hopes that women's groups will more and more come forward regardless as 'political actors and leading advocates of women's rights'.[27]

The activities of NGOs thus tend to be ambivalent: on the one hand, they are instrumentalized in ways that are self-exploitative and let the state off the hook; on the other hand, they are forces for autonomous action and greater democracy. The growing corruption of state regimes, together with their loss of significance as agencies of social equality and provision, have led to the hyping up of NGOs in recent years as the great hope for developments towards social justice. The creativity and improvisation characteristic of women's groups has thus given rise to a myth about women's supposedly inexhaustible power of survival. As well as failing to appreciate that structurally adjusted women also have limited time and energy, this myth falsely romanticizes the feminization of responsibility.

Matrioshki of the Transformation[28]

Voluminous bridal clothes swing surreally in the autumn sky between the branches of a tree. At the next stand, leather jackets and fur hats hang on scaffolding five metres high, and next to them a tower has been built of boots and padded shoes. The pitches are small in Moscow's Luzhniki Park, so it is only logical that the traders should build their displays skywards. A pitch costs 100,000 rubles (currently $15) a day, plus protection money. Luzhniki is one of the central trans-shipment points for imported goods, from cosmetics through clothing to food. Masses of people jostle one another in the narrow spaces between the stands, constantly squeezed aside by handcarts brimful of huge chequered plastic bags.

Chelnoki are a new type of trader who first appeared with perestroika. Commuting on jet flights to and from Turkey, Poland, India, China or Thailand, they may buy 200 kilos of goods, grease the palms of officials and customs officers, and then resell them at a fat profit. Seventy per cent of the *chelnoki* are women. Why? Natalya, who has been one for five years, does not bat an eyelid: women are simply cleverer and more supple in dealing with traders abroad and the authorities at home. Men could not handle money so well and would spend too much of it on booze. So Natalya's division of labour is that she commutes and he manages the selling at Luzhniki, with her help.

Those who, like Natalya, have developed good business contacts can also earn quite a lot. But their life is not without its dangers. Some of Moscow's thirty mafia circles are also involved in this commuter economy. And apart from women like Natalya who commute on their own account, others work on a commission basis for big merchants. Most of these women were originally victims of Russia's sea-change and the cull in public sector employment; they were among the 60 per cent of all economically active women who lost their job during the 'collapse'. But they anticipated which way the wind would blow and went into the lucrative import business. Highly skilled women engineers and technicians are also to be found in it.

The trading women who buy at Luzhniki commute at a national level. They transport the goods to small markets in Moscow, or by bus and train to more distant Russian cities. Throughout Russia the conspicuous chequered bags hold out a promise of imported goods and the expensive fragrance of the big wide world.

The third category of women traders stand guard at the metro entrance in front of Luzhniki Park; they are Muscovites who offer a dress, a child's snow-suit or a pair of socks as a bargain. They trade in what they have just snapped up at a favourable price, whether as a single item or by the dozen. For most of them it is a second or third job, coming after they have spent the early morning hours cleaning buses, or helped out with the mail, or put in a few hours as a secretary, telephonist or door-keeper. In the time of actually existing socialism, women earned on average 70 per cent of a man's income; today they pick up no more than 40 per cent at the end of the month.

There are also illegal traders; for example, the women who appear with shopping bags full of beer, cola and vodka, after the street kiosks with their ample supply of alcohol have closed for the day. They have no licence to sell and take to their heels as soon as they glimpse someone in uniform.

All these women are looking in the informal sector for ways to 'adapt' to the newly privatized conditions of market economy. According to official statistics, 39 per cent of those who obtain a licence to trade are women. 'The older the women are, the harder it is for them to adapt'; this was the rule of thumb discovered by Marina Malysheva, an expert at the Institute for Gender Studies. 'Those who don't adapt, sink into poverty.'

One who has not managed to adapt is Lena Lokteva. For thirty years she managed a club for amateur film-makers together with her husband, built a film library and travelled through the various republics of the Soviet Union organizing film festivals. 'My work was just everything to me, much more important than keeping house or consuming things. I was completely happy with the life we had.'

Perestroika brought a new way of judging her work: it had to be economically viable. And since the club had always existed to promote culture, not to make a profit, Lena and her husband were made redundant. At first she worked as a book-keeper, then got a job in a kindergarten for the equivalent of US$40 a month. In addition there was her mother's pension of $60. So there were $100 for four people, with $25 going on the rent and electricity.

In 1997 her mother died, and then quite suddenly her own husband. The funerals were expensive. Previously she had gone on holiday every year with her husband and son to the Black Sea; now she did not even have enough money to ring her friends there and tell them of her husband's death. How do they get by at all, in a country where most things cost as much as in Germany? Most of the time they eat bread and potatoes. 'We make the spuds nice and tasty.' She looks skinny and care-worn. What affects her the most is the fact that no one appreciates her thirty years of work. Cultural activity, her real specialism, is no longer in demand. She feels worthless.

Yulia and Tamara, on the other hand, are still young and would be quite happy to adapt. But Tamara's husband left her when he learnt that their second child was severely handicapped. Yulia has two children, a disabled husband, and a father-in-law in need of care. During the Soviet period, her husband worked as a restorer in the historical museum and sent letters critical of the regime to US radio and television stations. As a result, he disappeared into a psychiatric clinic and was treated with mind-altering drugs. He has been severely depressed ever since. Yulia gave up her teaching job when the second child came along. But she is certainly not lacking in energy. 'I am the horse that pulls the cart in which my family sits,' she laughs. She wants to return to her profession when the young ones are a little older.

Russian society no longer has any shock-absorbers for women like Lena, Yulia and Tamara, who have to live in the direst poverty. The number of poor people in Moscow is estimated at 50 to 60 per cent of the population. Single mothers, because of the collapse of state childcare facilities, are clear losers in the new Russia.

However, it is old people who have paid the highest price for the transformation. 'What society has done to them is criminal. No one can forgive and forget it,' says Marina Malysheva. They saved all their lives and then lost everything in the hyperinflation. The measly pension of $60 a month is not enough to live or die on. It is a cheated and deceived generation. Old people used to have power in the family, and enough money to help out the younger generation. Now they depend on the support of the young adapters.

The resulting loss of authority and respect, and therefore of self-respect, is a traumatic experience. Women are a considerable majority in the older generation, since the doubling of alcohol consumption has dramatically cut male life expectancy to just fifty-seven years, compared with seventy-one years for women. The size of this difference is unique in the world.

Often the pension does not arrive for two or three months at a time. Many female pensioners clean eight hours a day for $40 a month, so long as their bent backs allow it. In the metro a partially sighted woman is begging for alms, led by her granddaughter; on the Arbat, the old commercial street, a babushka sings a melancholy popular song; and everywhere in markets and metro entrances, one sees old women offering a kilo of apples, two bunches of flowers, or a saucepan looking much the worse for wear. Gradually all their household goods are fetched out for sale – plate by plate, sheet by sheet.

The bitterness on their faces is nothing other than the shame of having to beg. For years many have not been able to afford any new clothes or shoes. Every winter not only hunger but also illness, and particularly toothache, hang suspended over them like the sword of Damocles. Public health care is lamentable, private facilities far too expensive. Old women in need of dentures have to wait two years to be treated in the state dental clinic.

'Shock therapy from above' is how university lecturer Olga Vershinskaya describes the passage from the age of provision to the age of private initiative. Formerly the state was 'father and mother rolled into one' – an unsustainable system, she says in retrospect. But today those who, for whatever reason, cannot fend for themselves in the market economy are mercilessly excluded.[29] 'It is like a postwar period, like the period after the Third World War,' suggests Elena Balayeva, who has also been made redundant and cast aside. She used to be a researcher at the Academy of Sciences, but the state no longer has the money for research. Now she is self-employed in the global academic market, and happy to have got a study grant from the Ford Foundation.

The amount of unpaid labour done by women has been sharply increasing, both at home and in society at large. 'We used to have a double burden with state support; now we have it without state support,' complains Marina Liborakina from the Independent Women's Forum in Moscow. Marina has herself cleaned floors at the hospital where her children were being treated. She calls this extra women's burden 'compulsory volunteering'. 'We are slowly catching on that the rundown in social services is not a passing trend', for it is part of the deal negotiated between the Russian government and the World Bank.

This unpaid feminization of social provision is accompanied by the rebirth of a conservative image of women. In a general swing away from the values of actually existing socialism – against its collectivism, against the compulsion to work, and against the breakdown of family bonds – the media and the restrengthened Orthodox Church celebrate woman as mother and protectress of the home, as a stable pole in the midst of turmoil and collapse.

The penalty that women make society pay for the general loss of security is the falling birth rate, down by a half in the last fifteen years. Instead of 2.6 children, the statistically average woman now bears only 1.3. The number of abortions is twice as high as the number of births.

Men react to the new insecurity with growing violence against women in the family. At the workplace, sexual harassment is so common that many women seeking employment add to their small ads in the paper: 'No intimacies!' The daily hotline operated by the Institute for Gender Studies between 9.00 a.m. and 9.00 p.m. is never quiet for a moment. Women's groups are building a network of advice services throughout Moscow and in other Russian cities.

All these silent tragedies in every corner of the country – this erosion of old generational ties, this shrinking population, this increase in divorce, violence and crime – are known in the official rhetoric as 'unforeseen consequences of the transition to market economy'.

The growth of social inequality counts as another 'unforeseen consequence'. Ten per cent is the estimate commonly given for the dollarized class of 'new Russians'. This includes those *biznismeni* who, in the days of perestroika, made the leap into the market economy by buying raw materials cheap in the state sector and selling them dear on the free market – in the United States, for example – one of the raw materials on offer being women. The new economy was reflected in the growth of corruption, and in those mafia circles which now control city politics and dictate prices. While every old woman is ashamed of her undeserved poverty, this new bazaar bourgeoisie shamelessly puts its power and affluence on display. The way in which drivers of the latest limos ignore red lights is a symbol of this demise of the old laws and regulations. The women of the globalization profiteers live in gilded cages, able to go out only with a bodyguard. They shop with dollars at Pierre Cardin in the outrageously expensive art nouveau GUM department store on Red Square, buy children's clothes with deutschmarks at Karstadt's, and fly off on holiday to five-star hotels in Tunisia or Spain, if they do not already have a house of their own in the South of France.

Between the impoverished majority and the obscenely rich New Russians, only a relatively small middle layer has come into being. The social architecture is thus completely different from that which has characterized most European countries in recent decades.

Typical of the new middle layer are the class of traders like Natalya, who have achieved a certain routine of life together with high profit margins, but also the class of book-keepers, bank staff and secretaries earning three to five times more than a public employee. Foreign companies are especially valued as employers: that is, they pay in dollars or marks. This 'generation of book-keepers' is both achievement-motivated and consumption-oriented.

How people feel about their future prospects in the market economy is directly proportional to age: the younger, the more optimistic. Marina Malysheva feels quite sure: 'The market system offers women greater choice in education, jobs and travel. They have good prospects – but only if they are young, mobile and energetic.'[30]

One woman who has successfully adapted to the market is Tatyana Andrejeva. She is boss and part-owner of Iltis, a firm specializing in computer software, management training and marketing advice. There is currently a lot of demand for such services, and the competition is intense. The young businesswoman has five permanent employees and ten contract workers. She studied physics and specialized in laser technology at Moscow's prestigious Technical University, which did research for the space programme and cooperated with the military–industrial complex. In addition, she completed a professional course in patent law. Highly qualified, highly motivated and still in her youth, she could sense the change in the air and applied for a grant from the German Carl Duisberg Society. She finished her practical training at various German corporations and at the medium-sized Iltis consultancy firm in Rothenburg. Then in 1993 she founded Iltis, Moscow. The business is doing well.

Tatyana is well thought of as a businesswoman, 'because everyone knows that a woman has to be especially good'. She and fifteen other business-women in Moscow have formed an association to exchange views about their special problems. Most of these other women are active in typically female areas, producing such things as cosmetics or educational videos for schools.

Nearly everyone who was a fellow-student of Tatyana's is today without a job, for neither space travel nor the military–industrial complex is in good shape. The men cling much more than the women to their prestige and fear that they will have to take a humbler position. 'Add some alcohol, and his personality is finished.' The women, on the other hand, feel responsible for their family and accept deskilling in order to put some food on the table. When asked who have been the losers from Russia's sea-change, they are in no doubt: 'Men.'

Winner Takes All, or the Splitting of Society

'Investments in women's health are undergoing a tragic decline in an age of growing wealth,' complains Patricia Giles from the Commission on Women's Health appointed by the World Health Organization. One in-dicator of this is the worldwide increase in childbirth mortality. Not so long ago the WHO estimated that half a million women died each year from complications in pregnancy, childbirth or unsafe abortions, but now it seems that the figure needs to be revised upward, to nearly 600,000 a year. 'Many of these deaths are easily avoidable,' says WHO chief Hiroshi Nakajima, 'it is poverty and powerlessness that make the women ill.' Russia, China, India and Cuba today have higher childbirth mortality rates than in 1990, and the situation has not improved at all in a further fifty-one countries.[31]

As a result of ongoing privatization, concludes the Women's Global Network for Reproductive Rights, health is no longer considered a human right, but rather a commodity to be bought and sold on the market.

In African countries, cuts in the public health and education systems have led to two classes of provision. Those who can afford it send their children to private schools and foreign universities, go to a private doctor and a private hospital. Staff in the public system work without enthusiasm in wretched conditions, constantly driven by rock-bottom wages to look for additional income on the side. In the private sector, the earnings are higher, the motivation greater, and the equipment more modern. It is a dual system, which inscribes social polarization in people's bodies and heads.

Take Zimbabwe, for example. In the 1980s the country set itself the goal of significantly improving its schools and medical facilities. After fees were introduced between 1991 and 1993 as part of a structural adjustment programme, 40 per cent fewer X-rays were taken, 20–30 per cent of hospital beds were empty, childbirth mortality doubled in Harare, tuberculosis control broke down, average life expectancy fell by five years, 26 per cent of all school-age children stayed away from school, and doctors and teachers emigrated in droves to neighbouring countries that offered higher pay.[32]

It is true that a 'social development fund' in Zimbabwe is supposed to target poor people in special need, to relieve them of school and hospital charges, and, since the elimination of food subsidies, to support them with the princely sum of 75 cents a month. But it is so complicated to prove one's entitlement and to fill in the necessary forms that the approval procedure has become impossibly expensive and arbitrary. Fewer and fewer claims are made, and anyway there is not enough to go round for everyone. Oxfam explained: 'The experience of Zimbabwe calls into question the seriousness with which the World Bank has attempted to integrate poverty-reduction mechanisms into structural adjustment.'[33]

A take-up analysis of the social measures supposedly accompanying structural adjustment has established that it is mainly men who benefit from support. The largest wad of money goes into employment programmes for public sector workers who have been made redundant. In Bolivia 99 per cent of the beneficiaries were men, in India 84 per cent, in Honduras three-quarters. Only one of the thirty projects to promote small business in Zimbabwe has been directed at women. Food aid is the most that is still made available to them.[34]

It is generally the case that money from social assistance funds seldom reaches the poorest layers. One reason for this is the way that it is supposed to be demand-driven. Those in need, or an NGO acting on their behalf, must first make an application and often even submit a proposal for a project. The demand thus steers the supply in accordance with principles of market behaviour and individual responsibility. Often the necessary information does not even get through to the poorest people in remote regions. But if an NGO takes up a case, it usually does so in the interests of male applicants. At best, an accompanying social programme can limit the damage for a few poor women; it can by no means keep them out of poverty.

The fact that people are no longer seen as having a human right to life's necessities means a splitting of society between the rich (for whom they are an ordinary consumption good) and the poor (for whom they are an unattainable luxury). In Orissa, which in 1997 became the first Indian state to privatize its energy supply, the elimination of subsidies has led to a fivefold increase in electricity prices for private households, together with a 23 per cent reduction for industrial users. In the cities of India, poor people often filch a little juice for a light-bulb from their better-off neighbours. But when electricity suddenly becomes noticeably more expensive, the rich become more tight-fisted and put a stop to this informal subsidy.

The advantages given to big over small users are also apparent in credit dealings. The tiny sums borrowed by poor women in slums, or the loans taken out by small farmers for subsistence production, are charged at a higher rate of interest than large business loans. Small but expensive, is the law of the market.[35]

Water, too, is everywhere supposed to fetch its market price. For it is running dangerously short, mainly because of its use in agricultural irrigation and various industrial processes. Pricing policy is meant to check wastefulness. But most people in the rural regions of the South would never even dream of wasting water. Since time immemorial, women there have been the living aqueducts, carrying buckets and containers over long distances on their heads and shoulders. When a price is put on water – whether on a tap in an urban slum, or on the supply drawn by small farmers from the spring or tank of a landowning 'waterlord' – the women are the first to make a move by walking still further to fill their cans in a pond or a brook; without purification or filtering, of course.

The commercialization of essential supplies and social services raises the importance of money in countries where a large part of the economy has not previously been monetized. The poor are excluded from the new markets for lack of purchasing power. But, in a self-reinforcing circle of poverty and exclusion, their access to money or purchasing power is in turn limited by their lack of purchasing power to invest in their own 'human capital'.

UNDP, the United Nations Development Programme, has recently made a distinction between income poverty and 'capability poverty', the latter measured by undernourishment of young children, deficient medical care during childbirth, and the illiteracy rate among women. Accordingly, 21 per cent of the population in the South live below the income-related poverty threshold, but 37 per cent suffer poverty in human capabilities.[36] The World Bank defines any annual income below $370 as absolute poverty, and it is true that the percentage of people in the world with less than a dollar a day to live on has been declining. Yet the absolute numbers of the poor still grew between 1987 and 1993 from 1.2 billion to 1.3 billion, a quarter of humanity. Poverty and wealth go together; they are two sides of the same coin.

Seventy per cent of the world's poor are women; they are, in the development jargon, more 'vulnerable' than men. Traditional disadvantages, combined with marginalization through new forms of development, have been increasing the risk of poverty for women. Where food and employment, health and education facilities are all in short supply, cultural norms of selection and distribution work against women. The main cause of the feminization of poverty is the contrast between heavy work burdens and low earnings. This disparity is most blatant in the case of 'female heads of household' (accounting for 35 per cent of households around the world), where it directly triggers the slide into poverty. Single mothers, with no ifs and buts, have to perform a balancing act between care for their children and the need to earn a wage for the family. Constant stress and chronic overwork make them especially prone to illness. Their 'unprotected' social status increases the risk of violence.

According to UNDP figures, the shape of poverty has been rapidly changing since the 1980s. Women, children and old people are more at risk of poverty than men, people in towns more than in the countryside, and people in Africa more than in Asia.[37] The UNDP has had the merit in recent years of ruthlessly exposing the wealth gap that has opened up between rich and poor. In 1960 the wealthiest 20 per cent of the world's population disposed of 70 per cent of world income, but by 1994 the figure had risen to 86 per cent. The share going to the poorest fifth fell over the same period from 2.3 per cent to 1.1 per cent. In other words, those at the top owned thirty times more in 1960 and seventy-eight times more in 1994.

'Globalization has not so much reduced wages in developed countries and made people unemployed, as led to greater prosperity in large parts of the world.' This is how Martin Wolf, financial editor of the *Financial Times*, changes the angle of vision.[38] Clearly his absolute measure of prosperity takes no account of the extremely unequal distribution of that prosperity.

Assets are concentrated mainly in the accounts of transnational corporations. According to *Fortune*, the profits of the world's 500 largest companies rose in 1996 by an average of 25 per cent. Leading the pack was General Motors, with an annual turnover higher than the gross national product of Denmark. Ford's yearly business is greater than South Africa's, and Norway cannot keep pace with Toyota. So do the relations of power change between states and private corporations.

The UNDP remarks: 'As trade and foreign investment have expanded, the developing world has seen a widening gap between winners and losers.' Apart from the richest bracket, everyone else saw their income decline, so that by 1991 85 per cent of the world's population disposed of only 15 per cent of world income. The assets of the 358 richest people in the world are equal to the income of 2.3 billion people, 45 per cent of all those living

on earth. In short: 'The greatest benefits of globalization have been garnered by a fortunate few.'[39]

Social polarization has intensified within many countries. The gap
between rich and poor is widest in Brazil, Guatemala, Guinea-Bissau and
the United States.[40] But recently poverty has also been increasing in the
industrialized countries, where unemployment has reached record levels
and income differentials are greater than at any time in the last hundred
years. Everywhere the scale of poverty is headed by single parents and the
elderly. More than a hundred million people in the 'rich' countries live
below the poverty threshold: nearly 14 per cent of the population in the
USA, 11 per cent in Germany. Portugal and Britain head the poverty
tables in Europe.

A quarter of the British population is poor, 60 per cent of them women.
Why is this? Seventy per cent of women who go out to work are in the
low-pay category; four out of five women have a part-time job. 'Thatcher's
children' is the name given to those who fell into the social holes dug by
Thatcherite cuts in social services: a low level of education, a casual job
here and there, no proper roof over their head. At the same time, the
British economy is experiencing an upturn; here, more than anywhere else,
poverty is a phenomenon of growth. Gone are the times when growth
brought prosperity for all and social integration. Now it is the engine
driving social distinction and exclusion.[41]

In Germany, the society where everyone was supposed to be middle-
class has more recently been drifting apart. Less than half the population
earns roughly the average income, while the proportion of incomes less
than 75 per cent of the average has been steadily rising. The number of
people on income support has grown by 50 per cent in the last decade and
now stands at 2.8 million. Over the same period, however, the numbers
earning more than DM10,000 a month have increased more than sixfold.[42]
The meltdown of the middle layers signals the end of the Fordist social
contract, which based itself upon the consumption and purchasing power
of a broad section of the population. For the French sociologist Alain
Touraine, what looms ahead is a 30:30:40 society in which no more than
40 per cent of the population live at a relatively high level of social security
and prosperity. Others fear that the tendency to social inequality is more
likely to result in a two-thirds or even a 20:80 society.[43]

One echo of these economic trends is the social democracy of Tony
Blair, in which neoliberalized politics aims at most to produce equal opportunities but no longer equal results. True, it has become easier for women
to take part in the social competition, through education and training,
flexible forms of work, and even special advancement programmes. But
when it comes to distribution, the results are little changed. In the split

society, women are not so often found in the ranks of the triumphant wealthy elite; but there are many indeed in the growing group of losers, of the redundant, excluded and poor.

Notes

1. Jeremy Rifkin (1995), *The End of Work. The Decline of the Global Labor Force and the Dawn of the Post-Market Era*, New York.

2. UNDP (1995), pp. 87–98.

3. *Frankfurter Rundschau*, 16 November 1995; Inge Rowhani-Ennemoser (1997), 'Die Folgen sind für Frauen katastrophal und existenzbedrohend', *Frankfurter Rundschau*, 7 April.

4. Ingrid Palmer, 'Gender Equity and Economic Efficiency in Adjustment Programmes', in Afshar and Carolyne Dennis (eds) (1992), pp. 69–83.

5. Diane Elson in *WIDE* (1995), pp. 13ff.; Veronika Bennholdt-Thomsen, Maria Mies and Claudia von Werlhof (1988), *Women: the Last Colony*, London, pp. 83; Hazel Henderson, 'Building a Win-Win World: Life beyond Global Economic Warfare', address to the Grenzen-los conference, Wuppertal, 21–22 November 1996.

6. Ursula Schröter (1992), 'Ostdeutsche Frauen im Transformationsprozeß', *Rundbrief des Deutschen Frauenbunds*, February, 1992, pp. 6–12.

7. DGB (1995b), p. 8.

8. Gunhild Gutschmidt (1997), 'Die gerechte Verteilung des "Arbeitsmarktrisikos Kind"', *Frankfurter Rundschau*, 4 August.

9. Patrick Liedtke, 'Some Keynote Issues of the Report to the Club of Rome', in HVBG (1997), pp. 37f.

10. Gerhild Frasch, report to the Frauenbündnis für Arbeit und gegen Sozialabbau, Bonn, 7 March 1996.

11. Loic J. D. Wacquant (1997), 'Vom wohltätigen Staat zum strafenden Staat', *Frankfurter Rundschau*, 12 July 1997.

12. *New York Times*, 30 June 1997.

13. Konrad Ege (1997), 'Wenn Drachentöter helfen wollen', *Freitag*, 16 May.

14. See Martin and Schumann (1997), pp. 61ff.

15. Deutscher Frauenrat, press statement, 7 May 1997.

16. *Frankfurter Rundschau*, 26 July 1995.

17. Deutscher Frauenrat, press statement, 7 May 1997.

18. Faiza Rady (1997), 'An Egyptian Feminine Mystique', *Al-Ahram*, 20–26 February.

19. Heba Nassar (1996), 'The Employment Status of Women in Egypt', American University Cairo and Friedrich Ebert Stiftung, December.

20. Heba El Laithy (1996), 'The Economic Status of Women in Egypt', American University Cairo and Friedrich Ebert Stiftung, December.

21. Chossudovsky (1997), pp. 191–214; Bea and Jules Rampini Stadelmann (1994), 'Auswirkungen des Neoliberalismus in Peru', *Finanzplatz Schweiz* 2.

22. IPS, 25 February 1997.

23. Gabriele Zdunnek, 'Strukturanpassung und geschlechtsspezifische Differenzier-

ungen am Beispiel Nigerias und Ghanas', in M. Braig, U. Ferdinand and M. Zapata (eds) (1997), *Begegnungen und Einmischungen*, Stuttgart, pp. 160f.

24. See James and Susanne Paul (1994), 'Die Zerstörung der Altersversorgung', *Informationsbrief WEED*, 5 December.

25. FAO (1995), *World Agriculture: Towards 2010*, Chichester, p. 272.

26. Gudrun Lachenmann (1994), 'Ansätze der Transformation und kreativen Fortentwicklung traditioneller und informeller sozialer Sicherungssysteme in Afrika', *Nord-Süd aktuell* 2, pp. 283–94.

27. Wichterich (1996), pp. 74ff.

28. *Matrioshki* are the dolls within dolls that symbolize the unfathomable Russian soul.

29. Olga Vershinskaya, 'Gender Aspects of Socio-Economic Transformation in Russia', manuscript of a talk given to the conference on Employment and Women, ICRW, The Hague, 18–19 September 1996.

30. Marina Malysheva (1995), 'Gender Identity in Russia', *Canadian Women's Studies* 16/1, pp. 22–7.

31. IPS, 28 February 1997.

32. Thomas Siebold (1995), 'Die soziale Dimension der Strukturanpassung – eine Zwischenbilanz', *INEF Report*, vol. 13, Duisburg, pp. 37ff.

33. Jean Lennock (1994), *Paying for Health*, Oxford, p. 35.

34. Jessica Vivian (1994), 'Social Safety-Nets and Adjustment in Developing Countries', UNRISD, Geneva, pp. 11ff.

35. Claudia v. Braunmühl, 'Thesen zum Umgang der Entwicklungszusammenarbeit mit den Herausforderungen von zukunftsfähiger Entwicklungspolitik', in Germanwatch (1997), *Zukunftsfähige Entwicklungspolitik – Vision oder Illusion?*, Bonn, p. 43.

36. UNDP (1996).

37. UNDP (1997), pp. 53ff.

38. Quoted in *Le Monde Diplomatique*, June 1997.

39. UNDP (1996), pp. 2ff.; UNDP (1997), p. 9.

40. UNDP (1996), pp. 16–17.

41. Werner Schiffauer (1997), 'Kulturdynamik und Selbstinszenierung', *Tageszeitung*, 4 March.

42. *Tageszeitung*, 1–2 November 1997; *Berliner Zeitung*, 17 September 1997; Uwe Jeans Heuser (1997), 'Wohlstand für wenige', *Die Zeit*, 24 October.

43. See Martin and Schumann (1997), pp. 1–11.

5

Variants of Modernity

Consumption as Global Culture

When I was living in India in the early 1980s, my friends always handed me a list of things they wanted me to bring back from a trip to Germany: a hand-mixer, tampons and rock music were usually at the top. At the time the Indian car industry was producing just two models in two different firms – Ambassador and Fiat – with a total annual output of 40,000 cars. Billboards everywhere urged those with the money: 'Be Indian, Buy Indian!' A bank clerk in the financial metropolis of Bombay managed no more than thirty to forty entries a day. Coca-Cola had been expelled from the country by Prime Minister Indira Gandhi and replaced with a sweet brown imitation called Campa Cola. At the language faculty of Jawaharlal Nehru University – the most advanced in India – a single duplicator was available to run off stencils. A telephone call from Delhi to Bombay was a test of patience that could last hours, and was not always rewarded with success.

Today the children of those friends wear made-in-India Reebok models that I have never seen. New CDs by their favourite hip-hop band can be had at music stores in the South Extension grid square on the same day as in Berlin. On television they watch the same CNN news that I do, and as in Germany children advise their parents which camera is the best buy and which word-processing programme is the most user-friendly.

The long period of seclusion from the world market had a boomerang effect on people's consciousness. All foreign products carried with them the myth that they were better than local ones. McDonald's in the wealthy Vasant Vihar district cannot complain about its flow of customers, although Indian cuisine has a large number of fast-food meals on offer. Benetton has several branches in Delhi, Copy Shop is on every street corner, familiar mauve bars of chocolate lie in supermarkets amid a plethora of other goods, a rooftop parabolic aerial is a symbol of openness to the world and its media messages, business yuppies carry a mobile on their belt or a pager in their pocket, the city is permanently clogged with traffic.

Far from the metropolis, too, the markets and grocers' shops today offer a much wider variety of consumer goods, whether made in India or, increasingly, abroad. Abundance is replacing shortage. In a remote village in the Himalayas as in the deserts of Rajastan, you can phone anywhere in the world from a digitalized call-box, including Europe for US$1.80 a minute.

Fifteen years and a massive opening to the world market lie between Delhi the city of four million and Delhi the city of ten million. In the early 1990s, the big cities witnessed the formation of a middle layer with real purchasing power and a class of *nouveaux riches* living in the lap of luxury from the new import–export businesses. But liberalization also sent waves of goods, advertising and news into the poorer regions and aroused new expectations in everyone not totally ground down by the daily struggle for survival. Happiness and prosperity are now being redefined even by small farming families. Needs are not static; they develop.

First it was men who joined the consumer world by purchasing a transistor radio, a wristwatch or a bicycle. Now, even in the lower middle classes, spending on cosmetics has gone up in leaps and bounds. Motor scooters, consumer electronics, refrigerators and washing machines are the tokens of rising consumption and status. What is happening used to be completely alien to the Indian caste system: social hierarchy is increasingly tied to the possession of consumer goods. A video recorder, electronic equipment and computer games are the vehicles of social differentiation.

Women or the bride's family are often used as a way up to the next rung on the consumption ladder. Dowry demands, in particular – from a television in the lower middle classes to a small Maruti car in the upper middle classes – exceed all the bounds of decency. Consumption lechery is buttressing the commercialization of marriage.

Earlier, Indian culture had no concept of leisure time. There used to be only two reasons for travel: a special family occasion or a pilgrimage to a holy site. Now the Indian middle classes go off to see the cultural sights of the country and, in summer, to enjoy the pleasant upland climate. 'We want to show our children why so many foreign tourists come here,' say a couple from Delhi, both earning a salary, on a crowded tourist bus with two children one Christmas day. The new lifestyle geared to leisure and consumption creates a new class consciousness, a new social identity over-lying but not yet displacing the old. 'Caste', they say, 'is no longer so important in the city.'

Rich kids in the pedestrian zone of Vasant Vihar put this new class membership on display. They wear T-shirts, jeans and trainers, with their hair in modern styles. Jeans are more than an item of clothing; they represent a particular lifestyle. Levi's on a woman go together with a certain type of sexualization of the female body, but they also signal mobility and independence. Since the 1980s, the daughters of the middle classes have been wearing jeans to college or to the cinema. Their peer groups reject a sartorial order which up until now was strictly gender-specific. Western male clothing symbolized modernity and progressive attitudes, while the woman with her sari and salwar kamiz had the task of preserving tradition. Even today, most women return to traditional dress after they get married.

The issue of dress-regulated female respectability exploded in a storm of protest – from Hindu nationalists, left-wingers and feminists – at the Miss World contest held in November 1996 in Bangalore. Conservative forces, led by Hindu chauvinists, used the event to swear women to cultural traditions and family roles associated with the Indian gender hierarchy. An alliance of women's groups opposed both this conservative image and the imported commercial physical norms of the beauty competition. 'Beauty is an industry,' read their posters. 'On the altar of capital, women's bodies are transformed into a commodity for sale.' They said that the image of women presented on the McWorld stage would generate a false view of liberation and modernity and forced women into a stereotyped subordinate role.

Images of women and men are indeed being universalized through the globalization of consumption, and tastes, behaviour and value orientations are becoming increasingly uniform. Advertising conveys an image of women that is completely new in India: the middle-class housewife holding a packet of washing powder. The cigarette industry is likewise targeting middle-class women, in the hope of changing the traditional reluctance of Indian women to take up smoking.

The media and migration are two crucial mechanisms generating value and goal uniformity. Thirty private television stations feed by satellite the customers of the brave new world of consumerism. The public channel Doordashan seems home-spun and unsophisticated in comparison with the flow of electronic pictures from Rupert Murdoch's Star TV based in Hong Kong, or from Channel V, the Indian variant of MTV. Lifestyle magazines featuring beautiful homes in the cosmopolitan style, as well as a dizzying range of other special journals, carry adverts for both Indian and foreign brands of goods. The multinationals have launched a huge offensive to occupy ground in the Indian market. Strategists rack their brains over whether it makes more sense to stick with worldwide campaigns (à la IBM, Volvo and Gillette) – which is obviously the less expensive option – or to commission from local agencies something that speaks more distinctively to Indian culture.[1]

Procter & Gamble's advertising campaigns in Eastern Europe and Asia have invented a new problem: dandruff. This had not previously carried a stigma but now has to be combated by means of a Procter & Gamble shampoo. That is demand management through advertisement. It creates universally effective signals for the arousal of needs, but it also creates universal needs.

At the same time, the migratory wave of the 1970s is setting up cultural feedback in India. Many families who emigrated to North America, Europe or Australia visit their native land once a year with children born in Toronto, London or Cologne. They bring with them not only the usual consumer goods but also more flexible norms and a mixture of values. When they arrive, they are regarded – rightly or only in people's imaginations – as 'the rich relatives from the West', and they operate as models and emissaries of changed modes of conduct.

It seems at first sight that a few stock items from the world of imported consumer goods – Western outfits, music and appliances – add up to a new culture. Is this cultural globalization? Is this the new cultural imperialism, the coca-colaization of the world, with Michael Jackson and Madonna as chief gladiators?

No doubt there really is a tendency towards uniformity of consumption patterns, with a partial devaluation of traditional lifestyles and values. But that is not the same as a Westernization which makes everything else flat and empty. The children of liberalization, the Indian generation of tomorrow, want both to be 'modern' and to remain 'Indian'. 'We are proud of our culture!' they say. For them, modernity is not simply Western; it is a combination of Western and local elements, an integration of convenience and mobility, comfort and technology into traditional ways of life and normative systems. Some might call it a cultural mish-mash or eclecticism, but it is actually a synthesis. Usually stock elements from the West are simply superimposed on conventional contexts, often remaining subordinate to the Indian way of life. The values of the West, which are based upon individualism and personal liberty, are still alien to most people. As so often in its history, India's cultures are proving to be at once absorbent and resistant. They incorporate new elements yet maintain their continuity.

In parallel to the globalization of the consumption and culture industry by Western corporations, large regional sub-markets are also developing in the countries of the South. These adapt to the synthesis or fusion of Western–modern and traditional cultures. Three influential centres are taking shape: Latin America, the Japanese–Chinese cultural space, and the Indian sub-continent. Alongside American soaps such as *Dynasty* or German crime series such as *Derrick* or *Der Alte*, the market is also expanding for Latin American *telenovelas*, kung fu films from Hong Kong or *manga* cartoon films from Japan, and various Indian series and films with their accompanying Hindi-pop. Currently the Chinese television industry is riding high in the international media market, especially in East and South-East Asia, with its monkey-king cartoons, costume dramas and combat spectaculars.

Products of India's gigantic film industry – movies about gods or gangsters from Bombay's 'Bollywood', as well as cock-and-bull stories, mythological staples and assorted pulp in various South Indian languages – attract devoted audiences from among Malaysians of Indian origin and migrant workers in the Gulf States. But Indian stars are also idolized in Africa, from Egypt to the Cape. In Arab cultures, it is Hindi videos that women bring home for the evening's entertainment, while the men are out enjoying themselves in tea houses and elsewhere. On the Swahili coast of East Africa, the finding and watching of fresh supplies of the video–drug is an important activity for female groups of relatives or neighbours.

Daytime radio or television soaps are mainly directed at women, since they are able to listen or watch while they do the housework. The patterns of female dreams and fears that are played out there in virtual realities, the tangled never-ending chain of longings, mean tricks and blows of fate garnered from the fantasy life of the middle classes, are clearly so stereotyped and transcultural that a Mexican *telenovela*, for instance, can run for a whole year with great success on Kenyan television.

The consumption and culture industries mould people's needs to the shape of the market and satisfy them on a market basis. The commodity form clings like a sticky film to the traditional range of economic activities, cultures and sexual relations. Dominated by the brand-names of Western corporations, the global market greedily sucks out local elements and converts them into an ethno-look, 'world' music or 'ethnic' food. Differences are good for business.

Decadence and Independence

At weekends it is impossible to get through to Jalan Cihampelas, the famous jeans street in Bandung. Buses from all over Java block the access roads. Young people, students and office workers spend hours being driven here to participate in the world of the big brands. The old tree-lined avenue is a kilometre-long cheap goods table piled with textiles and shoes which, though produced for export, were rejected as flawed or not finished in time. Nowhere in Indonesia are Levi's, GAP and Liz Claiborne as cheap as they are here. An endless succession of boutiques boom with rap and rock, while huge cardboard figures of Superman or Rambo point the way into the shops and James Bond raves about the special offer of the day.

The small groups of girls and boys are visibly excited as consumption fever takes them over. They flick through one revolving stand or bargain counter after another, move from one side of the street to the other, show each other the trophies they have acquired, collapse on the roadside exhausted and loaded down with bags, and eat ice-creams. In the evening they go back to Jakarta and other places.

A pair of Armani jeans, a Benetton T-shirt; these are the symbols of belonging to the world of brand-names. The transnational corporations have succeeded in splitting up the world of consumption: there are top-notch consumer goods (that is, the genuine proprietary articles) and there is the rest. Leading brands are the entry ticket to the global shopping-mall and the global fun-society. They have become the mantra for quality and social status, stretching right across continents and cultures. Brand awareness is replacing class consciousness. Brand is what creates class.

Indonesian families used to club together to purchase *kebaya*, magnificent clothes in which their daughters could dance at village festivals. Today students at a women's hostel, or young people in a neighbourhood, pool their pocket-money to buy some branded goods. They take turns to wear them when they go for a couple of hours to a *dangdut* bar (where bands play a hybrid of techno, Malay and Indian music), or even when they just want to poke their head inside the Hard Rock Café in Jakarta. Young people take up the tradition of pooled savings and loans, so that they can visit a disco, mall or fast-food restaurant in a top-brand outfit.

Upwardly-oriented working women also try to cover up their *kampung* (village) origin with a certain outfit and style of behaviour. To share an Esprit T-shirt three ways or to borrow one for the sake of effect, to walk around with a plastic bag from a luxury store or with a top brand logo – this is real 'as if' conduct. A standard of living is often simulated, symbolically consumed, so that it becomes what might be called a virtual lifestyle.[2]

Up and down the street, the West is flooding public space with English-language publicity, advertising boards and company signs. In 1995 the Indonesian government tried to combat this by decreeing that English names had to disappear from shops, restaurants and hotels. When the owners did not themselves paint over or remove the offending sign, squads of government enforcers went out into the towns and villages to repel the foreign-language invasion. Conservative reactions have also been apparent in the streets, schools and universities, where there has been a marked increase in the number of young women wearing *jilbab*, the black cloak, and girls wearing headscarves.

The Vietnamese government followed the Indonesian example of protecting the nation from linguistic imperialism, but it went still further. In 1996 not only were advertising signs compulsorily altered; a defensive battle was also waged against the decline in values and the encroachment of 'decadent Western culture that poisons happy family life'.[3]

In fact, everything that the communist regime prohibited after victory – from sinful night-life through drugs to the widely popular games of chance – has been celebrating a triumphant comeback rooted in the opulent supply of imported consumer goods. *Ao dai*, the tight-fitting women's national costume banned by the communists as a feudal relic, is undergoing a renaissance. The 'iron butterflies', who fought alongside men in wartime in unisex clothing, have been resexualized in their new public appearance in the cities. In the market economy, femininity is redefined in accordance with old models that emphasize the difference between the sexes.

In 1996 a palace of consumption and leisure was built in Ho Chi Minh City by a firm from Singapore. This 'Saigon Superbowl', which cost more than $11.5 million, is an El Dorado for the young rising class of high-earners. Karaoke bars, where Western music can be practised, are the epitome of the new-style fun. For the cool cats who had the good fortune to be born late, the city's hottest nightclub is called Apocalypse Now. The former prison for captured GIs in Hanoi, ironically baptized the Hanoi Hilton, has been converted into a shopping centre. Not to be missed is the street advertising in which the red of Coca-Cola is displacing the red of the Communist Party.

The Vespa, the Honda and the television set are key icons of modernity. As everywhere, progress is measured in terms of horsepower. The transition from bicycle to moped in the 1980s, and now from moped to motorbike, marks the gradations of consumerism. Five hundred new motorcycle registrations a day are quite normal in Hanoi.[4]

The new wave of buying has been accompanied by a new form of payment, for it is on credit that people move up the floors of the global warehouse. Many are unable to afford a refrigerator or gas cooker on their own earnings, so they get a little extra along the winding paths of bureaucratic corruption and everyday palm-greasing. Mass consumption and mass corruption go hand in hand.

In a spirit of repression, the government tries to overcome the moral evils and market excesses by periodically confiscating videos, closing down bars and insisting on adverts in Vietnamese. National pride is planted in opposition to value and commodity imperialism from outside.

Contradictory trends are also observable in neighbouring Laos: Buddhist temple culture is flowering again after years of politburo repression, but so are the imported consumption and culture industries. Apparently, the more isolated a country used to be, the greater is the consumption hunger today. In Laos the brave new world enters across the 'Friendship Bridge' with Thailand, or else by satellite. Six Thai stations beam their addictive

TV series to the Mekong's sleepy other shore, where the government vainly anathematizes 'decadent Thai pop culture' (which in China would be called 'pollution of the intellectual environment'). The market-driven, media-steered lifestyle, with its insatiable thirst for consumption and leisure, continues to advance and to exert an enormous fascination. At the same time, however, there is a process of retraditionalization that values originality and independence against the steamroller of Westernization.

Looking West, Turning East

In 1997 Malaysia's prime minister, Mahathir Muhammad, was seized with horror at what was happening to the *bumiputra*, the sons and daughters of Malay extraction. Various studies and statistics showed that it was precisely these products of a Muslim upbringing who were the most likely to become addicted to drugs, as well as to frequent nightclubs or to become *bohsia* girls (teenagers who, after school or work, earn some extra money from prostitution to raise their level of consumption).

Although the state had done all in its power to promote economic growth and prosperity, it had always been assumed that profit and the Prophet were compatible with each other, and that Islam would be the moral backbone of the younger generation. In the early 1980s, rapid export-oriented industrialization was complimented by the motto 'Look East' as a guardrail that could protect the national culture. The model in this respect was Japan, where a way was supposed to have been found of reconciling the logic of capitalist industrialization with traditional values.[5]

In the course of the 1980s, young women working in export factories became a public bone of contention. They had their own money, which gave them a new mobility and interest in consumption. Advertising, workplace beauty contests and trips to villages by 'Avon Ladies' spread the Western ideal of womanhood and beauty. Although most working women did not experience the new freedoms in their own lives and still felt bound by village values and parental expectations, they came under fire for alleged 'immorality' and 'sexual permissiveness'. This 'shame' brought conservative Islamic forces on to the scene. Village elders controlled what young women did in their spare time, or instructed foremen to keep an eye on them in the factory.[6]

In the Malaysian state of Kelantan, a decree was issued that Muslim women in both public and private employment should cover their whole body including hands and face, and even members of other religions were forbidden to wear mini-skirts. Fines were prescribed in the event of non-compliance with this order. In order to prevent extramarital affairs, married women were encouraged to allow their husbands a further spouse.[7] Pro-

Islamic and revivalist (*dakwah*) groups offered women Koranic instruction and housekeeping courses after working hours, and encouraged them to stand up to 'Western materialism and individualism' by observing 'Muslim' dress and morals. Even if they do not wear the veil, many young women from the villages responded to this appeal. They are looking for something secure to hold on to in alien surroundings, and for a way out of the dilemma caused by the conflict between their own demands for emancipation and family expectations and public contempt. The religious courses offer them points of reference with things they find familiar, as well as ideas about how to reference their new role at work with traditional images of women and recognition of male and religious authority. It is the appeal of an identity in a situation of general insecurity.

It is not only workers who take up the Islamist offer; the number of 'new Muslim women' is also growing in high schools and universities. These young women, usually the first in their family ever to have a higher education, are consciously deciding to live in accordance with the teachings of Islam and to wear either a headscarf or the *hijab* covering the whole body.[8] This makes them feel freer and more secure in an unfamiliar environment, allowing them to assert themselves legitimately in the public fields of education, administration and politics. The veil functions as a protector against the outside world and signals a demand for respect. What they wear beneath the cloak may well be jeans rather than traditional clothing. Eroticism is here explicitly reserved for the private sphere.

Self-assertively, sometimes even seeing themselves as a new elite, they present the image of 'educated Muslim women'. Interpreting the Koran in their own way, they fight for women's rights and especially for the right to take part in public life. They do not withdraw into the home with a copy of the Koran, but use the available Islamic education and entertainment, on the Internet as well as on radio, television and video. Their re-Islamization should thus be understood not as a return to the middle ages, but as a modernization of Islam itself and of the role of women. They bring to it their own conceptions of the private and the public, a new Islamic women's identity plainly different from what conservative males would like to see.

In Bangladesh, too, where religion tends to have a liberal hue, conservatives have mobilized against the younger generation of women who go out to school, office or factory and bring home education, an income and a new self-awareness. When the writer Taslima Nasrin started to attract the attention of a politicized public with her texts against the subjugation of women by Islam, Islamists attempted to make their mark by organizing huge demonstrations in the cities and by pronouncing a *fatwa* death sentence on her. Girls' schools in the countryside were set on fire, NGO-sponsored women's projects were attacked, and death threats were made against women doctors who actively promoted birth control. Mulberry plantations on which women practised sericulture to supplement their income were destroyed. Women's education and autonomy were perceived as a threat to existing power relations.

'When women are educated, they start to make their own decisions,' remarks Sandra Kabir, founder of the Women's Health Coalition in Bangladesh. 'Fundamentalists are against education and health for women, because both make them stronger. And that is precisely what they do not want.' More and more parents send their children to government or NGO schools, instead of to religious schools in the village. They go to health centres instead of traditional healers. The influence, and the income, of religious leaders are on the wane.

'This is a power struggle which is not only political and economic but also a struggle to secure patriarchal rule,' argues Rounaq Jahan from Bangladesh, currently a professor in New York. This assessment can also be applied to the tirades of Sheikh Nasr Farid Wassel, Egypt's foremost authority in theological law. The state-appointed mufti hit the newspaper headlines in January 1997 when he insisted that women were too sensitive and indecisive by nature to hold high office, that men were 'more rational, wise and logical in difficult situations'. A thorn in the flesh of the theologian is undoubtedly the three female members of cabinet, who seem to run their respective ministries – economics, science and social affairs – no worse than did their male predecessors. His attacks are also intended to maintain the wretched unwritten law that no woman should ever become a judge. For years, women lawyers who nevertheless put themselves forward have been fobbed off with the flimsiest excuses.

In Egypt, as in Turkey and a number of other countries, Islamist currents find women supporters among the poorest layers of society, because their clinics, nurseries and emergency services fill some of the gaps left by the collapse of state provision, and because their group activities allow women to broaden their circle of contacts. With the high value it attaches to their role as wives and mothers, political Islam also strives to compensate for women's lack of prospects on the labour market.

Throughout the Islamic world, the funding for this kind of social work comes from the Gulf States. Further momentum is provided by migrant workers who have worked in the Gulf for several years and brought home in their luggage, along with the obligatory home electronics, a recipe for modernization consisting of state religion plus economic growth and prosperity.

But in some countries – Malaysia, for example – political Islam also finds takers among newly educated people who see themselves as a counterweight to the drive-in generation. In 1993 the children of Cairo's 'fat cats', as rich people are called, celebrated the first MTV broadcast on Egyptian screens with a big festival at the American University to usher in the new 'cool' age. Sociologist Karin Werner has observed how educated women in an Islamist youth group construct a lifestyle and subculture as an alternative to Westernization. The veil and bodily purification are paraded in opposition to the 'sexy mini-skirt-wearers' and the cliquish mixed-sex culture of Westernized Egyptian youth. On the one hand, this is a defensive strategy against instrumentalization of the female body as a sex object, but it is also an offensive modernization strategy in which the personality is presented as morally pure and self-governing, rather than heteronomous. To the Western-style eroticization of the female body for public display, these young Islamist women counterpose a publicly displayed rejection or barricading of the erotic dimension.[9]

It is over women's bodies that the conflict is being fought out between East and West, modernization and traditionalism. And yet, the real dilemma is not between tradition and modernity but between two rival concepts of modernization.

This is equally true in Turkey, where headscarf and cloak have, since the 1980s, again been at the centre of political controversy. In the 1920s Kemal Atatürk tried to ban the wearing of the fez or headscarf in public and to secularize the country through a strict separation of state and religion, and equality between the sexes. The fez disappeared, but the headscarf remained in Anatolian villages and in the *gecekondus*, the unofficial urban settlements. In the 1980s, the rural exodus meant that it also found its way back into higher educational institutions. Students who wear headscarves are made to feel insecure in two senses: they stand between their world of origin and new educational horizons; and they are subjected to discrimination. At university exams and in the civil service, they are not even admitted with a headscarf. Political Islam offers them crucial help in role conflicts, as well as a thread to guide them through identity crises. In return for exclusion from secular society, it attaches greater value to women's education and the roles of housewife and mother, as well as to other areas of public activity.

The Islamist Welfare Party of Necmettin Erbakan owed a large part of its success to the 'footwomen' who conducted its electoral campaigns at the base. They went from house to house in the *gecekondus*, organized picnics and theatrical performances, looked after sick people, and above all brought out the poor women's vote. Female activists in Erbakan's Refah Party protest against forced Westernization and demand toleration of their dress and identity choices. The *turban* or headscarf, which lay politicians treat as a signal of repression, is turned by them into a symbol of liberation.

'Turban feminists', as the Turkish media call them, do not want to have Western criteria of emancipation laid down for them.

Visibility in public is a key element in their concept of modernization. Both political recognition and a separate labour market offer them considerable scope in this respect. Yet the Refah Party excluded women from its leadership and from standing as candidates in the parliamentary elections of 1995. Up to now the 'turban feminists' have swallowed this restriction, but it remains to be seen how much longer they will do so.[10]

Identity Politics

Hundreds of thousands of Afro-American women gathered in October 1997 on the streets and squares of Philadelphia, mostly in response to appeals over the Internet. After the mass demonstrations in Washington by black men in 1995 and white men in 1997, black women were finally doing the same – exclusive and separatist, basing themselves on gender and colour.

'The march is a declaration of independence from ignorance, injustice, poverty, abuse, and everything negative that divides us from one another as black women and damages us as people,' stated the organizers.[11] The conglomeration of demands for affirmative action and a war on poverty, drugs and crime seemed rather random, but the goal was quite clearly the building of an Afro-American women's community. The marchers celebrated a new readiness to tackle their problems and to take responsibility for themselves; the keyword was 'empowerment', strength through common action. Social segregation was given a positive twist and made the basis of an autonomous paradigm of survival.

Here a socially declassed minority is constructing an identity against the dominant culture. This kind of identity politics is a side effect of globalization. The processes of globalization assimilate societies and make it appear that the world is becoming one 'global village' and humanity one 'global community'. In this context, nation and state lose much of their identity-grounding significance, and so a collective quest begins for an identity beyond national citizenship, or for a second nation such as the Nation of Islam among Afro-American men.

The formation of a collective identity, such as that of Afro-American women in the United States, not only founds a community but also produces a new self-understanding both inwardly and outwardly. Precisely when socio-economic exclusion and redistributive struggles grow more intense, self-definition in terms of culture, religion or ethnicity becomes increasingly important. Demonstrations of otherness and originality involve the formation of cultural capital within a competitive society. But group formation is also a response to consumerist individualism and the neoliberal push-and-shove society.[12]

In Kenya women scrub, starch and iron their white frocks every weekend, before they go to the Sunday service that a redemptionist sect holds beneath a tree. That is their community: they are part of a larger meaningful whole. The group is their source of understanding and strength, their retreat and shelter. In the Abyssinian Baptist Church in Harlem, schoolgirls and students proudly and emotionally account for how they have used the grant given them by the community. Especially in the case of the Christian sects and communities, it is evident that activity at the base – beneath the level of the male leadership – almost entirely rests upon the shoulders of women. The group's identity, with its public demonstrations of belonging, is used by women as a means of enhancing their social status. It gives them self-esteem.

People who migrate from countryside to town, or from one country or continent to another, are in a sense 'extraterritorial' figures. They bring part of their cultural heritage with them; however, the new place in which they live no longer directly constitutes their identity.[13] This identity has become geographically unattached and must be given a new location. For young people born in the Kreuzberg district of Berlin who attend a Koranic school there, Turkey is mainly a holiday country to which they go every summer with their parents; the *umma*, the Muslim community, is their real home.

Identity politics, as it is practised by marginalized groups, is an anti-disparagement politics, an attempt to build a countervailing power. This is what those blacks did who took up the term 'nigger' and tried to turn it around, or the gays who positively inflected the term 'queer'. For immigrants in the United States, the construction of ethnicity or cultural identity as Women of Color, Latinas or Asian Women was a similar attempt at self-assertion against the tendency of the white women's movement to take decisions for them.[14]

Separate identity is also a central theme of the young 'third wave feminists' in the USA, who see themselves as following the first wave of the late nineteenth and early twentieth centuries and the second wave of the 1970s. In contrast to the feminism of their mothers' generation, what binds together their often strange and shrill attitudes is 'our negotiation of contradiction, our rejection of dogma, our need to say "both/and"'.[15] Much in the spirit of this post-ideological and post-orthodox age, such approaches spurn the certitudes and stabilizing truths of the older feminism; now ambivalence is warmly welcomed, great play is made with contradiction, pleasure and diversity are erected into political concepts. 'Third Wave women and men talk a lot about pleasure. This could be because we're young or because we're such well-trained consumers [...] or because we watched too much TV growing up.'[16]

In India, Muslim and *dalit* ('untouchable') women are organizing independently of the Hindu-dominated women's movement, and in Latin America indigenous women are founding organizations of their own. In Germany, too, women immigrants mainly organize separately and keep their distance from the white women's movement and its racist tendencies; least of all do they join the trade unions. For many, solidarity with men from their culture of origin is more important than gender-based solidarity with white German women.

The return to what distinguishes oneself from others, even when traditions have to be invented anew, the putting of one's own culture or ethnicity on display – this making visible of 'who we are' is a way of insisting on recognition by the dominant culture. Authenticity is constructed, traditions and distinctions are invented, and in this way a difference from the majority society is manifested in the public arena.[17]

The same mechanism is at work when young people in the industrialized countries find ways of marking themselves off within the global consumption and culture industries. Punks, skinheads, ravers, skaters, girlies, and goths, or even the fully kitted-out fans of a football or ice hockey team, identify themselves through certain dress codes. Trends are set by young people asserting themselves as 'special', whose group membership thus demarcates them from others.

Such ways of standing out may be found both within individual countries and in the international political arena. Unlike ten or twenty years ago, many African and Asian women no longer wear a suit with starched blouse as a kind of international conference uniform, but stress their cultural difference through a return to 'authentic' or 'traditional' dress. In Britain and the United States, women from ethnic minorities also use clothing to make the same return to authenticity.

For the Berlin ethnologist Werner Schiffauer, these collective stagings are an appeal for perception and recognition by the dominant culture. Outfit and dress codes are possible vehicles of the presentation of self; violence and aggression are two others, which guarantee a relatively high degree of attention and are obviously practised more by young men than young women.[18]

Every society with a significant amount of immigration faces the question of what will bind together the various classes, ethnic groups, religions and cultures, in the absence of a common national feeling. The concept of a multicultural society promises to bring about integration while respecting the right to cultural difference. In April 1997, an issue of *Der Spiegel* announced the collapse of this project in Germany with picture illustrations of, on the one hand, headscarf-wearing Koranic students, rising crime and violence among immigrant groups, and, on the other hand, xenophobia and national-chauvinist revival among groups of Germans from Mölln to Solingen. Even Kreuzberg, the district in Berlin held up as a model of integration, appears to be a failure: 20 per cent unemployment rising to 50 per cent among young people, a tense and threatening juxtaposition of ethnic groups, no real mingling and fusion of cultures.

Is this the war of cultures predicted by the US theoretician Samuel Huntington as the shape of things to come?[19] Is violence the inevitable response to unsuccessful integration, as the Bielefeld expert on youth questions Wilhelm Heitmeyer argues with his thesis of 'the allure of fundamentalism'? Such analyses, which fall back upon cultural difference as the cause of social conflicts, divert attention from the growing social and economic divisions in society.

Globalization processes give rise to multicultural and multiethnic societies, but also to multiracist, ethnically hierarchical and socially polarized structures. The global market is only a limited mechanism of economic integration, for it also excludes and marginalizes and does not bring about greater social equality. The 'global cities', from New York through Paris to Tokyo, are high-visibility concentrations of societies segmented both vertically (from top to bottom) and horizontally (along the economical and cultural coordinates of inside and outside). The global cities are conglomerates of various ghettoes, at whose points of contact more frequently aggression breaks out, cars are set alight, youth gangs wage war on one another, and property crimes and violence against women are on the increase.

'Crossing' and 'connecting' between cultures are the basic principles of globalization, and migrants are their living embodiment. It is they who are consciously at home in two worlds and who reflexively combine different traditions and value systems. In recent years, some of them have taken on leading roles within the international women's movement. Cultural anthropologists call them hybrids, and analyse their culture as a hybrid culture, because they unite different elements in a new synthesis.

The globalized societies of the future will need such a hybrid civilization that combines respect for difference with solidarity – one which, on the basis of cultural difference, is able to develop a common culture of social rights and economic opportunity and security.[20] To build bridges that everyone can use without eroding historically grounded difference – that is what Vinay Bahl in India sees as the way out of the conflict between 'global homogenization' and 'local cultural identity'.[21]

Notes

1. *Financial Times*, 30 June 1997.

2. Solvay Gerke (1995), 'Symbolic Consumption and the Indonesian Middle Class', Working Paper no. 233, Bielefeld University.

3. *Süddeutsche Zeitung*, 17–18 February 1996.

4. *International Herald Tribune*, 7 June 1997; *Handelsblatt*, 19–20 January 1996; *Nachrichten für den Außenhandel*, 24 January 1996. Cf. Heinz Kotte and Rüdiger Siebert (1997), *Vietnam, Die neue Zeit auf 100 Uhren*, Göttingen, pp. 22ff.

5. Ong (1987), p. 149.

6. Ibid., pp. 181ff.

7. Mona Abaza (1996), 'Die Schwestern wollen einen modernen Islam', *Der Überblick* 4, pp. 40ff.

8. Renate Kreile (1997), *Politische Herrschaft, Geschlechterpolitik und Frauenmacht im Vorderen Orient*, Pfaffenweiler, pp. 336ff.

9. Karin Werner (1995), 'Infitah und weibliche Identität in Ägypten: Auswirkungen der verstärkten Weltmarktintegration Ägyptens auf die Lebenspraxis junger Mittelklassefrauen in Kairo', Working Paper no. 230, Bielefeld University.

10. Interview with Nilüfer Göle, in *Tageszeitung*, 6 March 1996; Heidi Wedel (1996), *Frankfurter Rundschau*, 23 August; Birgit Cerha (1996), 'Ausweg aus den Rollenkonflikten', *Der Überblick* 4, pp. 32–7.

11. Quoted (and retranslated) from *Tageszeitung*, 27 October 1997.

12. Werner Schiffauer (1997), 'Kulturdynamik und Selbstinszenierung', *Tageszeitung*, 4 March.

13. See John Tomlinson (1996), 'Cultural Globalisation: Placing and Displacing the West', *European Journal of Development Research* 8/2, December, pp. 22–36.

14. Ilse Lenz, 'Grenzziehungen und Öffnungen: Zum Verhältnis von Geschlecht und Ethnizität zu Zeiten der Globalisierung', in Lenz et al. (eds) (1996), pp. 206ff.

15. Jennifer Drake (1997), 'Review Essay: Third Wave Feminisms', *Feminist Studies* 23/1, p. 104.

16. Ibid., p. 106.

17. Jean-François Bayart (1997), 'Umwege des Fortschritts?', *Tageszeitung*, 24 June; Eckart Dittrich and Astrid Lentz, 'Die Fabrikation von Ethnizität', in Reinhard Kößler and Tilmann Schiel (1994), *Nationalstaat und Ethnizität*, Frankfurt/Main, pp. 23–45.

18. Schiffauer (1997), 'Kulturdynamik und Selbstinszenierung'; Wilhelm Heitmeyer (1997), *Frankfurter Rundschau*, 7 March.

19. Samuel Huntington (1996), *The Clash of Civilizations and the Remaking of World Order*, New York.

20. Ghai and Hewitt de Alcantara (1994).

21. Vinay Bahl (1995), 'Cultural Imperialism and Women's Movements', *Economic and Political Weekly*, 28 October, pp. WS-50–59.

6

Globalization of the Women's Movements

Movements and Networks

Huairou, a provincial town 60 kilometres outside Beijing, became for ten days in September 1995 the women's 'global village' and the burning glass of the worldwide women's movement. Fearing what NGO women might get up to, the Chinese leadership had moved the NGO forum at short notice out into the prairie. Thus, while government delegations at the UN Women's Conference in Beijing were haggling over every word and comma of a policy platform for the coming years, the NGO women had an agenda of their own based upon experiences of struggle and directed towards feminist organization and women's politics in the shadow of globalization.

No film could reproduce vividly enough the colour and diversity of that gathering.[1] It was a rainbow encompassing the most diverse structures and politics, from local rank-and-file and self-help groups to well-funded international lobbies and umbrella organizations: Women's World Banking alongside Canadian pro-life activists, the National Council of German Women's Organizations opposite Kuwaiti women widowed by the Iraqi invasion, Latin American lesbians and Indian peasants. And all conceivable shades between participant and representative politics were there in the marketplace.

Women from villages and slums came in larger numbers than ever before. Their grassroots initiatives organize survival for many women – the daily struggle over small freedoms and new rights. Such 'local feminisms' derive from everyday problems, adapted to local possibilities of cultural and social action and directed at pragmatic immediate goals.[2] Their struggle for personal loans, secure housing, childbirth assistance or a battered wives' refuge is based on the realization that gender is one, but not the only, dimension of discrimination and violence. They have learnt to see their individual suffering as the symptom of a wider structure of injustice, to make links between the micro- and the macro-level. Especially in the South, such groups tend to have a material core in 'survival feminism', because women there bring feminist perspectives into their elementary struggles for food, health and water supply, as well as for further education and physical integrity, even if this is not the term that they themselves use.[3]

Between the local groupings and the international organizations, national unions formed a broad middle ground of women's rights and care organizations, ranging from mothers' federations or anti-discrimination activists to professional associations of midwives or business women.

For the first time, Christian sects, pro-lifers, pro-regime Iranian women and Islamic groups from the USA and Britain were well represented and well prepared. Confidently directing their fire against the liberal Western understanding of emancipation, they argued instead for a biologically complementary definition of female and male gender roles and defended the patriarchal family as the basis of moral order in a world turned upside down. Most of the participants, however, identified this new political and religious conservatism as the greatest threat to the gains of the women's movement. It drew the only violent denunciations of the whole event.

Otherwise, differences were recognized on all sides at Huairou; conflicting concepts lay undebated beside one another, and only a few disputes were really thrashed out to the end. The old North–South polarization was a thing of the past, as themes and controversies cut right across the geographical line between the two. Nevertheless, women from the North were often there in the role of listeners and learners, as the main issues were overwhelmingly introduced by women from the South. It is they who have given the Women's International its vitality, they who have put their stamp on its debates, analyses and perspectives.

The reference points in Huairou were no longer common positions and strategies, but rather a recognition of difference in the global framework of women's politics: 'Diversity is our strength.'[4] In Huairou, then, plurality was raised into a structural and strategic principle, so that the diverse movements on the ground could enhance the strength of women's politics.

It is not surprising, then, that there is neither a women's political united front nor a global feminism. South African women, for example, distancing themselves from Western claims to dominance, spoke of their own 'indigenous' feminism as a local, pragmatically adapted variant. East European women, for their part, reported that Western feminism had had an inspiring effect on them, but that they thought it too dogmatic and too centred on the USA and Europe. Now they wanted to go their own way.

Dominating the debates in Huairou was a quest for common elements derived from experience and a desire for mutual understanding and co-operation. Unifying themes – especially the 'cross-sectional' issues of globalization and human rights – served as pegs for the various political approaches. Structural similarities were apparent both in the matters of concern and in the experience of problems. Women from small farming families in Switzerland, New Zealand and Africa exchanged views on which of the hurdles erected by officialdom or agribusiness they had to clear in the processing and local marketing of their produce. Women belonging to associations of domestics in Colombia, India and South Africa discussed the forms of resistance they might develop. Organizations from countries that both supplied and received prostitutes coordinated their AIDS education programmes. In all these exchanges, grassroots problems were often traced back to structural causes, and local and global elements were analysed together.

'We are the nucleus of global civil society en route to the twenty-first century.' The women's NGOs clearly understood themselves as a third force apart from governments and private business. Several times before the event in Huairou there had been some suggestion that the highly decentralized international women's movement needed an organizational umbrella so that it could act as a force of global civil society *vis-à-vis* the United Nations and the corporate 'global players'. But this proposal was not taken any further, nor was the idea of a women's UN as a counterforce to the United Nations, which on its own admission has been a failure.

So there was no discussion about whether a common representative structure might make the movement politically stronger in relation to governments and market forces. The huge diversity of approaches was not brought together into clear action strategies, political concepts and co-ordinated forward-thinking.

Instead, the women made Huairou a festival of networking. Experiences were exchanged, alliances were formed between women from different regions or continents, between single-issue groups such as peace activists, and between women from minorities (immigrants, lesbians, disabled people, indigenous groups) who were fighting against discrimination and to construct their own identity. One novelty was the forging of a large number of South–South alliances. Especially for women who have previously been isolated, networking offers insights into how things are connected, as well as a pool of inspiration and new political horizons. To maintain contact with one another, the women hoped to use the global information systems (e-mail and the Internet) which are independent of postal censorship and control – a point stressed particularly by women from parts of the former Yugoslavia.

Thus, the women's movements gathered together in Huairou themselves reflected the process of globalization. They have spread to the farthest corner of this patriarchal planet and succeeded in forging closer links with one another, but at the same time they have remained diverse and fragmented. The Women's International moves between the poles of

globalization and localization, networking and splitting. Networks appear to
be the organizational and political form most appropriate to globalization.

Alliance for the Right to a Few Square Metres of Housing

'Do you know how many people use a watering place? Or a toilet?'
'Fifty,' one woman answers. 'A hundred,' says another. 'So you don't know!'
concludes Sona. 'But you have to know, if you are to demand water pipes
from the town council.' Then Sona leads the women and men into Block
C of Piesang River Township in Natal and starts to count. How many
people live in each of these terrible places? How long have they been here?
Who goes out to work? Where is the nearest shower, the nearest school,
the nearest health station?

Sona comes from India and is not a highly paid expert in the development aid business. What qualifies her to teach the inhabitants of Piesang
River in South Africa are her own wretched pavement shack on Bombay's
Apna Road and her experience as a barefoot housing-planner. She belongs
to a women's group on Apna Road organized by SPARC (the Society for
the Promotion of Area Resource Centres), and she is involved in an unusual
international cooperation project between homeless and slum-dwellers'
organizations. Since 1991 there has been a regular shuttle between Bombay
and South Africa: ideas and experience are exchanged across the Indian
Ocean, between SPARC and the Slum-dwellers Union on the Indian side,
and People's Dialogue and the Association of Homeless People on the
South African side. The workers call their cooperation simply 'the Alliance'
– a grassroots network from slum to slum, from pavement to pavement.

Most of them are women. For it is mainly women who have to pay for,
and try to cushion the effects of, the injustice and incalculable risks present
in makeshift housing. Whether in Johannesburg or in Bombay, they struggle
to turn even the flimsiest hovel into a 'cosy home'. 'We women', says
robust Thandi from the Cape Region, 'are the mortar that holds the home
together.' It is up to them to ensure that water and fuel are available, even
when there are no water pipes or electricity cables. They catch the rain-
water that drips through the rotten corrugated-iron strips of the so-called
roof, and they try to catch family disasters before they get out of control.
They feel responsible if the children cannot stay 'at home' and go out on
the prowl, if the daughter comes back pregnant at fifteen or the son brings
home drugs and stolen loot.

The women from Indian slums and African townships have more in
common than a longing for firm ground under their feet and a roof over
their heads. They also share the humiliating experience of injustice and
eviction. Lakshmi from Bombay and Ruth from Johannesburg have several

times been through the nightmare of eviction: 'It's like an assault on your whole existence.' One morning, when the local authorities can be sure that the men are out at work or looking for a job, the municipal bulldozers roll in to 'clean up'. The women are just able to collect a few pots and their screaming children before all their worldly goods are crushed and thrown into waiting lorries. The women are left behind with the pitiful remnants of their existence, and with their despair.

It is impossible to escape the municipal 'cleansing operations', because the occupation of pavements and land is simply against the law and the wrath of 'decent' citizens is sure to follow. In Bombay, however, SPARC has developed strategies to overcome the powerlessness of those who have no rights. A court order was obtained that required notice to be given of an impending eviction. But when the destructive custodians of the law are eventually closing in, hundreds of women now gather in a flash and themselves pull down the targeted shacks. Instead of a few wailing and defenceless residents, the police encounter a few hundred singing women. Their community action not only saves the possessions of the families in question, but also removes the isolation and impotence that are the most traumatic feature of the event.

The women from SPARC have more experience than South African township residents in struggling to get a share of the municipal housing, land and infrastructure resources. Their advice is not to wait and see what the authorities will do, but to insist on their rights and to go on the offensive by making demands of their own. In this spirit, the Association of Homeless People in Johannesburg formulated its own housing policy in 1994. 'It is a democratic right of poor people to plan their own development,' states its opening sentence.

As Sona demonstrated in Natal, SPARC has for years been collecting its facts and figures to use as the basis for political demands. With her help, the residents of Piesang River took only a few hours to conduct their own census of the township's population and infrastructure; then they went to the authorities and began to negotiate over the work that needed to be done. Their 'own' figures provided them with a solid basis and real bargaining power.

In 1992, when People's Dialogue members first went to Bombay, they were overcome with bewilderment at the long rows of patchwork hovels put together from cardboard boxes, plywood and plastic sheeting which clung to house walls and railway embankments. Half of the metropolis's 13 million inhabitants lived in slums and other desperately poor districts. Could such a density of housing deprivation be what lay in store for South Africa too?

The townships have certainly been hardened in struggle, and their experience gives them some lead over Bombay in terms of organization,

solidarity and resistance. Nevertheless, the political strategies that worked
in the liberation struggle are not suited to conflicts with the democratically
elected government.

They had hoped that liberation and democratization would solve overnight the existential problems of the poor but, in the new South Africa,
there has not yet been any major alleviation of housing need and land-
lessness. Although the government has made many a promise to build new
homes, the official wheels turn not only slowly but also reluctantly for
those at the bottom of the city heap who have no political lobby to speak
up for them. At the same time, the construction and housing markets have
become a hotbed of corruption. At least two million houses need to be
built in South Africa. But 1.2 million families earn so little that they are
not creditworthy in the eyes of the banks, and state subsidies target families
with a monthly income of at least 1200 rand (500 rand more than the
average). 'We can't and won't wait for the government to get moving,' says
Mama Iris Nomo from People's Dialogue.

Instead of exercising patience, another People's Dialogue delegation
went to Bombay and this time learnt a lesson about building societies. The
SPARC women in Bombay had set up their own society, and on the basis
of their own pooled savings they had been able to obtain loans and to
negotiate with the city authorities over the allocation of building land.
With the help of an architect, they also learnt how to build their dream
house – if at first only as a cardboard model. They found out how high
the rooms should be, whether it made sense to have extra sleeping space
between floors, where the windows should go, whether the toilet should be
inside or outside. They even had a hand in the building work, helping a
couple of hired workers to mix the mortar, to lay the bricks for their four
walls, and to put the roof-tiles in place.

Following the Indian model, People's Dialogue founded a savings society
and a network of building, information and training centres. Within a few
years, people living on the margins of civil and municipal life had saved
a couple of million rand – a clear sign of their willingness to contribute
constructively to a solution of the housing problem. In March 1995, when
some savings societies laid the foundation stones for the first houses, this
represented the first move by people in the township towards a future
designed by themselves, 6.5 metres square. The group that completed the
model house had learnt how to produce bricks and roof-tiles commercially,
and thus outwitted the building sharks who had quoted a price of 24,000
rand instead of the 9100 rand they ended up paying. Several hundred
owner-occupied homes have since been built throughout the country under
People's Dialogue supervision. More are being added to the total every day
– a thousand a year, they say.

Having seen that 'illegal settlers' manage to build more houses than the housing ministry, the government has changed its course to one of alliance and cooperation. Self-help thus kills two birds with one stone. It takes some of the burden off the government's shoulders, and it satisfies the desire of the township residents to take control of their lives.

Nelson Mandela watched the women building houses, Construction Minister Nthembi-Nkondo injected 10 million rand into their organization's housing fund and in 1996 appointed three of its members to South Africa's delegation to the UN Habitat Conference in Istanbul. It was all a reasonable success, such as no other NGO in South Africa had yet achieved.

Without the 'Alliance', People's Dialogue would not be where it is today. The experience of SPARC in Bombay became its starting capital in the struggle over the distribution of resources. The Indian tactics and ideas cannot, however, be simply copied and repeated. Just as the township residents in Cape Town and Durban have devised different model houses, they must also adapt their strategies to South African conditions. 'We don't have ready-made recipes in our luggage,' said Celine D'Cruz of SPARC. 'In each country people have to find their own way.' The Alliance has certainly brought plenty of inspiration for both sides. 'We can also be very different from each other – for example, in gender relations. But we have the same problems and can learn from each other.' SPARC found it more difficult to see eye to eye with the women who came to Bombay from the slums of Bogota. 'They considered every man as their enemy.' The Indian women do not understand such a confrontational gender politics.

It is not easy to win donors for this original form of collaborative work. That 'experts' should jet from continent to continent and from conference to conference is treated as a matter of course. But it is thought a waste of money for slum-dwellers to fly eight hours so that others can learn from their experiences and avoid their mistakes. The 'allies' in India and South Africa can only shake their heads in puzzlement. 'Governments and businessmen cooperate internationally, so why shouldn't we?' 'There are illegal settlers everywhere,' argues Sheinaz from SPARC, who has also been with the Asian Women and Shelter Network to Bangladesh, Thailand and the Philippines. 'We have to help each other. We are not demanding anything outrageous; we have a right to somewhere to live.'

The New International Women's Politics

It is Sunday evening. The fax-machine starts up and ejects a report from a women's rights organization in New York. The Nepalese Prime Minister, Sher Bahadur Deuba, said on a trip to the United States that his government had more important things to do than trace Nepalese girls carried off to Indian brothels or carry out rehabilitation programmes for prostitutes who returned to the country. 'Write protest letters to the prime minister, the interior minister and Nepalese embassies in every country,' the fax recommended.

Simultaneously, women's organizations are putting the finishing touches over the Internet to a joint letter to World Bank chief James Wolfensohn. In 1995, at the Fourth International Women's Conference in Beijing, he promised the NGOs that he would do what he could to secure greater gender equality in his institution and in World Bank programmes. However, a study conducted by a number of women experts (contactable at awid@ igc.apc.org) revealed that after nearly two years hardly anything had been done to follow through on the fine words. They requested formulations for the letter to the World Bank to be sent to AWID, the coordinating organization in Washington.

There is another message in the mailbox. The NGO coalition urgently needs proposals about how women's interests should be taken into account in the tasks laid down for an international court of justice. 'If we do not make any proposals, crimes against women will be disregarded,' warns the International Women's Tribune Center in New York.

Exchange of information and rapid coordination by e-mail, cries of outrage over individual cases and Amnesty International-style protest actions, the influencing of UN politics and international institutions – these are what characterize the new international women's politics. The previous era, which reached its height in the 1970s in the industrialized countries and in the 1980s in Asia and Latin America, had been one of 'autonomous' social protest by national women's movements operating outside the established parties, ideologies and political processes. Then the mobilizations died down and the movements became more differentiated. They left the streets as the central locus of organization and fragmented into various NGOs – a process similar to that which affected other social movements such as environmentalism. A host of new groupings, initiatives, projects and non-state organizations took shape and developed along various paths of institutionalization and professionalization. The networks formed by these national, mostly single-issue, organizations are today the backbone of the international women's movement.

There were already international women's associations in the last century, mainly representing particular occupational, religious and trade-union interests. But since the First International Women's Conference in Mexico in 1975, more and more network structures have been created among single-issue groups. In particular, the NGO Forum at the Third International Women's Conference in Nairobi in 1985 helped to crystallize the newly forming Women's International. It marked a twofold change.

First, the earlier sisterly dispute between North and South over thematic differences and questions of emphasis – body politics and male violence in the North, poverty and imperialism in the South – largely gave way to a will for understanding and solidarity. DAWN, a South–South network of women academics and activists, took shape as a vanguard in matters of political programmes. Second, the focus widened from so-called women's issues – the international trfficking in women, mortality in childbirth and so on – to include world political and economic questions, from the nuclear arms race to the growth of poverty.[5]

Both these tendencies were foundations for a new international women's politics from below. But this was really the child of globalization, for it is unthinkable without the new information and communications technologies, which are not only its key tools but also a field of action that forms and shapes the movement. At the same time, its political substance is the realization that the definition and experience of problems are increasingly similar in different countries, and that they can generally be traced to global structures.

When the United Nations, following the collapse of the bipolar world order, launched a series of mammoth conferences between 1992 and 1996 for governments to work out a new world 'internal' politics, a platform also appeared for the forces of civil society to 'think globally, act globally'. Taking their lead from business, governments and civil society thus also got down to intensifying their transnational cooperation.

Perestroika and the wave of democratization in many countries of the South and East had already triggered a change of direction towards institutionalized politics on the part of national women's movements. The end of the African single-party systems and the Latin American military dictatorships were seen by women as a historic opportunity to define their stake in participation and the development of a new politics within a democratic framework.[6] They took their degree of involvement in both political and economic decision-making as an indicator of democracy – 'No democracy without women's participation' – and criticized the exclusion of women as 'incomplete democracy'. In the face of an increasingly corrupt political culture, the transparency of politics and the accountability of governments became key demands of women's movements.

In the industrialized countries, autonomous women's movements had already learnt from experience that they could have only limited influence through protest actions, projects and campaigns. They came to see work at grassroots level as a lower political form, and conceived the passage from movement politics to established institutional politics as a march from the margin to the centre of power.

The sextet of UN conferences from the Rio Earth Summit to the

World Habitat Conferences in Istanbul offered the chance of participation at international level and of a democratization of transnational politics. Women also hoped to achieve a gradual breakthrough by influencing the broad agenda of the six conferences. If they demanded a place at the negotiation tables, it was not only to assert 'women's issues' and questions of equality, but also to affect the structure of world politics and economics.

The beginning of the new international women's politics can be dated quite precisely. In 1991, in the run-up to the Earth Summit, WEDO (the Women's Environment and Development Organization) held a women's congress in Miami which unanimously adopted a position paper for the gathering in Rio. The acronym WEDO is already a programme: We Do. Its profile reflects a new type of organization: an international network with headquarters in New York, strategically close to the United Nations; an office staff mainly composed of young immigrants living in the United States with a bridging function between North and South. The political culture has a strongly American stamp, geared to media effect and often carried along by a wild optimism. The founder, the former Democratic Party congresswoman Bella Abzug, has applied her decades of mainstream political experience to the institutionalized arena of power, bringing onto the executive some of the world's best-known women activists in the areas of ecology and development: from the Indian academic Vandana Shiva through the Kenyan ecological activist Wangari Maathai to the Brazilian women's rights activist Thais Corral.

Other nodal points in the process of international women's networking include the Centre for Global Leadership in New Jersey, which coordinated preparatory work on the human rights conference in Vienna, and the International Women's Health Coalition in Washington, which drew the threads together before the population conference in Cairo.

To introduce women's themes, to demand transparency and accountability, and above all to participate – this is the strategy pursued by the global network of women at UN conferences. 'From WEDO we have learnt what a caucus is, and also how to do lobby work and how not to be afraid,' praises Noeleen Heyzer, head of the UN's women's fund UNIFEM. And indeed, WEDO did succeed via the Internet in establishing itself as the nerve centre of international women's lobbying in the circles around UN conferences. It organized the women's caucus – originally an American Indian word for gathering – for the ad hoc fine-tuning of conference tactics, and trained women from all over the world to be on the alert for opportunities to get in touch with government delegations. WEDO women jetted around with laptops and mobiles from one summit to the next, carrying in their luggage a line-by-line alternative to the document up for discussion.

The Rio conference of 1992 was the crucial test of this political strategy

– and a success. Women's themes were placed on the agenda, and were incorporated into the final document, *Agenda 21*. Not only did women's NGOs become visible and audible on the floor of UN diplomacy, they also developed a conference culture of their own. In Rio, and at the human rights conference in Vienna, women's politics from below still concentrated entirely on lobbying for the final documents. It soon became clear, however, that final documents improved in the sense of women's politics are not automatically translated into action; that they may, just like any other, become a victim of political Alzheimer's and be laid aside by the responsible authorities. Work to influence negotiations and action plans is therefore only the first step in this field. Political pressure for action to follow it up in various countries is a necessary long-term trial of strength.

The conference-centred political process subsequently developed in four stages. First, assessments were made of the situation of women and the state of women's politics at national level, and demands for future action were made on this basis. Second, regional pre-conferences strengthened understanding and networking and helped to pool and synthesize proposals. Third, national and regional approaches were woven together during the UN conferences leading to action programmes. Fourth, pressure was brought to bear in each country for the implementation of internationally-agreed documents. It is true that such documents are not legally binding, but they are regarded as normative frameworks and can be used by forces of civil society as a moral point of reference.

Hopes that the steady conference rhythm would yield linear progress for women, both in thematic content and in levels of participation, proved to be an illusion. There was no escalator carrying them up to equality. And at the population conference in Cairo, women's politics found itself marking time in the face of obstruction and backlash by conservative forces. The chief aim of the women's NGOs at the last three conferences has been to prevent a relapse after the events in Cairo.

With regard to participation, the NGOs have been dancing a kind of tango with government delegations: forward and back, near and far, opening up and holding back. The limits of influence have become ever more clearly discernible. It is true that the NGOs gained a foothold in the negotiating structures, but they remain excluded from the inner circles of decision-making power. Governments and the UN took up the problems and issues raised by women's NGOs; their style of speech was adopted by UN rhetoric and government programmes, critical concepts were coopted and softened; and their ideas gave an impulse to modernization and reform. Even governments, in the concluding document of the Beijing conference, paid tribute to what 'NGOs, women's organizations and feminist groups' were able to achieve as a 'driving force for change' in civil society. But the vision of the Miami Congress, which had sought to steer world politics in new directions, slipped ever further into the distance.

Although the political software has been modified in these various ways, women have been kept out of the 'hard core' of politics that concerns economics and finance. In Beijing the governments made it quite clear that, in line with their cost-cutting social policies, no extra funding would be available for measures associated with women's politics. And in Singapore in December 1996, when the World Trade Organization debated economic growth, trade issues and the next steps in globalization, the NGOs were locked out and left kicking their heels. It was quite symbolic that one had to risk one's life to cross the six-lane highway separating the congress centre from the NGOs' meeting-place.

In terms of content, the conference oriented the women's movement more strongly to what was politically feasible. Not only did they get closer to 'big-time politics', they also had to labour under its constraints. In the dilemma of adaptation and counter-strategy, lobbying work exerts a constant pressure to fit into the existing practice of politics. Torn between the integration of women's issues into the negotiating framework of the final document and the vision of structural change at once radical and global, conference politics has inevitably tended to move in small steps towards the mainstream. Grand alternative designs serve at best as very distant lodestars of political action.

After the UN conferences, the lobbyists passed the ball back to the national women's organizations, which then had the task of translating the final documents into practicable proposals and putting pressure on governments to implement them. 'Monitoring' became the keyword in the follow-up process. Women's NGOs tried to gain acknowledgement as watchdogs over state actors and multinational institutions. In Beijing they brought their political muscle into play: they wanted to monitor the World Bank, to monitor the UN, to monitor national governments. So far, however, there have been few concrete strategies for long-term pressure and supervision.

It is true that the essential content of Beijing was given a national footing through a host of lectures and other events by participants from NGOs. But there has been a lack of ideas, strategies and reliable instruments for women to step up political pressure on governments in the face of global competition hysteria, social cutbacks and downsizing, and to turn the international resolutions into political will and political action. The link-up between global and local, between major world events and day-to-day women's politics, is still only in its early stages.

Up to now, anyway, mostly lip-service has been paid to the implementation of conference decisions from Rio to Istanbul. The balance-sheet conference held five years after Rio, in June 1997 in New York, was a summit of disillusionment at which one government after another declared its failure.

In the course of this six-stage marathon conference, women's NGOs perfected their lobbying techniques and appeared all round as exceptionally well prepared and organized. Their often outstanding specialist knowledge and professional behaviour won them political recognition and legitimacy, both from governments and from the wider public. Most of the time it was a US-based group which exercised leadership, but women from ethnic minorities and from the South had at least as high a profile as white feminists. This professionalization has brought to the fore a new trans-national and transcultural class of lobbyists, who appear really on top of their subject and tools, competent and eloquent, who tour the world with a high salary, a high expense account, and an equally high appraisal of themselves.

This has led to a hierarchical differentiation among the women's NGOs, with a clique of professional lobbyists at the top and a large crowd of supporters at the bottom. Beijing witnessed the launch of 'Equipo', an international elite force of lobbyists. Non-professional NGOs with weak structures and finances cannot possibly match that professional level. At the head of this internationally active women's movement are the North American 'BINGOs' (Big NGOs) such as WEDO. It is therefore no accident that all three of the previously mentioned examples of feminist e-mail solidarity operate via the United States, the nodal point of the globalized world.

The new international women's politics, like the NGOs as a whole, must ask itself whether output really matches input on the summit heights, and whether the lobbying form of political intervention should continue to be pursued at the international level. Up to now the global women's movement has had two spheres of action: the corridors of UN conferences and the Internet. In June 1997, at the New York balance-sheet conference on Rio, a return to local level was clearly in the air. If politics takes place only in the international arena, it becomes a matter of tilting at the windmills of spoken, written and broken words. The women's NGOs have now tested this field of politics. And not only are they as weary of conferences as government delegations are; they have learnt from experience that, even in the age of globalization, international lobbying is not a foolproof scheme for success but simply one of many possible forms of politics.

Countering Powerlessness

At the NGO Forum in Huairou in 1995, neoliberal globalization was a central issue and a portmanteau notion at many of the debates, as complex as it was vague. It was identified as a market-centred rather than human-centred process, which subordinates people's needs and rights, and which has been generating growth without jobs in the North, structural adjustment in the South, privatization in the East, and public spending cuts everywhere. It is a process which unites through market integration and new information technologies, while at the same time dividing through the growth of social polarization. For women's movements in Latin America it is largely synonymous with neoliberalism. The Philippines group Gabriela considers it to be one and the same as imperialism – a new stage of colonialism and capitalism. For the Brazilian women's federation, it means hunger and poverty. African women mainly think of it as structural adjustment.

On the one hand, then, globalization has been regarded as a threat to exploit women as an unpaid or underpaid resource and a threat to social justice and women's rights, while on the other hand, it has been described as an opportunity for democratization and solidarity, for the strengthening of the forces of civil society. The critique of globalization has, of course, been the springboard for many lively debates. But clearly no comprehensive alternative has emerged from within the ranks of feminism, nor has one path asserted itself as the single beckoning counter-strategy.

Nevertheless, women are trying to break through the myth that there are no alternatives to the globalized market. The more it extends its grip, and the more power is concentrated by transnational corporations and international financial institutions, the more difficult it becomes to devise feminist alternatives and the stronger is the feeling of impotence and hopelessness.

In what follows, some outline will be given of the variety of responses to globalization that are beginning to emerge in women's politics. One response, of course, is to focus on the new life opportunities, new freedoms and individual options. The processes of globalization, in this view, offer women new occupations and careers on the flexibilized labour market, unprecedented choice on the consumption and culture markets, and routes to mutual understanding through new channels of information and technologies of communication. Women should use all these for themselves.

The critical approaches may seek instead to take a hand in the shaping, or reshaping, of globalization, or to build up counterweights and countervailing forces. But the different approaches are not sharply distinguished and may flow into one another in political practice.

Transformation through participation Integration and transformation were for a long time a pair of opposites about which women's movements fought and split with one another. The concept of transformation through participation, put forward in 1995 by the South network DAWN, over-comes the blockage of the either-or.[7] There is no longer seen to be a mutually exclusive choice between being inside and outside the dirty coopting business of politics and the capitalist economic system. No path seems to point political participation towards the taking of power. Yet not only are women seeking to participate in greater numbers and in higher positions; they are also aiming at a structural change in politics, economy and development. Decision-making power is for them a means to the end of changing course.

Equal participation in politics and the economy is a very old demand of women's movements that places systemic reforms at its centre. Its priorities are the struggle against exclusion and discrimination, for affirma-tive action in favour of women, and for the introduction of women's issues into all fields of social action.

This stance of participation within the system has been integrated into alternative growth models and the concept of 'empowerment', which was the main inspiration of NGO debates at the women's conference in Nairobi in 1985. It was then that DAWN counterposed empowerment for women to policies of equality and integration. The aim was to bring about a global, national and sexual redistribution of the power to take decisions and shape the world, a social transformation with a new paradigm of development that was no longer tied to growth and the world market.

This concept of women's empowerment and systemic transformation was expressed in 1995 by DAWN in a diagram in which state, market and civil society formed three sectors of participation and change at the three corresponding levels: macro, meso and micro. 'Restructuring of the market', 'reform of the state' and 'strengthening civil society' were to be the three simultaneous and interconnected objectives.[8] Horizontal and vertical alliances would develop an overarching strategy for the transformation of 'institutions and processes' – a strategy geared to the needs of the weakest section in society, most of whom are women.

As an aid to empowerment in institutions at every level, women's movements demanded a quota system of positive discrimination. These were supposed to ensure that, in the long march through the institutions of political and economic power, women formed a 'critical mass' of at least a third. For there is simply no way in which individual campaigners can set structural changes in motion, and it is extraordinarily difficult for them to avoid being coopted and instrumentalized.

In Africa, for example, it was only through a reservation system that women were able to break in significant numbers into the political chambers. In South Africa, after the end of the apartheid regime, a 25 per cent quota helped women to force their way into the male reserve of parliament and to take part in the drafting of a new constitution. In India, women have over the last decade gained a one-third quota for elections to village and municipal councils. By 1997 women in both India and Pakistan were fighting for a quota in parliament – not yet successfully, because of fierce cross-party resistance by men jealous of their power. Still, the Scandinavian example is doing the rounds as a means of securing greater female representation.

Whereas DAWN focuses on transformation, WEDO lays the greatest stress on participation, especially in international institutions such as the UN, World Bank, IMF and WTO, so that it can gain influence over global developments. Following the series of UN conferences, reform of the UN itself has become a goal of WEDO's lobbying and 'mainstreaming' politics. At Rio in 1992, women's NGOs were still discussing, as the key strategic question, whether women should fight for the abolition of the World Bank or whether a struggle should be waged for more women to hold leading positions within it. Since then, the answer has been given in favour of participation.

For years now, while NGOs from various spheres of society have been placing democratic thorns in the side of the UN and the World Bank, and women's NGOs have been conducting a World Bank watch campaign, the World Trade Organization has stubbornly resisted calls for greater demo-cracy and transparency. Nevertheless, women are still demanding space for negotiations to introduce their own themes and requests into the institution: for example, the creation of barriers to the international trade in women for prostitution. In 1996, when the European women's network WIDE (Women in Development Europe) asked the WTO to send a representative to its conference in Bonn on 'Women and Global Trade', the world arbiter of free and fair trade shamefully declined on the grounds that it had 'no mandate for women'.

In the private sector of the economy, affirmative action is still harder to achieve than in the public sector. What levers can be moved to change global economic structures when the trade unions are becoming less and less powerful? How can the neoliberal market system be, if not split from within, then blunted and made more humane? Reform-oriented approaches seek to restructure the world market so that it is more socially just and tolerable to women and the environment: soft instead of hard loans, ethical instead of no-holds-barred banking, fairer trade, greater corporate trans-parency and democracy, social clauses, public awards for socially- and ecologically-minded companies.

Women's organizations often directly negotiate with corporations, banks and multinational institutions. The state, however, is increasingly the object of their demands, even though feminists criticize its patriarchal character.

Governments and UN agencies are called upon to re-regulate the de-regulated markets (through new tax policies, for example), instead of sacrificing their citizens' rights upon the altar of cut-throat competition.

At the microlevel of politics, women are currently trying to use Local Agenda 21 as the forum for a dual strategy of participation and trans-formation. The implementation of Agenda 21 – the timetable for a new world order agreed by governments at the Earth Summit in 1992 – is gradually getting under way at the grassroots, with the involvement of all the forces of civil society. The central concern is to link up local economic, ecological and social issues with the maintenance of global justice. For women this is an opportunity to kill two birds with one stone: to make their interests count at local level and to gain influence over community affairs, thereby 'democratizing' local democracy.

The actual key issues vary a great deal with the locality, ranging from regional development and transport planning to projects for craftswomen. Thus, if one takes the 170 or so initiatives under way in Brazil – many of them carried along by women – the central issue is health problems due to environmental damage, water pollution, and inadequate hygiene and refuse disposal. Women in Harlem, in New York, have made the manage-ment of solid and liquid waste part of their local agenda. They also want to involve the community in the repair of derelict housing and in various economic projects.

In Hagen in Westphalia, women are using Local Agenda as a forum to arouse public interest and to increase the pressure for the implementation of long-pursued demands: for example, employment initiatives for single mothers, compulsory insurance contributions for the lowest-paid jobs, backing for the Clean Clothes Campaign, removal of pedestrian tunnels and other urban features especially feared by women, and protection of children on their way to school. In some areas – Lüchow-Dannenberg, for example – women have themselves pushed the local authority into adopting a local agenda. In Heidelberg, 'future-search workshops' have been equipped for residents to develop their own ideas about the sustainability of their part of town.

It is often at local level that women can most readily gain a foothold in the structures of negotiating and decision-making power. It helps a lot if they are organized in grassroots groups, for at this level their reproductive and voluntary work is directly visible and comprehensible, and political decisions are most strongly oriented to life's immediate needs. In countries of the South, women have learnt from experience that collective bargaining-power in the village or slum is more easily achieved than individual bargaining-power within the family.

At the microlevel of the market, women's demands for participation, especially in Africa, are currently focused on access to personal loans. Since the Grameen Bank in Bangladesh, with its concept of a bank that 'goes out to women', has been held up as a model in sectors of world opinion concerned with development policy, small loans are everywhere seen not only as a way of bringing people into the money and market economy, but also as a means of combating poverty. Typical of the new concept of women's action is the fact that organizations such as the CEEWA, the Centre for the Economic Empowerment of Women in Africa, combine the principle of 'A loan for every woman' with a demand for the social remodelling of structural adjustment programmes. The micro- and macro-levels are here brought together in one conception, and multitrack measures are supposed to make life more secure for women on the global-ized market. In order to make structural adjustment appropriate to local conditions, however, women must win the power to make decisions at the macroeconomic level. This is what completes the political–conceptual circle between the local and the global.

In their search for strategies that combine participation with transforma-tion, women's organizations are trying to find a path between autonomy and adaptation. This balancing act aims at an alliance between women 'inside' (that is, within the established political structures) and women 'outside' (in the non-state sector). Only through such a functioning alliance can women's movements become a force to shape and change society.

Women's rights are human rights Over the last decade, national and international women's organizations have drawn major inspiration from the discourse of human rights. Descended from the European Enlighten-ment, this approach is well suited as a frame of reference for internationalist politics. It effects a universalization of norms within a globalized world.

The core of human rights is a concern for human dignity and basic rights, irrespective of individual and cultural differences. With the slogan 'Women's rights are human rights', women's rights activists have managed to overcome the stigma that comes from regarding women as a special case and their rights as special rights. This changed both how women saw themselves and how they were seen from the outside, so that now women no longer appeared primarily as petitioners in special need, but rather as bearers or subjects of a general right. In this way, it became possible not only to make injustice and victimization more visible, but also to transcend the role of victim as such.

Basing themselves on this line of argument, women's organizations opened a way for themselves into the United Nations and related to its normative foundation in human rights. Various issues such as violence against women, which had always been avoided as 'private' or culturally specific, could thus also be introduced, as a central factor in gender relations, into the generally accepted discourse of the UN and individual states.

Furthermore, women's understanding of themselves as subjects of rights altered the ways in which political action was conceived: that is, not mainly as calls for help to victims, but as ringing demands for the respect of human rights and involvement in negotiating its social and political pre-conditions. This shift of emphasis to political, economic and socio-cultural participation signals one of the most important changes in the discourse of women's politics.

The driving force behind the 'women's rights are human rights' debate has been the women's movement in the United States. But the approach has also been taken up by continental networks such as WILDAF (Women in Law and Development in Africa), the RIAF/DLVF network in franco-phone Africa, and the AWHRC (Asian Women's Human Rights Council). These organizations start from a knowledge and respect for their respective cultures, but do not allow this to obscure the respect due to women. The concept of universal human rights has led them to relate in new ways to their cultures and traditions.

A number of tribunals have been held in and around UN conferences to break the culture of silence surrounding human rights violations against women. Individual women have given moving evidence there of violence and other abuses, both physical and economic, and thereby asserted the collective importance of what happened to them. The awareness that they have suffered injustice and are fighting for their rights has proved to be a powerful impetus to solidarity over and above political and cultural differences.

The Western paradigm of human rights refers to a relationship between the 'free' citizen and the state, and places at its centre civil freedoms and political rights. Human rights and women's rights activists from the South, however, put greater emphasis on collective rights and goods such as food, health and employment, or the right to development.[9]

By adopting an international approach and capturing media attention through the work of tribunals, the global network of women's movement has successfully developed a holistic human rights concept in which in-dividual and civic–political rights are combined with social and economic rights. Governments, on the other hand, have not achieved such an integration. In their negotiations, the conflict between collective rights and individual autonomy, between socio-economic claims and civic–political freedoms, has retained its explosive charge.

The Asian women's rights network AWHRC, for example, attaches great importance to the right to development, but rejects any idea that women's rights should be sacrificed to it. Countries that rely on tourism as a source of hard currency and an engine of development may well factor in prostitution as a structural condition for economic success, which means that they systematically plan for violations of women's dignity.

In a context defined by the UN conferences of recent years, the international debate concerning women's rights has concentrated on their cultural relativism by authoritarian states such as China and by religious fundamentalists. While several UN conferences have nearly collapsed as a result, the international women's rights movement has had to answer the delicate question of whether human rights are culturally definable, and therefore restrictable, or whether they have general validity. The dominant conception in the movement has certainly been a universal one, but women have tried to develop it within different cultural contexts. They stress, for example, that all cultures, traditions and religions have had within them, and still have, both conservative and liberal currents, both repressive and emancipatory forces with regard to women. The point, then, is not to impose a Western schema of universal norms, but to fulfil liberal demands on the basis of each distinctive tradition. This opens up a broad field of action between universal levelling and cultural relativism.[10]

As things stand today, women's rights are subordinated not only to culture, religion and politics, but also to the globalized market. Women have to keep taking up the struggle for their rights against attempts to minimize and truncate them. Women's rights are not a title-deed, but an unsecured cheque towards a future that even in the age of globalization still has to be secured. What is involved here is a process of catching up. In its respect for cultural difference, the globalization of an ethics of physical integrity, social rights and civic freedoms must not simply match the globalization of neoliberal markets; it must also call a halt to that process.

Delinking, regionalization and localization In 1996, under the slogan 'Women say no to imperialist globalization', the Philippines women's association Gabriela waged a campaign against the Asia–Pacific Economic Community in which the USA and Japan are struggling for pre-eminence.[11] Gabriela wants to stop foreign companies from acquiring mining rights and control over land and resources in the Philippines; to defend the country's economic and day-to-day self-reliance by resisting the domination of foreign capital.

Where women have learnt from experience that world market integration means dependence and insecurity, they often wish for a return to transparent regional economies. Farming women in East Africa, who have endured the collapse of coffee prices, want to plant less coffee and cotton for the world market and to use more land to grow their own food. They think that their work should be rewarded in cash, in security and in control over means of production. They want loans for trade that they can control themselves within a regional framework, using river transport instead of aeroplanes that carry their produce halfway round the world.

In the countries of the South, women still practise subsistence forms of direct exchange, reciprocity and collective use, and out of sheer necessity they may also develop new modes of cooperation or union. Poor grassroots women are especially likely to look for ways of making a living not on the world market but in areas where they are strong: in the informal sector, in local and regional trade, and in barter trade. They do not, to be sure, reject the market out of hand, but they want to see transparent and controllable structures in which there is still room for elements of moral economy and for communal use of such resources as water and land. This also implies a recovery of self-reliance and the potential to provide for themselves. This regional conception is thus opposed to globalization, which involves maximum alienation and distance between production and consumption, and minimal transparency and local control.

In the North, too, more and more niches and small economic circuits are developing outside the globalized market: for example, the direct marketing of organic farm produce; local exchange trading systems (LETS), which exchange skills or services without cash, calculating in units of time or inventing local currencies such as 'peanuts' in Frankfurt, 'neutrals' in Wittenberg or 'piafs' in Paris; recycling workshops, second-hand stores, the sharing of cars and other goods, and eco-villages.

The strengthening of regional and local forces and circuits is also a crucial element in the criticisms of globalization that feminist economists have been developing in recent years. They draw their concepts of economics from where it originates: from the household economy and the sphere of reproduction.

In their view, production and trade should be oriented to basic needs and provision, not to profit. Accordingly, feminist theorists such as Antonella Picchio in Italy formulate the goal of economic activity as needs satisfaction and improvement of the quality of life, not the achievement of maximum financial gain. This entails a different way of interrelating with nature.[12] The Finnish theorist Hilkka Pietilä similarly argues for a 'cultivating' and 'preserving' economics, in contrast to one based upon short-sighted over-exploitation of resources.[13] The Indian environmental activist Vandana Shiva, for her part, calls for a 'relocalization of the economy and decision-making'. Instead of 'cultural and biological uniformity and monocultures', the 'diversity in nature and society' should be protected; and instead of the human 'colonization of nature by men', there should be 'ecological democracy' and 'partnership with nature's intelligence and creativity'.[14]

While the German–Swiss network 'Providing Economics' (Vorsorgendes Wirtschaften) stresses the three principles of provision, cooperation and life-necessities, Carola Möller's key concept is an orientation to the common good.[15] The starting-point for most of these theorists is the relationship between paid and unpaid labour, between economies based upon commodities and markets, and economies based upon care and reproduction. A redistribution and revaluation of paid and unpaid labour is for them the lever with which to reshape the gender hierarchy and the whole economic system.

Ideas tend to differ about how to relate to market rationality. The British economist Diane Elson has proposed a strategy of 'claiming markets back', on the basis of grassroots initiatives such as producer and consumer cooperatives and new types of banking and investment.[16] Subsistence theorists argue instead for a 'turning away from the expansionist economy' based upon money and commodities. For the ecofeminists Maria Mies and Veronika Bennholdt-Thomsen, subsistence economics does not rest 'upon the colonization of women, nature and other nations'; it places 'life and life's necessities – not the accumulation of totems, of capital – at the centre of all economic activity'. It is a perspective 'good not only for village women in Bangladesh but also for Hillary Clinton'.[17] Totally oriented to small-scale farming, it rejects all industrial production and highly developed technology, as well as condemning approaches based upon equality and participation. It thus offers the most radical departure from the global market and communications society.

All approaches based upon a return to the local and the regional aim to ensure sustainable livelihoods, as well as a reappropriation of resources and of spaces defined by local people themselves. Whether they abandon the ground of market reality and the state, or whether they seek to use regional counterweights to force back global neoliberalism, they see in the local a possible way of recovering autonomy. At the political level, this is also the perspective of Local Agenda 21, although it aims to operate within existing structures rather than to withdraw from the system. Through a return to self-determination, individuals or groups posit themselves as subjects within global processes – processes that increasingly turn them into objects. Their idea is to build up power from below, in order to renew politics on the basis of the local and the household economy.

Globalized Woman

The heads of government who met in 1996 at the G-7 summit in Lyons reaffirmed the claim that globalization is a 'success from which everyone benefits'. Employment gains and detraditionalization are thought to provide evidence that women profit from the liberal removal of barriers to markets and cultures.

It is true that young, skilled, flexible women have better opportunities than ever before to decide the shape of their life, to improve its quality and to advance in their career. But the group of winners is not exactly large. It makes its way on to the vibrating springboard of the new knowledge, finance and technology markets that eventually hurls a select few upwards. But all that most women manage to grab from their bargain-hunting in the employment market are the really cheap and nasty jobs. As society grows more polarized, they remain the losers, excluded from prosperity and a secure existence. New forms of subordination lie cheek by jowl with the new life opportunities. In the fierce undercutting that pits one country against another, 'globalized woman' is burnt up as a natural fuel: she is the piece-rate worker in export industries, the worker living abroad who sends back foreign currency, the prostitute or catalogue bride on the international body and marriage markets, and the voluntary worker who helps to absorb the shock of social cutbacks and structural adjustment. The strategic function of 'globalized woman', within the broader project of globalization driven by economics and politics, is the execution of unpaid and underpaid labour. This plays a significant instrumental role in the deregulation and worldwide restructuring of the jobs market, as well as in the cutbacks in social provision.

Neoliberal globalization results in contrasts and inequalities: it produces growth and prosperity, while at the same time eroding social certainties. The economy, thanks to huge productivity increases, is heading for a crisis of overproduction; and the redundancy of more and more labour has already plunged it into a crisis of overcapacity on the jobs market. 'Globalization', notes the International Confederation of Free Trade Unions, 'has become a synonym for joblessness, underemployment and growing inequality.'[18]

In a context where the general sense of security is being lost, women manage to create a number of little certainties – especially in the social domain, but also in the management of daily life and nourishment, in ecology, in culture and the politics of civil society. They achieve this through multiple and flexible action strategies, usually in the much-practised balancing act between paid and unpaid labour, between the private and the public. They maintain or rebuild a sense of community through voluntary work or self-help projects, at a time when old family ties are being eroded, the state and capital are forsaking their social responsibilities, and competition, male violence and social tensions are escalating. Where everyday contexts and cultural production are detraditionalized, women search for new identities among modernized traditions, social ties and autonomy.

Women show that they are prepared to bear risks, to develop initiatives of their own, to shoulder responsibility. Yet these virtues, so highly praised by neoliberal ideologues, are of little help to them on the globalized markets. In the universal risk society, their task of generating security becomes more and more Sisyphean in character. For the majority of women, neoliberal globalization does not live up to its implicit claim to justice and prosperity; it is not the promised win–win game, but is creating a future of inequality all around the globe.

A redistribution of work, prosperity and power is currently taking place, but it does not benefit either the poor and excluded or the mass of women. Now as before, women must carry on struggling for social justice, legal security and the power to make decisions and shape their lives. In the women's movements of the future, some will still fight for equality and rights within the existing global system, while others develop counter-strategies and feminist alternatives to that system. Dual strategies – both inside and outside, from the top and from below, local and global, gradual and visionary – will be necessary to gain strength in civil society. Only then can there be built not only power-sharing but a real countervailing power within the grinding mills of neoliberal globalization.

Notes

1. For a more detailed account, see Wichterich (1996).

2. Amrita Basu (ed.) (1995), *The Challenge of Local Feminisms: Women's Movements in Global Perspective*, Boulder, San Francisco and Oxford.

3. Saskia Wieringa, 'Introduction: Subversive Women and their Movements', in Saskia Wieringa (ed.) (1995), *Subversive Women*, New Delhi, pp. 1–23.

4. See Uta Ruppert (1996), 'Vielfalt statt Visionen?', *BUKA Agrar Dossier* 17, Hamburg, pp. 40–4; Birte Rodenberg, 'Die Kräfte sammeln … ', in ibid., pp. 33–40; Anja Ruf (1996), *Weltwärts Schwestern!*, Bonn.

5. See Wichterich (1995).

6. Gwendolyn Mikell (1995) 'African Feminism: Toward a New Politics of Representation', *Feminist Studies* 21/2, Summer, pp. 405–25.

7. DAWN (1995), 'Securing our Gains and Moving Forward to the 21st Century', a position paper by DAWN for the Fourth World Conference on Women.

8. See Wee and Heyzer (1995), pp. 152f.

9. See Corinne Kumar-D'Souza, 'A South Wind: Towards New Cosmologies', in GSI (1997), *Frauen für eine neue Weltinnenpolitik*, Bonn, pp. 33–60.

10. See Annie Bunting, 'Zur kulturellen Verschiedenartigkeit von Frauen in internationalen Menschenrechtsstrategien von Feministinnen', in Lenz et al. (1996), pp. 130–52.

11. Statement issued by Gabriela, 19 October 1996.

12. Antonella Picchio, in WIDE (1995), pp. 11ff.

13. Hilkka Pietilä (1997), 'The Triangle of the Human Economy: Household–Cultivation–Industrial Production', *Ecological Economics* 20, pp. 113–27.

14. Shiva (1995), pp. 28f.

15. *Politische Ökologie*, special issue 6, 1994; Adelheid Biesecker (1996), 'Lebensweltliche Erneuerung der Ökonomie – über alte und neue Formen weiblichen Wirtschaftens', *Bremer Diskussionspapiere zur Sozialökonomik* 8, University of Bremen, May; Müller et al. (1997).

16. See Elson, in WIDE (1995), pp. 17f.

17. Bennholdt-Thomsen and Mies (1997), pp. 10ff.

18. ICFTU (1997), *Annual Survey of Violations of Trade Union Rights 1997*, Brussels, p. 6.

Select Bibliography

Afshar, Haleh and Dennis Caolyne (eds) (1992) *Women and Adjustment Policies in the Third World*, London.

Altvater, Elmar and Birgit Mahnkopf (1997) *Grenzen der Globalisierung. Ökonomie, Ökologie und Politik in der Weltgesellschaft*, Münster.

Bakker, Isabella (ed.) (1994) *The Strategic Silence: Gender and Economic Policy*, London.

Bennholdt-Thomsen, Veronika and Maria Mies (1997) *Eine Kuh für Hillary. Die Subsistenzperspektive*, Munich [English translation, Zed Books, forthcoming].

Bündnis 90 and Die Grünen in Bayern (1997) *Frauen handeln. Krise – Kosten – Kompetenz*, Munich.

Cagatay, Nilüfer, Diane Elson and Caren Grown (eds) (1995) 'Gender Adjustment and Macroeconomics', *World Development* 23/11.

Chossudovsky, Michel (1997) *The Globalisation of Poverty. Impact of IMF and World Bank Reforms*, Penang and London.

DGB Bildungswerk (1995a) *Materialien 36: Informeller Sektor. Marktwirtschaft im Schatten*, Dusseldorf.

— (1995b) *Materialien 38: Hierarchie oder Emanzipation. Frauen in der europäischen Union*, Dusseldorf.

— (1995c) *Materialien 42: Sozialklauseln und Gewerkschaften*, Dusseldorf.

— (1996a) *Materialien 46: Freie Produktionszonen. Grenzenlose Gewinne!*, Dusseldorf 1996.

— (1996b) *Materialien 49: Kleider aus der Weltfabrik*, Dusseldorf.

— (1997) *Materialien 53: Spielzeug: Weltmarkt im Kinderzimmer*, Dusseldorf.

Elson, Diane (1991) *Male Bias in the Development Process*, Manchester.

Forrester, Viviane (1996) *L'Horreur économique*, Paris.

Forschungs- und Dokumentationszentrum Chile-Lateinamerika (1996) *Frauenarbeit in Lateinamerika. Gewinnerinnen der Globalisierung*, Berlin.

Frauen in der einen Welt (1996) 2, Dienstmädchen.

Ghai, Dharam and Cynthia Hewitt de Alcantara (1994) *Globalisation and Social Integration: Patterns and Processes*, UNRISD, Geneva.

Giddens, Anthony (1994) *Beyond Left and Right*, Cambridge.

Group of Lisbon (1995) *Limits to Competition*, Cambridge, MA.

HVBG (Hauptverband der gewerblichen Berufsgenossenschaften) (1997) *Dokumentation Zukunft der Arbeit*, Sankt Augustin.

IBFG (Internationaler Bund freier Gewerkschaften) (1996) ed. Natacha David, *Zwei Welten: Frauen und die Weltwirtschaft*, Brussels.

ICDA Journal (1996) *Focus on Trade and Development* 4/1, Brussels.

ila (*Informationsstelle Lateinamerika*) (1995), 185: *Maquila*, May.

Joekes, Susan (1995) *Trade-Related Employment for Women in Industry and Services in Developing Countries*, UNRISD, Geneva.

Joekes, Susan and Ann Weston (1994) *Women and the New Trade Agenda*, UNIFEM, New York.

Kreissl-Dörfler, Wolfgang (ed.) (1995) *Mit gleichem Maß. Sozial- und Umweltstandards im Welthandel* (book produced for the International Congress in Munich), November.

Lenz, Ilse, Andrea Germer and Brigitte Hasenjürgen (eds) (1996) *Wechselnde Blicke. Frauenforschung in internationaler Perspektive*, Opladen.

Martin, Hans Peter and Harald Schumann (1997), *The Global Trap: Globalization and the Assault on Democracy and Prosperity*, London.

Möller, Carola et al. (1997) *Wirtschaften für das 'gemeine Eigene', Handbuch zum gemeinwesen-orientierten Wirtschaften*, Berlin.

Musiolek, Bettina (ed.) (1997) *Ich bin chic, und Du mußt schuften. Frauenarbeit für den globalen Modemarkt*, Frankfurt / Main.

Ng, Cecilia and Anne Munro-Kua (eds) (1994) *Keying into the Future. The Impact of Computerization on Office Workers*, Kuala Lumpur.

Ökumenisches Büro für Frieden und Gerechtigkeit e.V. (n.d.) *Profit ohne Grenzen. Freie Produktionszonen in Mittelamerika*, Munich.

Ong, Aihwa (1987) *Spirits of Resistance and Capitalist Discipline: Factory Women in Malaysia*, New York.

Oxfam (1993) *Focus on Gender* 1/3: *Women and Economic Policy*, October.

— (1996a) *Focus on Gender* 4/3: *Employment and Exclusion*, October.

— (1996b) *Trade Liberalisation – At What Price?*, Dublin.

Peripherie 59/60, special issue: *Globalisierung*, December 1995.

Shiva, Vandana (1995) *Women, Ecology and Economic Globalisation*, New Delhi.

Sparr, Pamela (ed.) (1994) *Mortgaging Women's Lives. Feminist Critiques of Structural Adjustment*, London.

Sprenger, Ute, Jürgen Knirsch and Kerstin Lanje (eds) (1996) *Unternehmen Zweite Natur. Multis, Macht und moderne Biotechnologien*, Giessen.

Standing, Guy (1989) 'Global Feminisation through Flexible Labour', *World Development* 17/7, pp. 1077–95.

Südwind e.V. (1994) *Bürsten gegen den Strich. Frauen im Reinigungsgewerbe*, Siegburg.

— (1997) *Kleiderproduktion mit Haken und Ösen*, Siegburg.

United Nations (1995a) *1994 Survey on the Role of Women in Development. Women in a Changing Global Economy*, New York.

— (1995b) *The World's Women 1995. Trends and Statistics*, New York.

UNDP (1995; 1996; 1997) *Human Development Report*, Oxford.

Wee, Vivienne and Noeleen Heyzer (1995) *Gender, Poverty and Sustainable Development*, Singapore and New York.

Weibblick (1997), *Frauen im vereinten Europa*, Berlin.

Wichterich, Christa (1995), *Frauen der Welt. Vom Fortschritt der Ungleichheit*, Göttingen.

— (1996) *Wir sind das Wunder, durch das wir überleben. Die 4. Weltfrauenkonferenz in Peking*, Cologne.

WIDE (1995) Bulletin: *Towards Alternative Economics from a European Perspective*, Brussels, August.

— (1996) Bulletin: *Women and Trade: European Strategies for an International Agenda*, December.

— (1997) Bulletin: *Trade Gaps and Gender Gaps: Women Unveiling the Market*, November.

Widerspruch (1996) 16/31: *Globalisierung – Arbeit und Ökologie*, July.

Zeitpunkte (1997) 1: *Die mageren Jahre. Deutschland in der Klemme zwischen Globalisierung und Sparzwang*.

Index

abortion, 92, 122
Abyssinian Baptist Church, Harlem, 141
Abzug, Bella, 154
Ackermann, Lea, 65
Affirmative Action organization, 160
Afro-American women, march by, 140
Agir Ici organization, 15
AgrEvo company, 89
agriculture: excessive use of antibiotics, 90; industrialization of, 81; productivity of, women's role in, 70; small-scale, 166 (feminization of, 70); urban, 73–4; women's work in, 69–74, 108, 164
Ahmed, Redwan, 7, 8
AIDS, 115
Albania, 62
alcohol, consumption of, in Russia, 119, 122
'Alliance for Youth', 104
Amihan organization, 80
Andrejeva, Tatyana, 121–2
Anna, a sex worker, 62
Apisuk, Chantawipa, 63
Argentina, 111–12
Asia Monitor Resource Centre, 3
Asian Women and Shelter Network, 151
Asian Women's Human Rights Council (AWHRC), 163
Association of Homeless People (South Africa), 148, 149
Atatürk, Kemal, 139
Australia, 22
automation, 17

El-Badri, Youssef, 109
Bahl, Vinay, 143
Balabagan, Sarah, 59
Balayeva, Elena, 120
Bangalore, software industry in, 50
Bangladesh, 3, 4–9, 24–5, 27, 32, 62; Islam in, 137; malnutrition in, 79; prawn farming in, 75, 76, 78

banking, mergers in, 56
Baur mail order company, 6
Benetton company, 129, 134
Bennholdt-Thomsen, Veronika, 98, 166
Berne Declaration organization, 15
BINGOs, 157
Biocyte company, patent on blood cells, 91
biodiversity, 90
biopiracy, 87
birth rate, in Russia, falling, 120
blacklisting of women organizers, 28
Blair, Tony, 126
Blumen 2000 company, 43
Body Shop company, 43
body shopping, 52
brand awareness, importance of, 134
Brazil: genetically engineered tobacco crops in, 89; prostitution in, 63; soya production in, 88
Breyer, Hiltrud, 88
Brickell, Warren, 10
British American Tobacco company, 84
Brooke Bond company, 72
BSE disease, 83
building societies, establishment of, 150
Burma, 62
businesses, run by women, 43
Busse, Dirk, 3
Butegwa, Florence, 116

Cairo, waste sorting in, 107
call centres, 54–5
Cambodia, 3, 8, 27; and traffic of women, 61; demonstrations in, 29; UN peace mission and sex market, 61
care work, 41, 42–3, 98, 100; for elderly and sick, 101; performed by women, 102
career opportunities of women, unequal, 49
Cargill Corporation, 81
Caribbean, database keyboarding in, 45